The
CARIBBEAN:
PEOPLES, PROBLEMS, and PROSPECTS

SERIES ONE   *VOLUME II*

A publication of the
SCHOOL OF INTER-AMERICAN STUDIES
which contains the papers delivered at the second annual conference on the
Caribbean held at the University of Florida, December 6, 7, and 8, 1951.

ISSUED WITH ASSISTANCE FROM
THE WALTER B. FRASER PUBLICATION FUND

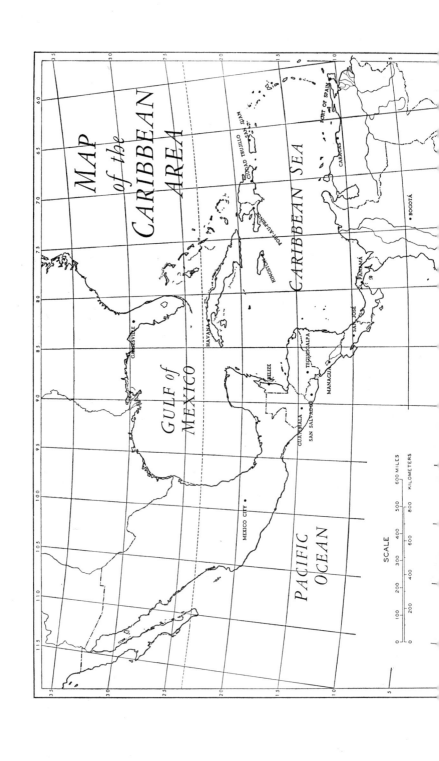

MAP
of the
CARIBBEAN
AREA

The
CARIBBEAN:

PEOPLES, PROBLEMS, and PROSPECTS

Florida. University, Gainesville
Papers delivered at the annual conf. 1951

edited by A. *Curtis* Wilgus

1952

UNIVERSITY OF FLORIDA PRESS

Gainesville

Copyright, 1952, by the

UNIVERSITY OF FLORIDA
ALL RIGHTS RESERVED

A University of Florida Press Book

L. C. Catalogue Card Number: 52-12530

Printed by

THE H. & W. B. DREW COMPANY
JACKSONVILLE, FLORIDA

Contributors

Francisco Aguirre, Secretary, Pan American Division, American Road Builders' Association

Frank K. Bell, Vice President, Alcoa Steamship Company

W. H. Callcott, Professor of History, University of South Carolina

Harriet de Onís, Translator and Author, New York City

José Guzmán Baldivieso, Honorary Consul of Bolivia to Indiana and Kansas

C. H. Haring, Professor of History, Harvard University

John P. Harrison, Latin American Specialist, National Archives

Mark D. Hollis, Assistant Surgeon General, Public Health Service, Federal Security Agency

Muna Lee, Bureau of Inter-American Affairs, Department of State

Alberto Lleras, Secretary General, Pan American Union

James G. Maddox, Assistant Director, American International Association for Economic and Social Development

Wilfred O. Mauck, Vice President, Institute of Inter-American Affairs, Educational Division

J. Hillis Miller, President, University of Florida

Ross E. Moore, Assistant Director, Office of Foreign Agricultural Relations, Department of Agriculture

Rafael Picó, Chairman, Puerto Rico Planning Board

William L. Schurz, Professor of Area Studies and International Relations, American Institute for Foreign Trade

Fred L. Soper, Director, Pan American Sanitary Bureau

Doris Stone, Archaeologist and Anthropologist, San José, Costa Rica

Arturo Torres-Rioseco, Professor of Spanish, University of California

REXFORD G. TUGWELL, Professor of Political Science, University of Chicago

A. CURTIS WILGUS, Director, School of Inter-American Studies, University of Florida

GEORGE WYTHE, Director, American Republics Division, Department of Commerce

Foreword

THE CONSUMMATE importance of an ever increasing co-operation among the Americas, and of a wider appreciation by the United States of its responsibilities in the family of American republics, daily gains greater recognition. Events of the year past, during which the creeping paralysis of totalitarianism afflicted even more of the once-free world, leave no doubt in the mind of the thinking observer that the Americas must become more unified in thought and deed if the New World is to enjoy tomorrow, as today, the democratic way of life.

In the spirit of service to this cause of unity among the Americas, the University of Florida each year sponsors an inter-American conference, bringing together area specialists and leaders from the ranks of business, government, and education to exchange views and information pertaining to the American republics. In December, 1950, the first of a new series of these scholarly conferences was held on our campus to examine "The Caribbean at Mid-Century." A volume bearing this title and containing the proceedings of this conference was published by the University of Florida Press in 1951.

The papers which form the body of the present volume were delivered at the Second Annual Conference on the Caribbean, held at the University in December, 1951. Plans for a third meeting are well advanced as this volume goes to press, and it is the University's intent to continue these conferences so long as they remain useful to the cause to which they are dedicated.

The University of Florida acknowledges its sincere appreciation to the Aluminum Company of America, through the Alcoa Steamship Company, Inc., for its cooperation in this conference.

J. HILLIS MILLER, *President*

University of Florida

vii

Contents

Part I—HEALTH

Part II—LAND

Part III—TRADE

Introduction

No HISTORIAN is so clairvoyant that he can predict the future. He can, however, view in retrospect a panorama of past events—a chain of events, each a result of a previous cause. To this extent he views the past with its own future. In this way he may look into the future and he may conclude that a certain set of past events may run through a series of predictable results. But past history does not repeat itself.

The Caribbean area viewed in retrospect as a human geographical unit has a full record of a variety of events—political, economic, social, cultural, intellectual, religious. These events when placed together in proper sequence constitute a historical trend which leads definitely into the future. People have been acting more or less in the same way for centuries. That is part of human nature, which in the Caribbean has been running true to form for generations. And it probably will continue to run true to form in coming generations.

Participants in this conference have been looking toward the past, and toward the future. They have viewed the Caribbean area in retrospect and in prospect. Let us look now for a moment at a number of events as the historian sees them—in retrospective perspective.

I. Health

Not long ago we stood in a public park in a small town in Mexico. The weather was springlike. Innumerable people of various complexions came and went about their important businesses. Some were businessmen. Some seemed to have no business at all. A few were sitting on the grass eating picnic lunches. It was the noon hour. In the center of the park a fountain was sending up a thin stream of water which looked clear and sparkling. But it fell into a large basin filled with leaves and sticks and other debris. As we watched, a small boy came to the fountain, sat on the edge, and dangled his feet in the water, splashing it about in all directions. A man with a dilapidated automobile got out a pail which he used to dip up water to carry to the radiator of his steaming car. Birds bathed themselves in the water. A dog came to drink. A passing urchin picked up a handful of dust and tossed it onto the surface of the water, watching it settle. As we looked, an old man, obviously an Indian, hobbled up to the edge of the fountain and put his hand into the water, splashing it to and fro. Soon he bent down, brushed aside the dirt on the water, and put his lips to the surface, taking a long drink from the fountain. While he was drinking, one of the picnickers brought a cup and plate to the fountain and washed them off. Soon a woman with a child came to the edge of the fountain. First she looked around her, then she dipped her hand into the water and washed the baby's face.

We stood watching this scene for fully twenty minutes. In that time half a dozen people drank the water of the fountain. No one seemed to be disturbed by the fact that the water was dirty. Each brushed the dirt away and took a drink. This fountain in this Mexican village was obviously a place which had a variety of uses, depending upon the person who passed by. It was perfectly evident that these activities or similar ones had been going on for generations. It was only natural to consider that the fountain had been erected for the benefit of the citizens of this community. A similar phenomenon can be observed in other towns in Latin America. Even in localities where good drinking water has been provided, many of the local populace continue to use the public fountain. Public health had undoubtedly been affected by the presence of this fountain in the community. A culture habit has been developed upon which all our modern scientific notions and improvements have had no effect. It is a cultural pattern which, viewed from the present in retrospect, seems almost tragic.

II. Land

One bleak day we were driving along the Pan American
Highway on the high *antiplano* of the Andes. The clouds seemed
almost to touch the ground, and the wind whistled past in great
streamers. Off to the right we saw a cloud of dust whirling
toward us. We stopped, and soon out of the dust appeared
a yoke of oxen drawing a wooden plow. The horns of the oxen
were entwined with colored ribbons, mirrors, and tinsel blowing
crazily in the breeze. The oxen moved in slow and heavy fashion.
Behind the plow was an Indian who was doing his best to steer
the wooden implement in a straight line. Alongside him and the
oxen and following behind with shouts of joy were children
and adults. It looked like a gala occasion. Marching along
beside the plow was a priest. Someone was playing a flute,
obviously for the purpose of making a noise rather than music.
As we watched this scene it appeared that the priest was blessing
the land and apparently sprinkling holy water on the newly
plowed earth. There were no fences, and when the oxen came
within a few feet of the road, several of the adults picked up the
plow and headed it in the opposite direction while others tried
to push and pull the oxen so that they would return from whence
they had come.

Land in this area is cheap. It is probable that the potato, or
a branch of the potato family, was first developed in this region.
Certainly it has been cultivated from early times to the present
in the same fashion that is used today. But the potato, like the
methods of cultivation, has undergone no improvement whatsoever. The land produces little, and at times it produces nothing at all. Since human beings here are dependent upon what
the land yields, there are intermittent years of starvation between
the years when production rises slightly above the margin of
starvation. But life goes on; babies are born and die. Land
is cheap, though it is worth no more than it costs. Nature is
often uncooperative and the elements often unfavorable. Hence
the intercession of deity seems to be necessary. Superstitions regarding land and its productive ability are commonly accepted
characteristics of thinking in this region. Science, of course, is
gradually coming to the help of such backward people. But

first they must realize that they must do something to help themselves. Then nature perhaps will smile more frequently and more effectively. But today the retrospective panorama here is bleak.

III. Trade

Trading in Latin America is frequently a highly personalized affair. When one wishes to prepare a meal one usually goes to the public market. These markets vary from town to town in size and quality and odor. One hot, steaming day in a Central American country, we accompanied our hostess on a food-purchasing expedition in the city's market. First we visited the outdoor stalls where people could sit in the hot sun or in the cool shade and bargain all day long. Dogs and children were everywhere under foot, each making characteristic noises and reacting characteristically to the environment. As we entered the building, we saw that the narrow aisles were virtually footpaths occupied by people and animals sprawling on the ground. Some individuals were engaged in eating what appeared to be a variety of refuse. A few had braziers on which meat and fish were cooking. The floor was slippery in a slimy fashion with pieces of decayed vegetables and fruit. An uncommonly strong stench arose from the stalls and booths along the aisles. Our hostess stopped here and there to ask the price of food. Occasionally she made a purchase, but only after a violent argument had ensued over the price. As one haggled with one shopkeeper, others in the vicinity screamed at the tops of their voices to come and buy their wares. Prices varied with different customers, depending largely on how they were dressed. Fish and meats of all descriptions were exposed to the air where they lay on counters or hung from hooks covered with flies and unidentifiable vermin. Cakes and cookies disintegrated under the attack of insects. Candies and sweets quietly melted in the heat. The faces of the people, largely Indians, were morose and distressed. Only the young people seemed to be enjoying themselves. We hastened on from booth to booth along blocks of aisles, half-filled with humanity. Finally, our purchases complete, we headed for the open air and the sunlight.

Markets like these have been in existence since earliest colonial days. In some localities sanitary conditions have improved none at all; perhaps they have even become worse. Buying and selling activities continue as they have for centuries. At certain times of the day trade is brisk. On some days there is virtually no trade at all. Yet many of those who have produce to sell have come from miles away to the social center of the market place where their gossip substitutes for the newspaper, and public opinion is fickle and fluctuating. Thus, as one looks back at this and other markets in hundreds of Latin American communities, one wonders why large groups of the population have not been swept away by disease and plague.

IV. Culture

The scene is the plaza of a small Indian village in Yucatan. The noonday sun is hot. A microscopic breeze barely stirs the dust in the public square. Thousands of yellow butterflies are everywhere, and these and other insects go about their customary business in their own individual ways. Rangy, mangy dogs are listlessly sniffing the ground or lying in an apparent state of exhaustion in the dust of the road. On one side of the square near the corner is a white building. As one looks closely one sees that the roof is thatched and that the walls are made of mud covered with white-wash. On the side facing the square a door and two windows are visible. But these are closed. Above the door one makes out the word *Escuela* in small, faded pink letters. There seems to be a number also, which indicates that this school once had a prominent place in Mexican cultural life. We walk up to the entrance and try the door. It wobbles weakly on its hinge and opens with a groan. Inside it is dark. In a few seconds, however, we can see that this indeed has been a school. There are benches. There seem to be the remains of a desk and chair once used by the teacher. A piece of slate must have been a blackboard. But where are the children? Where is the teacher? What has happened to this school?

We know that for a number of years, now, the government of Mexico has been building rural schools and encouraging the in-struction of the Indians, especially in reading and writing Spanish and in working with their hands. But little evidence of this exists today in this little school beside the public square in the Yucatan village. We learn that the school has been closed for several years. The teacher has moved away. The children have gone uneducated. But nobody seems to miss the school. Life continues as it has since Mayan days. Across from the school there is a church which seems to be used only on Sundays. But even then there is no service in the church. In the home of one of the Indians beside the square is a weaving machine where native handicrafts are practiced. We learn that only a few people in the community can read and write. No one apparently seems to mind that education here is at a standstill. It is quite possible that the Mayas, who occupied this area ages ago, reached a higher cultural level than the people today.

We can see in retrospect, as we view the nearby ruins of an ancient civilization, that this was once a thriving community and that the prospering people developed a comparatively high cultural pattern which their descendants have all but lost today.

V. Diplomacy

Hardly had we arrived at the airport of a thriving West Indian capital than we realized that something was afoot. National flags were everywhere, furiously flapping in the trade winds. A radio was blaring martial music. People seemed to be in a gala mood. A boy was selling newspapers at the top of his voice. Was this a national holiday? Had a president been newly elected? Had some special divine blessing descended upon the country? On leaving the plane we learned that national troops had just avenged the national honor, insulted by foreigners moving across the common boundary. The "invaders" had been repulsed. The national army had even crossed the border to follow the foreigners in defeat. This was indeed a day for universal rejoicing.

When we arrived in town we saw what forms national rejoicing could take when a boundary dispute had been enthusiastically and joyfully terminated by military might. There was a fiesta spirit everywhere. Shops were closed. Many people were in the churches giving thanks to the deity for helping to repel the enemy. A military band was playing in the public square. Schools were closed, and students flooded the streets carrying banners and placards, and singing national songs. Orators on street corners were screaming defiance to the foreign invaders. The president-dictator soon proclaimed three days of rejoicing. The national honor had been vindicated. Let the invader return, and he would see what was in store for him!

As objective observers of this scene, we inquired what had happened. Sifting the innumerable answers, we concluded that settlers from the neighboring country had been crossing the border for some time, possibly without realizing it, until their presence had been magnified into an armed invasion, which must be repelled by force at all costs. Here was practical, personalized diplomacy at work. More often than not in a Latin American country bloodshed and tragedy have followed such events. As one looks back over the past century, one sees literally dozens of boundary disputes settled by threats, intimidation, and the use of arms. More than a hundred years ago Bolívar believed that such controversies were needless, and through unilateral understandings and mutual cooperation, armed disputes over common boundaries could be prevented. In recent years statesmen in the United States and in Latin America have attempted through cooperation to prevent the repetition of such incidents as we observed in this nation of the West Indies. The retrospective view of boundary disputes shows that often they have proved disastrous, and have resulted in national calamities which could have been prevented by full and free mutual cooperation and the cultivation and maintenance of common friendships throughout the hemisphere.

VI

These somewhat discouraging vignettes of the problems of health, land, trade, culture, and diplomacy of the people in the Caribbean all have one thing in common. They have been witnessed by innumerable observers over and over again in the past. They form a part of the intimate history of the Latin American republics and they constitute one of the mores of Latin American life. They represent experiences common to millions of people in the past and they may possibly continue to be common to millions of people in the future.

The experts participating in this conference have viewed the peoples and problems of the past in a retrospective fashion, and they have diagnosed what they have found with the object of suggesting cures. They have also looked toward the future and their prospective views of Caribbean problems seem to indicate that while much of the past is still a part of the present, the future will certainly be a period of change, improvement, and progress. The participants in this conference have not been unduly pessimistic, nor have they been overly optimistic. They have, however, attempted realistically to view the future in the light of the past and to see how present conditions can and will change. A retrospective view is necessary before prospects can be clearly seen.

A. Curtis Wilgus, *Director*

School of Inter-American Studies

Part I

HEALTH

Mark D. Hollis: ENVIRONMENTAL HEALTH NEEDS IN THE CARIBBEAN

MAY I SAY that it is a rare pleasure to be here today. The pleasure of attending this conference is all the greater because the business of public health has been put first on the program. It is always gratifying to find that others feel that the first order of business in any community program is to attend to the matter of public health.

I

If it is a question of what comes first in the field of public health, of course, most of us would favor our own specialty. My doctrine is that a healthy environment is basic to any public health movement. There are many valuable specialized activities in public health work, but in one way or another all are related to the basic environmental factors that sustain life. All are related to man's need for and man's use of air, water, food, and shelter. These needs are common to all people, whatever their birth, occupation, or status. The environmental health problems of some people may be more complicated than the problems of others, but their problems do not differ basically.

Basic environmental health needs for Brazil have been classified by Maria B. de Carvalho as water supply, sewerage and sewage treatment, waste and garbage disposal, drainage and reclamation, malaria control, and rural sanitation. These are basic environmental health operations that may be required also by peoples of the Caribbean or almost any other area, both in theory and in

3

practice. In speaking of environmental health needs, it is always a necessity to balance theory with practice. On the practical side of the balance, it is necessary to find money for health work. On the theoretical side of the balance, it is a question of understanding what health measures are most effective.

The first consideration in health work is not money, of course; it is life. But even life has its economic equations. Consider the issue of saving the lives of babies in a poor village where today half of the newborn children die before they are a year old. Some would say there would be little advantage in saving the lives of these children if they have to compete for a limited supply of food. This type of reasoning is that the extra mouths to feed would simply reduce the whole village to starvation. But it has been demonstrated that improvements in health also improve the ability to produce and procure food. And it appears also that the birth rate tends to drop as general living conditions improve, so that the population can level off eventually. The problem is to improve living conditions and the food supply as rapidly as health measures increase the population.

Consider also the question of whether it is effective to apply public health measures to a limited area. It seems almost a physical impossibility to control disease in every slum, every village, and every island. But it is equally difficult to prevent disease from spreading from infected areas to protected homes. Disease can be extremely democratic. It hits the rich as well as the poor. Infections today travel with the speed of airplanes, and reach from the public market place into secluded villages and estates. Quarantine services, to check the spread of disease, have limitations. The most effective defense against disease is sanitation services applied universally.

Another question is whether it is effective to concentrate on specific diseases to eradicate yaws, venereal disease, and smallpox, without regard for general sanitary conditions. Granting the value of such categorical programs, more lives will be saved and strengthened if the health program directs its first efforts toward environmental sanitation. In most communities, contaminated food and water and diseases carried by insects are the major causes of illness and death.

Sometimes it is a question of attacking an individual insect-borne disease, such as malaria, yellow fever, Chagas disease, typhus, trachoma, or filariasis. Generally, it appears that it is more effective to aim at control of insects in strategic locations rather than at the control of individual diseases carried by insects.

These remarks are not intended to deprecate the value of categorical health programs. Such programs are effective. They have a great impact on opinion and on attitudes as well as on health, especially in communities which have had little previous acquaintance with the power of modern preventive medicine. But I do wish to make it clear that it has been firmly established that a categorical approach to disease is most successful in communities that observe sound environmental health practices.

These questions are posed for those who wish to devote attention to the fundamentals rather than the refinements in environmental health. It is never easy to justify spending time and money on refinements when the great majority of the population live in open huts and when they do not even have access to a glass of clean water. In many a rural village, each morning at daybreak a family has a task of hauling water for as long as two hours before other work can begin. And even this water often comes from a polluted source, or is polluted in transit. In such a village, health work can be effective only if it starts with satisfying the fundamental need for clean water, safe disposal of human waste, and a protected food supply.

II

Health workers use several different approaches to determine a community's health needs: epidemiological studies; medical statistics; the advice of public health authorities; and the will of the people who are directly affected.

Epidemiological studies have demonstrated that many diseases can be controlled effectively by environmental measures. You are all probably aware that hookworm is prevented by proper disposal of excrement. The trichinosis cycle is broken if hogs are not fed uncooked garbage or offal. Proper disposal of garbage and excrement reduces the breeding of flies and other insects which transmit a host of diseases, including trachoma, filariasis, and dysentery, particularly the dysenteries that affect babies. Filtering and chlorination of water reduce the danger of worms, typhoid fever, cholera, and dysentery. Pasteurization of milk, or the use of dry powdered milk, reduces the danger of tuberculosis, brucellosis, and typhoid fever. Proper handling and storage of foods lessen the threat of gastroenteric infections or poisonings. Control of rats, rat fleas, and lice checks the danger of endemic typhus, epidemic typhus, and plague. Mosquito control reduces infections of yellow fever, dengue fever, malaria, and encephalitis. The disease named for the Brazilian physician Carlos Chagas is prevented by control of the biting bugs which carry the infection.

Epidemiology blames malnutrition for another Caribbean disease that goes by many names. It particularly affects infants and children and is characterized by listlessness and irritability. The environmental measures that combat malnutrition are improvements in the diet, such as are recommended by the Food and Agricultural Organization of the World Health Organization, and the sanitation that permits a community to produce more healthful food. For example, the control of malaria in Greece and other tropical areas has permitted the farmers there to bring in much heavier harvests. Of course, it is premature to speak with confidence about specific causes of malnutrition in the Caribbean countries. These causes, and the remedies, are under study at the University of Puerto Rico, which has published a handbook on tropical nutrition; at the Guatemala City laboratory of the Institute of Nutrition for Central America; and in the Section on Nutrition of the Pan American Sanitary Bureau.

But it seems clear that the epidemiology of most of the diseases of the Caribbean emphasizes the basic importance of environmental health measures. Even those diseases not directly related to environment are to some extent limited where the environment is clean and wholesome.

Along with the epidemiological studies, statistical studies help to explain which health conditions are in most urgent need of attention. As I have said, statistics indicate that the most common cause of death in many Caribbean communities is disease that is caused typically by contaminated food or drinking water. Now there is no denying that many of the Caribbean countries have achieved remarkable advances in recent years in the development of water supplies. Local efforts in this direction have been assisted by the formation of the Pan American Sanitary Bureau by treaty among American republics in 1902, by the Rio Conference of January, 1942, when twenty-one nations planned health operations as a phase of hemisphere defense, and by the activities of the Institute of Inter-American Affairs and of the World Health Organization. In eighteen or more American republics, health programs have been organized by the Institute of Inter-American Affairs for direction by a *Servicio Cooperativo Inter-Americano*, concentrating on the construction of health centers, including hospitals and dispensaries, development of water and sewage systems, malaria controls, and education. Other programs have developed in Caribbean territories under European governments.

The extent of the sanitation task is typified perhaps by conditions in Puerto Rico, of which I happen to have some first-hand knowledge. Most of the urban population has a central water supply. But two-thirds of the Puerto Rican population live in rural areas. And only one-fourth of this rural population is supplied by the Puerto Rican Aqueduct and Sewer Authority, although two-thirds of the Puerto Rican rural population are within reach of the water lines. But it is not necessary for these villagers to wait for expensive installations from the central system. A simple well, with a pump properly constructed, would be a vast improvement over their present system and it would cost less than water of questionable quality obtained from present sources.

Despite the progress that has been made under such organizations as the Puerto Rican Aqueduct and Sewer Authority, the Department of Hydraulic Resources in Mexico, the United Fruit Company, and other agencies, the statistics of morbidity and of water and sewage works indicate that safe, clean water supplies are still the most critical environmental health problem of the Caribbean areas. It may be that the statistics are far from complete or perfect, but they suggest this provisional conclusion.

A third approach to environmental health needs to study the statements of scientific authorities and political leaders. One such statement worth quoting is by The Honorable Miguel Alemán, President of the United States of Mexico: "The fundamental duty of a government that strives for the development and progress of its nation is to prevent, rather than try to cure, endemic diseases of its peoples. The water and sewerage works of all municipalities constitute the basic element in the fight against disease."

Another authority is the World Health Organization. Its official record (18-72) in 1949 states: "No permanent advance in the general health program can rest upon a substructure of poor sanitation. Any improvement in the disposal of excreta, in the protection of drinking water, and the destruction of the fly and the mosquito brings health and social advantage to man, woman, and child." A year earlier, the chronicles of the first health assembly of the World Health Organization (2-177) reported the statement that, with certain qualifications, nutrition was the most important single environmental factor in health. It is observed that malnutrition prejudices the health of 85 per cent of the population of the world. These two statements on environmental sanitation and nutrition remind us that disease and famine ride together as the horsemen of the apocalypse.

As late as June, 1944, Colonel Harold B. Gotaas was obliged to say that in general "sanitary engineering has not yet played an important part in public health work in Latin America." One reason, he said, was that it was given little emphasis in social thinking. Another reason was the scarcity of engineers, which I am sorry to say continues to this day. To overcome some of the personnel problems, Colonel Gotaas this year helped to organize training courses for sanitary engineers at the University of Mexico. Several Latin American universities have courses for sanitary engineers. Another training program is promised for 1953 in Panama, where the World Health Organization intends to conduct a course for operators of waterworks in Central America. An outstanding influence in environmental health work has been the organization of the Inter-American Association of Sanitary Engineers, which reported at its second meeting in 1950 in Mexico City that it already has 1,489 members with national sections in eighteen countries. With proper support this organization could be a great influence on environmental health progress in the Americas.

I would like to quote one more authority, Herman G. Baity, professor of Sanitary Engineering in the School of Public Health, University of North Carolina, who spoke last month at a meeting of the World Health Organization in Geneva:

Among preventive measures the most effective, the quickest, the cheapest is basic sanitation of the environment. By this we mean those simple, elemental things such as getting human excrement off the surface of the ground, giving the people clean water to drink and uninfected food to eat, and protecting them from the bites of disease-carrying insects. First things should come first.

One of the practical problems of public health administration at all levels, and affecting all professions, is to keep people down to earth and doing the fundamental things. This is as true of engineers as of the medicos, and not materially different south or north of the equator. We find people who know all about electronics and supersonics and radio-isotopes and complex formulae who feel that it is not dignified or professional to work in anything less than palatial offices and ultra-laboratories on high-flown theoretical problems, and who decline to see and do the simple and vital things that count most.

It would provide a most helpful orientation for public health workers the world around if they could understand the logical steps by which human betterment takes place. It has now been well demonstrated in many places that the beginning point in human progress is in the sanitary improvement of the environment. This sets in motion a chain reaction which first produces an improvement in health, then economic development, and then the social and spiritual betterment of the people.

III

As one reviews the literature on environmental health activities in the Caribbean countries, it becomes clear that there has been a remarkable degree of flexibility on the part of the official agencies and that they have adapted their ideas to local requirements. This adaptability is illustrated by the work which has been done in Panama to develop water supplies by digging horizontal wells in a terrain which is particularly suited to that form of construction.

In Venezuela, malaria control has moved far ahead of other environmental health measures and the death rate there for malaria has been reduced from 112 per 100,000 before the war to only 12 per 100,000 in 1948. In Guatemala, an urgent need for healthful housing is in the foreground, and in El Salvador, sewage treatment is prominent.

This adaptability and flexibility reflects the fourth approach to health needs—the democratic approach. The democratic approach does not begin and end with the business of counting noses and accepting a formal majority vote. The possible error in that idea was expressed by Leonardo da Vinci, who poked fun at the notion that, though a wise man may make mistakes, a thousand fools cannot be wrong. The democratic approach must be based first of all upon devotion to the general welfare, a genuine devotion and not one that pretends that a selfish interest and the general welfare are one and the same thing. The test of the reality of this devotion to the general welfare is the readiness of the majority to participate in and support a given program, not merely with votes and lip-service but with deeds. The complaint has been made against some communities that after the professional engineer has installed a water system, the system is not maintained or operated effectively. To me, this complaint is not a criticism of the community. It is a criticism of the failure of health workers to understand in advance the need for educating and training local people to carry on the work in sanitation. The installation of water-works equipment is neither a beginning nor an end in sanitation: it is only one phase of a continuing process. This process includes the task of demonstrating that sanitation is desirable, and also of demonstrating that it pays.

Two engineers, Luis Wonnoni and Edmund G. Wagner, in Venezuela have calculated the monetary value of safe water systems in that country and the savings such systems will effect for the people of the communities. These savings not only repay the cost of construction but increase the per capita water supply from ten to seventy-five liters per day. The savings are based both upon the reduction of working time lost because of illness and on the reduction of the daily costs of obtaining a supply of water. The estimate of reduction in illness was based upon the experience of the United States of America. Between 1900 and 1940, while the proportion of our population receiving safe water supplies increased from 40 per cent to 90 per cent, the incidence of water-borne disease was reduced 90 per cent.

Dr. M. von Pettenkofer once calculated that sanitation saved the city of Munich 25,000,000 florins in twenty-five years, and that was at a time when a florin would buy as much sausage as a

dollar buys today. Such studies as these supported by fact help
a community to understand that it can and it should support
sound health programs. The democratic approach requires also a
constant review and revision of health programs. Those responsible
for administering health programs must be alert to keep ahead of
new health problems that develop with the changing technology,
or with changing population patterns. At the same time, they
must not lose sight of the need for carrying on the health programs that have been well established. In the United States,
for example, we have on the one hand an emerging concern with
the increasing uses of synthetic chemicals, the increase in pollution
of the atmosphere, and the potential danger of ionizing radiations
from radiation-producing machines and from man-made radio-
isotopes. At the same time, we have to get on with the unfinished
business of basic sanitation.

A critical appraisal of the status of environmental health in the
United States will observe that in the larger cities progress in
basic sanitation has kept pace reasonably well with national growth.
The quality of public water supplies, extent of sewerage services,
and suppression of disease-carrying insects generally are satisfactory;
at least the gross health implications of these environmental factors
have been brought under control. To a much lesser extent have
been met the national need in milk and food sanitation, control
of excessive stream pollution, and sanitation of metropolitan fringe
areas. Similarly in need of improvement are the sanitation services
for schools, smaller communities, and rural areas. As yet un-
diagnosed is the full health significance of substandard housing,
excessive noise, refuse disposal problems, inadequate recreational
facilities, and air pollution.

IV

This appraisal makes it clear that the task of sanitation never
ends. As countries progress, their health programs simply take on
new aspects and new responsibilities. All of us in our respective
countries must bear in mind the necessity of changing with the
times to serve the total health needs of all the people. Only with
that attitude is it possible to keep driving ahead of problems in
each area of need.

That attitude is implicit in the democratic approach. It recognizes that officials working on public health and preventive medicine share their responsibilities with all the people. There is still a great deal of truth in the old axiom that a sound public health program provides 80 per cent of what people want and 20 per cent of what experts know the people need. Any serious deviation from that 80 per cent is likely to result in failure. A successful operation in the public health field depends on the understanding and active support of all elements in community life. If I may speak for my colleagues in all the Americas on general environmental needs, I should like to leave you with the thought that in basic sanitation we know what to do to improve the environment and we know how to do it. All we need is effective public support —which you all help to develop—in order to do an effective job.

Fred L. Soper: YELLOW FEVER
IN THE CARIBBEAN

THE OCCURRENCE of scattered cases of yellow fever in Panama, in 1948, 1949, 1950 and the first half of 1951, followed by a wavelike epidemic during the past six months in Costa Rica, moving from southeast to northwest, has focused attention on the yellow fever potentialities of the Caribbean area, as the equally significant occurrence of the disease under similar conditions since 1933, almost continuously in Colombia and less regularly in Venezuela, had failed to do. Until the occurrence of cases in Panama and Costa Rica, there was a tendency to consider Colombia and Venezuela as epidemiologically part of the South American continent rather than of the Caribbean area, where North, South, and Central America and the West Indies meet. It is fitting that the yellow fever potential of the Caribbean area, previously the most important stronghold of yellow fever, be considered in the light of present-day knowledge of this great historical scourge of the American tropics.

I

Yellow fever is a very modern disease, the first recognizable description of which dates back only three hundred years to the Yucatan Peninsula in 1648. Apparently many other places in the Caribbean, including Barbados, St. Kitts, Guadaloupe, and Havana, were infected about the same time. Just twenty years later, in 1668, yellow fever appeared for the first of many visits in the

13

port of New York. This was sixteen years before its first recorded visit to Brazil in 1684.

From the middle of the seventeenth until the early years of the present century, the history of yellow fever is very closely linked to the history of the Caribbean area. So important was yellow fever as a handicap to European exploitation of the Caribbean, especially through the destruction of newly arrived European troops, that it came to be called, in many places, *La fiebre patriótica* or "The Patriotic Fever." It is easy to imagine that, had the Finlay theory of the transmission of yellow fever by the *Aëdes aegypti* mosquito been accepted when first proposed in 1881, Cuba might well be a Spanish colony and the Panama Canal a French possession.

Besides being the site of the first reported outbreak of yellow fever, the Caribbean area was the great stronghold of the disease from which summer excursions to the United States and Europe originated during two and a half centuries and was the scene of the dramatic events leading to the first successful measures for the control of yellow fever.

It was in Havana that the theory of mosquito transmission was developed by Finlay in 1881, convincingly demonstrated by Reed in 1900, and put into operation by Gorgas in 1901. The Havana anti-mosquito campaign convinced the epidemiologists, and another Caribbean campaign, that in Panama, made possible the digging of the Canal and convinced the world in general that yellow fever could be conquered through mosquito-control measures in urban centers. This conviction lasted for thirty years, during which yellow fever was known as an epidemiologically simple, urban, and maritime disease, transmitted from man to man by the *Aëdes aegypti* mosquito which, in the Americas, is found breeding only in artificial water-containers, in and about human habitations.

All are familiar with the stories of Gorgas in Havana and Panama, Oswaldo Cruz in Rio de Janeiro, Liceaga in Mexico, White in New Orleans and others, who, armed with the secret of the mosquito transmission of yellow fever, performed miracles in the broad light of day and became the prophets and saints of the public health movement overnight.

Anti-mosquito campaigns in the important centers of yellow fever endemicity were followed by the disappearance of the disease not only from these centers, but also from large tributary regions.

By 1915 only a few recognized endemic centers of yellow fever remained in the Americas, including Guayaquil on the West Coast and Bahia and Pernambuco on the East Coast of South America. The then recently organized Rockefeller Foundation embarked on a program of collaboration with the governments of the countries in which yellow fever still might be found, in an attempt to eradicate the disease completely from the Western Hemisphere. Campaigns in the Central American countries, in Mexico, in Ecuador, in Peru, and in Colombia were completely successful and, by 1925, yellow fever was apparently limited, in the Americas, to a small coastal area of Northeast Brazil, where promising results were being reported. This attempt to eradicate yellow fever from the Americas was based on the belief that yellow fever was limited to man and on the observation that it could be eradicated from all infected cities by the single measure of reduction of *aegypti* breeding, following which the disease would not long remain in the smaller towns and villages.

II

Following the initial observation of yellow fever in the Valle de Canaan, Brazil, in 1932 as a rural disease occurring in the absence of the *Aëdes aegypti* mosquito, the true picture of yellow fever as basically a disease of animals (monkeys and marsupials), transmitted in the tropical and subtropical forests of the Americas by mosquitoes other than *aegypti*, and involving human infection only secondarily, has been filled in. Outbreaks of this so-called jungle yellow fever, which has been shown to be a source of virus for the re-infection of previous yellow fever centers and hence a permanent obstacle to the eradication of yellow fever as planned by the Rockefeller Foundation, have been observed in all of the countries of South America, except Chile and Uruguay, and in Panama and Costa Rica.

Blood tests on monkeys shot in Mexico early this year have shown that jungle yellow fever has been in the forests of Mexico during the lifetime of the animals tested. There is every reason to assume that jungle yellow fever occurs in all the countries of Central America except, possibly, El Salvador, where deforestation is well advanced.

It is noteworthy that *aegypti*-transmitted yellow fever has not been reported from any of the cities of the Caribbean since 1937, when a few cases occurred at Buena Vista, a small town on the Magdalena River in Colombia. Likewise, no jungle yellow fever has been found in the West Indies, although one of the early references to the possibility of monkeys having a part in the life history of yellow fever, published in 1914, referred to illness among monkeys in the forests of Trinidad during epidemics of yellow fever. It is believed that this freedom of the island zones from jungle yellow fever is due to the fact that the monkey population of the islands has been liquidated and that suitable conditions for it no longer exist in the remaining forests.

A line can be drawn, then, from between Yucatan and Cuba, south and east to a point just north of Trinidad, dividing the Caribbean into mainland and island zones. The mainland zone has the double threat of jungle yellow fever, as an important disease for forest inhabitants and laborers, and as a source of virus for the re-infection of such cities and towns as remain infested by the *Aëdes aegypti* mosquito.

The island zone is apparently subject to the threat of *aegypti*-transmitted yellow fever only if, and when, the yellow fever virus may be re-introduced from the mainland. The potential threat of the movement of yellow fever virus from forest to urban areas grows with the increased rapidity and facility of passenger traffic. However, the threat of urban yellow fever, originating from jungle yellow fever, is greatest at those urban centers infested with *aegypti* most closely in contact with infected jungle districts. If these exposed danger points are kept clean of the *aegypti* mosquito, there is very little opportunity for the disease to jump long distances.

The unrecognized introduction of yellow fever into urban communities from nearby jungle districts is the most probable mechanism by which persons preparing to travel to other countries might be infected close to the date of departure. This danger disappears with the eradication of the *Aëdes aegypti* mosquito.

III

Fortunately, about the time that jungle yellow fever was being demonstrated as a permanent source of yellow fever virus for the re-infection of urban areas, methods for the complete eradication of *Aëdes aegypti* were being developed in Brazil. Once the larger cities of Brazil were cleared of *aegypti,* it was found more economical to eradicate this mosquito from the suburbs and from the interior towns, and even rural areas, than it was to attempt to maintain *aegypti*-control services in the larger cities. Eradication of *aegypti* has proven to be an ever expanding program and, since 1947, when Brazil proposed its eradication as a continental program, the Pan American Sanitary Bureau has been dedicated, under a mandate from its Directing Council, to collaboration with the governments of the Americas in the eradication of *Aëdes aegypti* from North, Central, and South America and the West Indies. The eradication of *aegypti* will eliminate all possibility of surprise returns of yellow fever to old endemic centers of infection, such as occurred in Rio de Janeiro in 1928. Although it is impossible to eradicate the yellow fever virus from the Americas as was planned by the Rockefeller Foundation, it is possible to eradicate completely the urban vector and remove all threat of all but jungle yellow fever.

The program for the eradication of *aegypti* is well advanced in South and Central America and Mexico and has begun in some of the West Indies. It is of the highest importance, for the comfort as well as for the safety of the Caribbean, that the *Aëdes aegypti* mosquito be eradicated, not only from both the mainland and island zones of the Caribbean, but also from the United States and the rest of the Americas, thus eliminating possible sources of re-infestation in the Western Hemisphere.

José Guzmán Baldivieso: HEALTH PROBLEMS
IN VENEZUELA AND BOLIVIA:
A STUDY IN CONTRASTS

I AM FORTUNATE, honored, and proud to be seated at the same round table of this Second Annual Conference on the Caribbean with such great and distinguished gentlemen as my good friend Dr. Fred L. Soper, director of the Pan American Sanitary Bureau, and General Mark D. Hollis, Assistant Surgeon General of the United States of America.

I have a special greeting for Dr. Soper from Bolivia. Dr. Valentín Gómez, Secretary of Health of the Republic of Bolivia, in the name of the whole country and in his own name, sent me a cablegram of salutation on this first day of the Caribbean Conference.

About a year ago, from Dr. Soper's home town in Kansas, I, too, sent him greetings in my capacity as an Honorary Bolivian Consul to that state. You probably wonder just what an "Honorary" Bolivian Consul does in Kansas. In Bolivia we have two methods of disposing of political enemies: the "quick method"—hanging them from a lamp post, and the "slow method"—naming them Honorary Consul to some remote place like Kansas!

I have also, in a small way, something in common with you, Dr. Hollis. I was Assistant Surgeon General of Bolivia during and after the crucial years of the Chaco War.

18

I

For the next few minutes I should like to inform you from my own experience and studies about some contrasts in the health problems of Venezuela and Bolivia.

Some of you, perhaps, would remark that Bolivia is too far away and too high up from *el precioso Caribe*. I am sure, however, that the things I shall say may suffice to prove what I sincerely believe. I envy countries close to yours because of the great benefits they have received and continue to receive. I wish that my country could have been closer geographically to yours!

I am convinced that even though this conference is regional, a comparison of the great country of Bolívar and *la hija predilecta de Bolívar* is entirely appropriate here. I shall not enter, at this time, into detail to prove the geographical similarities of the two countries. A rapid glance at the map will be sufficient evidence that Venezuela and Bolivia have been endowed with the most beautiful *montañas y llanos*. Authorities like Dr. Soper will agree that many of our health problems are similar, especially if we are to consider definite problems, such as control of tuberculosis or of malaria.

The Orinoco *llanos* have their parallel in my country with the *llanos* of Santa Cruz, Beni, and Pando.

As far as climate is concerned we find striking similarities. Even the fabulous stories of *El Dorado* in Venezuela have a parallel with the not too well-known stories of the *paraíso terrenal* near Sorata and not too far away from the city of La Paz.

In both Venezuela and Bolivia nature and the Indian inhabitants of the regions have proved stronger than many white people eager for adventures, and even today great sections of the Orinoco in Venezuela and parts of the *hoya del Amazonas* remain uncharted and unknown.

As far as the flora and fauna are concerned, Bolivia and Venezuela could have been twin daughters of Bolívar: roses, orchids, gardenias, jasmine, and all the beauties of this world grow wild there.

Both countries have rich storehouses of the most precious types of woods. Both grow coffee, cacao, corn, tobacco, and cotton—and they both have plenty of oil!

Both are rich in animal life—in fact there are a great number of animals not even known to the zoology department of the University of Florida. I would like to volunteer to go to *Green Hell* in order to prove this assertion!

II

I have mentioned the geographical similarities of the two countries because they are so important if one considers their sanitary problems. However, there is one great difference: Venezuela has a "bank roll"; Bolivia, is "broke." And since money is the basis of health, it is impossible not to mention it. Later, we shall see what I mean. There has been, and still is, one strong ray of hope: the health and sanitary program of the Inter-American Institute which today benefits one of every six Latin Americans.

Someone has said that there are two very important dates to be remembered in North American history: 1942 and 1492. No more true statement could be made if one is referring to health and sanitation. Of course, we all know what happened in 1492. But a great majority of North Americans do not know what happened in 1942—that was when the North Americans discovered the Latin Americans at the Rio Conference.

The greatest of all programs, so far as I am concerned, prior to the Point Four Program was the health and sanitation program of the Institute of Inter-American Affairs. This was set up to save and protect the greatest of all values—human values—so disregarded today. It was in the year 1942 that the United States government, through the Institute of Inter-American Affairs, established the health and sanitation program which has been carried on in Bolivia, Brazil, Chile, Colombia, Costa Rica, the Dominican Republic, Honduras, Mexico, Nicaragua, Panama, Paraguay, Peru, Uruguay, and Venezuela. This program has aided twenty-three million Latin Americans to this year of 1951.

Venezuela has achieved a great deal. As far as the United States is concerned, the help to Venezuela has been halted. But Venezuela marches on with gigantic steps! Bolivia, however, still is in need of assistance.

Under this program, "controls have been extended over disease by extending controls over the environment." It has been said that "this is a program fundamentally to help people help themselves, to give them a hand along the road of health and economic development."

Figures are eloquent. Let us consider some of them. The budget for the Department of Health of Venezuela during the period 1946-47 was 55,295,773 Bolivares. During 1947-48 it was 86,403,092 Bolivares—an increase of 31,000,000 Bolivares. At the end of last year the increase was approximately 50,000,000 Bolivares over the previous budgetary period. When a government like that of Venezuela gives such an emphasis to *la inversión en la defensa de nuestro capital humano y en assistencia médica de manera planificada y eficiente,* we must agree that it is a great work. The Venezuelan government, of course, still has an important problem to face in the problem of nutrition of its masses. This no doubt will be solved in not too distant a day.

I know Bolivia's story well, especially before 1942, when Dr. Abelardo Ibáñez Benavente, the Surgeon General, and I organized a program on a scientific basis for the purpose of fighting malaria and tuberculosis. Dr. José Tejada Sórzano, President of the Republic, and Dr. Enrique Baldivieso, Minister of Defense (even though they understood the gravity of the problem), could not give more than $10,000—a "drop in the bucket"—for this purpose.

However, the Bolivian health and sanitation program has done wonders in the last few years, especially in industrial sanitation and in work with the health problems of the tin miners. There is still considerable room for improvement, especially concerning the budgets for hospitals, preparation of personnel, and sanitation of the many Indian villages; and even La Paz, as Dr. Soper will agree, could stand *más sanidad.*

This paper could be quite extensive if we attempted a parallel of each *servicio de la sanidad.* In such a short time I could not hope to cover all of them. However, I shall mention a few more which I consider important.

Since I was one of the founders of the only school for nurses in the city of La Paz, I am very much interested in this program. We need more schools for nurses in other sections of the country. Venezuela has ten times more trained nurses than Bolivia. In comparing the two countries further, I find another situation which could be remedied. While at La Paz the selection of doctors, sanitary engineers, nurses, and other health workers is still a political matter, in Venezuela the individuals are selected on the basis of their own merits. The budget for national hospitals alone in Venezuela is over 50,000,000 Bolivares. The largest hospital at the city of La Paz has less than twenty American cents per day per patient!

The greatest difference I find is between the attitude of the Venezuelan and Bolivian people toward their health services. Ingeniero Cristóbal Morales, now a guest of this University under the Point Four Program, remarks with great pride that the health situation today in Venezuela is "very good." He has also given me the latest data as to the birth rate and mortality rate during the last six months of 1951. Bolivia still has the second highest infant mortality on the continent.

III

I believe that the great ideals of Christianity and democracy are not achieved overnight. I believe that they too have stages of development. The first stage is the castor-oil stage. Some countries take to Christianity and democracy like one who takes castor oil—only when it is needed. The second stage is the breakfast-food stage. One takes wheaties, corn flakes, rice flakes, and all the other flakes which taste like cardboard or Celotex, but which are easy to swallow if mixed with cream, strawberries, or peaches! The third stage is the ice-cream stage: the more you have, the more you want. Only your country, my North American friends, has achieved this last stage, while mine, I hope, has passed the first stage!

I cannot finish without pointing out what one of the leaders of the Point Four Program has said: "Happy people are healthy people. I cannot see much prospect for peace and prosperity in a people racked with malaria, plagued by flies, besieged with lice, ticks, mites and fleas!"

I am glad that I have been able to point out to you two different patients. One is well on her way to recovery—Venezuela; another is still a *pueblo enfermo* that even yet needs the care and help of her kind relatives, as well as of her own will power, to get well.

First as a Bolivian, then as a Latin American, and, above all, as another *Americano Ciento por Ciento*, I want to say to you what is said in Matthew 10:7 and 8:

> *The kingdom of heaven is at hand.*
> *Heal the sick, cleanse the lepers,*
> *raise the dead,*
> *cast out devils:*
> *freely ye have received,*
> *freely give.*

Part II

LAND

James G. Maddox:[1] THE MAJOR LAND
UTILIZATION PROBLEMS OF THE CARIBBEAN AREA

THE PURPOSE of this paper is to suggest the main objectives toward which land utilization policies in the Caribbean countries should move. At the same time, some of the obvious techniques for achieving these objectives are discussed. The emphasis is on clearing a few main trails through the jungle, and not on making a careful survey of the whole complex terrain. All of the suggested lines of approach need much more study and discussion before they can become safe guides to action in particular countries. However, a definite attempt is made to put forth the main issues in a simple, straightforward manner, and to maintain a focus on these issues, without reference to the problem of political expediency which is always a component of policy-making.

I

The general nature of the problem can be stated in very simple terms: *How can the land in the Caribbean countries be most wisely used in order to raise the level of living of the people?* In other words, the center of emphasis is on improving levels of living.

[1] The views expressed in this paper are those of the author, and should not be construed as official statements of the American International Association.

Robert C. Cauthorn, Assistant Program Analyst in the New York office of the Association, has been extremely helpful in assembling statistical material and library references used in the preparation of the article, as well as in giving useful criticisms and suggestions respecting the presentation.

27

Our examinations of land-use practices, problems, and policies is for the purpose of finding ways and means by which this can be done.

The basic idea behind the shorthand symbol "level of living" is, like Gaul, divided into three parts:

First, it includes a series of material things, such as food, clothing, houses, furniture, roads, hospitals, schoolhouses, automobiles, and a million-and-one gadgets which people utilize in the process of living.

Second, it includes a group of non-material things, such as the services of doctors, lawyers, teachers, writers, musicians, and artists, which are services that people also make use of in the process of living, and which, therefore, have to be constantly replaced just as do the material things such as food and clothing.

Third, it includes a series of psychological attitudes and emotional feelings which are exemplified by the degree of security, the freedom from fear, and the individual liberty which people enjoy.

This third category of items presents some extremely thorny problems of analysis. For the most part, this paper centers attention on the first two groups—those goods and services which are utilized in the day-to-day processes of living.

The amount of these goods and services available for consumption in any given country is dependent upon three things: (1) the total amount of goods and services produced; (2) the way in which they are distributed among the people; and (3) the division of the total output between current consumption items, on the one hand, and items that will be used for purposes of future production, on the other. If, for example, country A produces twice as much per capita in any given year as does country B, and distributes this production equally as widely among its people, and does not use any greater amount of it for building new production facilities, which can only turn out goods or services in future years, then each inhabitant of country A will have twice as many goods and services to consume during the year as will each inhabitant of country B. In other words, two of the three important components of the level of living in country A will, for the year under consideration, be twice as high as in country B.

II

The countries touching on the Caribbean are notoriously low producers. Moreover, their economies operate in such a way that a relatively large proportion of what is produced flows to a few people in the upper-income groups. Although reliable data are scarce, it is probable that the proportion of current output which is used for future production facilities is not an important factor in explaining the existing low levels of consumption.

Even though the maldistribution of income is serious, it is fairly clear that the big and important explanation for the low levels of living in the Caribbean area is the low production per man. An index of this low productivity is given by the national incomes of these countries. National income is the total of all income payments for productive services, including wages, salaries, profits, rent, and interest. It is, therefore, closely equivalent to the total value of all the goods and services produced in the country. If the national incomes of countries such as El Salvador, Haiti, the Dominican Republic, Honduras, Nicaragua, and Guatemala were divided equally among all the people in these countries, the amount would be below $100 per person.[2] Indeed, not a single country touching on the Caribbean has an average per capita income one-half as high as the state of Mississippi, which usually ranks at the bottom of the list among the United States.[3] Thus, regardless of how the total pie is cut, it simply is not big enough to provide all the people with a decent level of living.

Therefore, a major element of our problem is clear: What can be done, in the way of changes in land use, to raise the per capita productivity of the Caribbean countries? It is important to realize that the focus is on raising the output of the whole economy—not just the output of the land or of the agricultural industry. We are interested in changing land utilization practices in each country so as to increase the total production of all goods

[2] Statistical Office of the United Nations, *National and Per Capita Incomes of Seventy Countries in 1949* (New York, October, 1950), Series E, No. 1, p. 28.

[3] The per capita income in the state of Mississippi for 1948 was $758. United States Bureau of the Census, *Statistical Abstract of the United States: 1950* (Washington, 1950), p. 266.

and services in that country. What are the general directions in which to proceed?

This is the basic question, and it forces us to recognize that there are significant differences in the relative proportions of productive resources among the Caribbean countries. Consequently, we cannot write one prescription to fit the needs of all the patients. Yet, without losing sight of the forest by getting lost among the trees, we can classify the Caribbean countries into three roughly similar groups and get a reasonably good answer to our question.

Countries of High Population Pressure.—For example, in the British West Indies, the French West Indies, El Salvador, Puerto Rico, Haiti, and the Virgin Islands, we have a group of countries in which the main problem is compounded of four factors. First, there is an unusually heavy population in relation to natural resources. Second, a very high proportion of the total population is engaged in agriculture. Third, the amount of land and capital equipment employed by the average farm family is small and of dubious quality. Fourth, the population is increasing rapidly. This adds up to a situation of extreme poverty for the great majority of the people, with little prospect for fundamental improvement until there can be basic adjustments in the relative proportions of land, labor, and capital used in production. Their economies are too heavily dependent on agriculture, and too much labor is used per acre of land operated.

In this group of countries there are from 150 to 650 persons per square mile, and in some of the individual islands the number is more than 1,000. This compares with about 50 persons per square mile in the United States, with 192 in France, 531 in the highly industrialized United Kingdom, and approximately 285 per square mile in India.[4] The latter is often thought of as the world's prime example of an overpopulated country, but several of the Caribbean countries have a higher density per square mile. Populations of this density can, of course, be supported at reasonably adequate levels of living in a highly industrialized setting, such as Belgium, Great Britain, or the northeastern part of the United States. In a country like Holland, with a highly rationalized

---

[4] United Nations, *Statistical Yearbook, 1949-50.* Figures have been converted at 2.59 km² per square mile, and rounded to nearest whole number.

agriculture producing specialty crops for sale to nearby urban areas, and with heavy flows of income from shipping, insurance, banking, and overseas investments, a population of over 700 per square mile has been maintained at a relatively high level of living. But all these things are lacking in this group of Caribbean countries. Industry is extremely meager, and income from foreign commerce and investments is practically nil. From 60 to 80 per cent of the people in these countries are occupied in agriculture.[5] Moreover, a large proportion of the land is mountainous and unsuited to farming. Such crops as are produced are of low value per unit, and are highly competitive with those of other countries in world markets. One man handles very little land, and his capital equipment is often not much more than a hoe, a machete, and a spade. This results in extremely low production per man, and an equally low level of living.

As an example, let us compare a West Indian laborer on a sugar plantation with a Mississippi sharecropper on a cotton plantation. The latter will cultivate ten to twelve acres of land, using mules and walking plows, on which he will produce six to eight bales of cotton, which, with the accompanying seed, will have a gross value of $1,000 to $1,500 in recent years. The former will handle two to three acres of sugar cane, which will produce six to nine tons and have a gross value of $500 to $800. Thus, the West Indian sugar worker produces about one-half as much as the Mississippi sharecropper, who is just about at the lower end of the productivity scale among workers in the United States. The fundamental reason for this is not differences in the productivity of the land, but in the number of acres handled per man. Indeed, it would be difficult to find land which produces in field crops *a greater value of product per acre* than good Caribbean sugar land.

The situation is essentially the same if we look at the small

[5] Estimates of these percentages for the countries concerned in this study range from about 40 per cent in Cuba to over 90 per cent in Guatemala, with the modal figure for the distribution probably close to 70 per cent. These high concentrations in agricultural populations contrast sharply with those in the United States and Europe, where the percentages averaged 19 per cent and 33 per cent, respectively, for the period 1939-1948. Food and Agricultural Organization of the United Nations, *Yearbook of Food and Agricultural Statistics* (Washington, 1950), Vol. IV, Part I, pp. 15 and 16.

peasant farmer. In these highly overpopulated countries, the thousands of small, more or less independent, farmers rarely operate more than two or three acres of land per family. Even if they are up in the hills producing coffee or fruit, and have fifteen to twenty acres, the value of their total output is often, if not usually, less than the value of the output of two or three acres of good level land.

It is absolutely fruitless to talk about ways and means of significantly increasing productivity, hence levels of living, in this group of countries without facing up to the necessity of transferring large numbers of people out of agriculture. Except for the small numbers of vegetable, poultry, and flower growers around the cities, no man—weak or strong, educated or illiterate—can make a decent living for his family from two to three acres of land. He simply has to be able to cultivate more acres, and this means that a large proportion of the present farm people, and their ever increasing progeny, must find employment outside the area or in non-farm occupations.

In general, I believe it means that a heroic effort must be made to bring industries to these countries. Some progress can perhaps be made in encouraging a greater use of the sea, both as a source of food and as a basis for a shipping industry. Moreover, there are some possibilities for out-migration, both to other Caribbean countries and to the United States. Although we run into the problem of immigration quotas and racial discrimination as impediments to out-migration, something might be accomplished toward loosening these barriers. Moreover, I am not unmindful of the fact that there is still unused land in most of these countries that can be brought into cultivation. The amount is probably smaller than is sometimes suggested, but every reasonable effort should be made to bring new land into cultivation, by clearing, draining, and irrigating areas that are adapted to farming.

Last, but by no means least, there are substantial opportunities for increasing the output of many of the acres now being cultivated. This is especially true of the lands outside the large plantations— the farms, in other words, of the small owner and tenant. Substantial gains along this line can be brought about through a more widespread use of modern insecticides and fungicides; through the use of organic compost and chemical fertilizers; through the development of higher yielding strains and varieties of plants; and through more timely planting and cultivating practices. There is ample opportunity for the modern-minded agricultural scientist to have a great and constructive influence in increasing production per acre. In a later section of this paper, the methods and organizational patterns which appear to be suited to this task are discussed.

Nevertheless, even with all these things—greater use of the sea, out-migration, cultivation of presently unused lands, and higher yields per acre from land now being cultivated—there will still be a surplus of people in agriculture in this group of countries. No real rationalization of land use can come about until families are able to operate substantially larger acreages than at present. I repeat, therefore, that the main direction in which to proceed is toward industrialization, thus drawing the rapidly increasing population out of agriculture.

The techniques by which to achieve the needed industrialization are beyond the scope of a paper which is concerned primarily with problems of land utilization. However, I believe that it must be an industrialization: (1) which is based on a cheap labor supply; (2) which finds both its principal raw materials and its main markets outside the area; and (3) which obtains most of its capital and managerial talent, during the first generation, at least, from the presently industrialized countries of the world.

Countries of Low Population Pressure.—Fortunately, only a few countries in the Caribbean region present such tough problems as those we have just been discussing. At the other extreme of population density, for example, we have such countries as Venezuela, Colombia, Honduras, Nicaragua, British Honduras, and Guatemala. In this group of countries, the population per square mile is relatively low—below twenty-five persons except in the latter two. There is, of course, much land in these countries that is not suitable for agriculture. Nevertheless, each has large areas of good undeveloped land. Taken as a group, these five countries represent "the great frontier" for future agricultural development in the Caribbean region.

Neither the extent, the quality, nor the economic potentialities of the untapped agricultural resources of these countries have been carefully evaluated. Nevertheless, all indications point toward

the conclusion that they are quite substantial. Moreover, in view
of prospective demands for agricultural and forest products in the
United States and Western Europe during the decades ahead,
together with the rapidly increasing population, urbanization, and
general economic development of Latin America which is already
underway, there are good reasons to believe that a properly
balanced program of public and private investment in the undeveloped resources of these countries would be both profitable and
socially desirable.

What then is the main direction in which land policy should aim
in order to increase national productivity, and, hence, levels of
living in this group of countries? In general, steps should be taken
toward opening up new lands for production, thus making possible
an increase in the amount of land operated by great numbers of
farm families. This, of course, implies an increase in working
capital and improvements in managerial skill on the part of
thousands of farmers so that they can effectively and efficiently
operate more acres per man.

In these countries, in contrast to the group with high population
densities, there is no need to draw people away from farming in
order to increase the cultivated land per family, because there is
good, unused land available. Moreover, they are primarily agricultural countries, both by tradition and by the pattern of their
resource base. Some modest industrialization is, no doubt, in order
for practically all of them. However, it is certainly not necessary
for any of them to have a rapid growth of industry, built on low
wages and imported raw materials, and depending on foreign
markets in which to sell their industrial products, as has been
suggested for the first group of countries. They can raise their
levels of living very significantly by making use of their greatest
natural resource—undeveloped agricultural land.

In the opening up of new land, there are, at least, two types of
problems within each of these countries to which serious attention
should be given immediately. First, practically all of them have
one or more areas that are heavily overpopulated. In other words,
there is a serious geographic maldistribution of population. Generally, this takes the form of all or a part of the highland areas being
seriously overcrowded, while lower-land areas, many of which are
potentially very productive, go unused. The pattern of land use

in many of the highland areas has essentially the same characteristics as that in the overpopulated countries discussed earlier. The farms are small, often consisting of not more than three or four acres. The land is usually badly eroded. The methods of land preparation and tillage are primitive, sometimes involving the use of nothing more than a hoe, a stick, and a machete. Farms of this nature are, of course, very unproductive.

The second type of problem needing immediate attention is that brought about by the semi-nomadic squatter—a small farmer who has neither ownership nor leasehold rights to the land he cultivates. He customarily "moves in" on any land available in his general area; clears two or three acres with a machete and fire; cultivates the new clearing for two or three years, and moves on to a new patch which he treats the same way. With this kind of farming, there is not only a wanton destruction of the soil and the vegetative cover which protects it from erosion, but also an extremely low output per man.

In view of these two problems, which appear to be of major, though of varying, importance in all these countries, there is a need for programs to develop new land areas in such locations and by such methods as to: (1) bring about the resettlement of many small farmers from the overcrowded highlands; and (2) decrease the number of the constantly shifting squatters by providing them with economic units to which they have stable tenure rights and facilities for efficient production. As the land development activities become effective in drawing families out of the overcrowded highlands, there will be the need for programs to consolidate the vacated holdings into the farms of those families who remain behind. In some instances, reforestation, instead of consolidation into larger farms, may be in order. The essential point is that the draining away of families from the overpopulated highlands should not only be a means by which the productivity of those who move would be increased, but should also result in those who do not move having increased resources at their command.

To design and carry through a sound land development and resettlement program of this general character is no easy matter. Yet, it is much simpler and requires less capital than the industrialization necessary in the overpopulated countries. Two of the most important steps are: (1) to free the areas selected for settlement from diseases, such as malaria and jungle yellow fever; and (2) to construct roads through them. In addition, however, there will be the need for some publicly-financed land clearing; for machinery pools so that new settlers will not be held to a hoe and machete scale of operations; and for credit and technical guidance for the farmers moving into the new areas.

The Latin American penchant for doing things in a big and dramatic way may have the tendency of making land development projects very expensive and complicated. It is to be hoped, however, that this tendency can be guarded against. A large number of relatively crude new settlements, provided the families have economic units and adequate capital and guidance, are much more important to the welfare of these countries than a small number of swanky ones. These countries do not have the resources, either technical or financial, to warrant heavy public investments in expensive new dwellings, fences, subsidiary roads, and community buildings during the early stages of land development. Many of these facilities can come later out of the efforts of the settlers. A certain amount of crudeness is to be expected in a developing frontier area. Indeed, there are situations in which it may be highly desirable. If, for instance, the developmental work has to be paid for from credit expansion or new currency issues, there should be a quick and voluminous flow of new farm products to market to offset the inflationary pressure arising from the land clearing and construction operations.

In establishing new land settlement areas, it will be extremely important to create units of such size that they will allow efficient operations, without at the same time turning them into a new group of haciendas to be worked by peon labor. This problem is not going to be easy to solve. Most of the settlers will be inclined to stick to their hoe and machete, unless they are given an adequate line of credit together with technical guidance and supervision. In this connection, it should be remembered that the ox and the mule still have a place in providing power for farming, even if most farmers in the highly developed countries are turning rapidly to tractors. The possibility of farm machinery centers, either privately or publicly operated, to do the heavy land clearing and preparatory work, while family-owned oxen or mules are used for planting, cultivating, and harvesting will probably provide an efficient source of farm power in a large percentage of the cases.

In having focused attention on land development, including resettlement, as being the main direction which land policy should take in these "low pressure" countries of the Caribbean region, I do not want to overlook the obvious fact that there are many opportunities for increasing the productivity of the land now in farms. Some of this land which is well suited for crop production is being held in large estates for cattle grazing. The recent International Bank Mission to Colombia made quite a point of this fact, and recommended a special tax aimed at forcing such land into more intensive use.[6] Although the recommendation was not received with high favor in some circles in Colombia, it nevertheless has some strong points to its credit. There may be more palatable ways by which the same end can be accomplished. Certainly, all governments should weigh carefully the costs of buying developed but unused lands for subdivision and resettlement purposes against the costs of clearing and developing new areas before choosing the latter course.

In addition to the cleared land which is being extensively used and which could be brought into cultivation, there is, of course, the real possibility of increasing the per acre output of land now being cultivated. The primitive, backward farm practices that are being followed in most of these countries offer a real and important challenge to all efforts to increase output per farm. Outside of the densely populated highland areas of these countries, there is usually the opportunity of increasing the scale of operations of many farmers, in addition to teaching them practices which will make their present acres more productive. In other words, while attention may be centered mainly on such practices as spraying and dusting to kill diseases and parasites, the introduction of higher producing varieties, the use of fertilizers, and better tillage practices, there is often also the possibility of adding a few nearby acres to many of the existing small farms, or of improving the present pasture area and adding one or two new animal units to the farm enterprises.

[6] International Bank for Reconstruction and Development, *The Basis of a Development Program for Colombia* (Washington, 1950), pp. 383-387.

Countries of Medium Population Pressure.—Up to this point I have discussed the general directions which land policy should take in two extreme groups of Caribbean countries. One group is characterized by heavy population pressure on the land; the other group by a paucity of population and relatively large areas of undeveloped land suitable for agriculture.

There is a third group which is between these two extremes, including Costa Rica, Cuba, Mexico, Panama, and the Dominican Republic. Each deserves separate treatment, but space does not permit it. Most of them do not have vast areas of undeveloped land. Yet, neither do they have the extreme population pressure of the first group. Their economies usually turn out a higher national product per capita than other Caribbean countries, except oil-rich Venezuela. In general, they are more industrialized and have a more efficient agriculture than their neighbors, though this is not true in every case. Panama, of course, has a substantial income stimulator in the canal, though neither its industry nor its agriculture is well developed.

In order to raise productivity per person in these countries, which, like the whole Caribbean area, have rapidly increasing populations, the general directions of their land utilization policies should combine in modest degree the principal elements suggested for both the other groups. In other words, increased industrialization is called for, along with land development and resettlement, and intensification of production on land already in cultivation.

Generally speaking, more emphasis should be placed on industrialization in this group of countries than in those with lower population pressure, but less than in the heavily overpopulated group. Moreover, there is more of a possibility of their industry using locally produced raw materials. With the possible exception of Mexico, where a large proportion of the total land is too dry for crop farming, there appear to be substantial areas of reasonably good land awaiting roads and the elimination of disease. In Mexico, there are still opportunities for increasing the acreage of land being irrigated. However, there are hundreds of thousands of rural families living in such thickly settled clusters in many Mexican highland areas that a substantial proportion of them must move into non-farm employments before there can be any significant improvement in land-use practices.

In this group of countries, as in the others previously discussed, there are substantial opportunities for increasing the per acre output of land now being farmed. Here, as in the other cases, the primary emphasis must be on getting farmers to use fungicides, pesticides, fertilizers, improved varieties of plants and animals, and to be more timely in their planting, cultivating, and harvesting practices. To the extent that local conditions permit, the number of acres handled by one man needs to be increased while, at the same time, he is increasing the output of the acres that he is already using.

III

In the preceding pages primary emphasis has been placed on the general objectives toward which land-utilization policies should aim in the Caribbean area in order to raise the total output of the countries involved. In one group of countries, those with extremely heavy population pressure and a large percentage of their people engaged in agriculture, it has been argued that great emphasis must be placed on industrialization. In another group, those with low densities of population, the development of new land and the resettlement of families from overcrowded areas has been suggested as the most urgent approach. In all the countries, however, it has been recognized that there are substantial opportunities for increasing the output per unit area of land now being farmed.[7] Enough has been said of the two latter objectives to indicate that the techniques for achieving them must reach a large number of backward, semi-illiterate farmers with a whole new set of ideas that can, and will, be put into practice on their individual farms.

What are these techniques, and how can they be brought to bear on the problems at hand? This is an extremely important aspect of the total policy problem under discussion, but only a few major points can be made in this paper.

---

[7] In many cases an approach which would put primary emphasis on obtaining greater output per acre among the thousands of small farmers in these countries would also have the opportunity of increasing the size of the farms of some of the more progressive-minded operators. This would be the case in all areas where overcrowding is not severe, or even in these areas if there were an out-migration to non-farm jobs.

It is well to recall that a successful approach along these lines will be aimed at getting thousands of farmers in each country to follow such practices as: (1) preventing crop losses by using a whole array of relatively new fungicides and pesticides; (2) increasing yields by using both organic compost and chemical fertilizers, if the latter are obtainable at prices that are not prohibitive; (3) planting improved varieties of crops and using high-producing sires to improve their livestock; (4) rotating their crops, terracing their rolling fields, and plowing, planting, and cultivating at the proper time and in the proper manner. To the extent that the size of farms can be increased, either by resettlement or otherwise, their operators will have a whole new set of management problems to which they have not been accustomed.

The very first problem that will be met with is the lack of the needed materials, and the paucity of proved answers to many of the practical questions involved. Supplies of the proper pesticides, fungicides, fertilizers, improved seeds, and well-bred sires are not available in thousands upon thousands of rural communities in the Caribbean area. There are too few experiment stations with results indicating the best times for planting and the most economic methods of preparing, planting, and cultivating the various crops in the different agricultural areas.

But even if these problems can in some way be slowly and haltingly solved, there remains the basic task of getting farmers to adopt new practices, and to use a part of their meager and hard-earned cash for the needed materials. Too often this is visualized as a problem to be tackled exclusively by the orthodox methods of agricultural extension education that have proved successful in the United States. But this, I believe, is not enough. Extension methods in this country have always been most successful with an upper-level group of educated farmers. It was not until the general educational status of farm people in this country reached a rather high level, and a generation of farm boys and girls grew to maturity under the tutelage of county agents and vocational agricultural teachers, that extension service methods began to show striking results. In the Caribbean countries, as in most other underdeveloped areas, the type of farmer that has been most responsive to agricultural extension methods in the United States simply does not exist.

To be successful in raising the output of extremely low-income, illiterate, small farmers, many of whom are part-time day laborers, sharecroppers, tenants, and squatters, there are, at least, three ingredients that must be integrated into one program and applied to the needs of individual farm families. They are: (1) education, (2) credit, and (3) security of tenure. Extension methods in the United States have rarely been individualized to meet the needs of particular farm families. Even more rarely have they tackled the problems of credit and tenure.

It is difficult to overstress the importance of combining credit with education. A little additional capital on many farms in these countries, if it is properly used, oftentimes makes a very big difference in farm output. Moreover, simply to be able to demonstrate new practices to the great bulk of the farmers in these countries, without being able to offer them loans by which they can obtain the supplies and equipment through which they can put the demonstrated practices into effect, is a distressingly difficult way to achieve results. Their incomes are so low and their living needs so urgent that only the most thrifty will accumulate enough in advance to buy the capital items that they need. Yet, a small loan to buy a few pounds of insecticides and a hand sprayer, or a few hundred pounds of fertilizer, or in some cases a relatively small quantity of improved seed, will often increase farm output by an amount two or three times as great as the loan. Funds for purchasing a team of oxen and two or three plows, or to add three or four cows to the farm business, can produce a big percentage increase in the scale of operations.

Credit used in this constructive manner is dependent, however, on sound judgments by farm technicians. There is nothing but harm to be done in burdening a farmer with a loan if he is going to buy some sort of insecticide that will not kill the bugs that attack his crops or cattle, or if he is going to put fertilizer on soil that will not respond to it, or if he buys some new, high-priced seed which is no better than that which is hanging in the corner of his kitchen. These and scores of similar problems which arise in using credit to increase production are concrete questions of fact, which cannot be answered by reference to general theories. They depend on judgments made on the spot by men who have the knowledge about the bug-killing power of a *particular* insecticide, who know the *particular* soil and its response to a *particular* fertilizer, or who know how a given variety will respond to the *specific* environment in which it is planted.

This means that a farm technician, backed up by experiment station results, or the carefully observed experience of other farmers, must be the man to extend farm production loans and guide their use as well. He must, in other words, carry out, as part of one operation, the twin functions of education and credit extension. This is no job for a banker who sits behind barred windows and looks at the resale value of the chattels included on the mortgage. The fact that the constructive use of farm credit to small farmers in these underdeveloped countries involves the use of farm technicians in making, supervising, and collecting loans means that the cost is much too high to be covered by the interest charged the farmer. It also means that these are educational functions and therefore legitimate parts of the cost of a really effective agricultural extension service. Unfortunately, the Extension Service and Farm Credit Administration grew up as two separate agencies in the United States. The Farm Credit Administration, moreover, was organized to go directly to the money market and borrow funds by pledging the security obtained from borrowers. This feature of its operation has precluded it from lending to the man who had no tangible collateral to offer when he needed a loan.

In the Caribbean countries, however, there is a good chance that these mistakes can be avoided. There are no organized markets for farm credit bonds, and governments ordinarily supply the funds for farm credit out of their treasuries, the same sources from which educational expenditures are made. If the farm credit and agricultural education functions could be brought together into one organization in these countries, their results would be multiplied several-fold in the general task of increasing the productivity of farmers by both increasing yields per acre and enlarging the scale of individual farm operations.

In addition to education and credit, there must also be some way of providing security of tenure on farms. The efficient use of farm credit and on-the-farm education will be impeded unless borrowers have a secure tenure to the land they operate and the right to reap the fruits of their efforts to improve it. Although tenancy systems can be devised to achieve the results desired—witness England and Australia—the practical solution in most Latin American countries is for the man who operates the land to own it also. In other words, along with a combined program of education and credit, there is badly needed a complementary program for increasing the number of owner-operated family farms.

The three essentials of a successful program for agricultural development, education, credit, and security of tenure, may be combined in varying proportions according to the need, but all of them must be present in order to achieve lasting results. By the same token, agricultural development based upon these ingredients is of seminal importance to the solution of the broader problems of land utilization throughout the Caribbean area.

Ross E. Moore: HUMAN FACTORS
IN LAND UTILIZATION

I

APPROXIMATELY one-third of the earth's surface is used for agriculture and forestry by the two and one-third billion persons who inhabit it. The effectiveness of such utilization varies widely. To an appreciable extent the effectiveness is determined by the endowments of nature, but to an even greater extent it is determined by the action of people. Over great areas of the world, physical factors such as soil, rainfall, and temperature have less bearing on effective use of land than do some of the social factors, such as the extent and effectiveness of social institutions, the access that farm people have to information, the availability of credit, and the security of tenure.

As we review the pages of history we find adequate examples of mankind's influence upon his lands. One page may tell of a people that industriously made the very deserts bloom. Another tells of a people that thoughtlessly denuded their forests and caused flooded rivers to carry away rich soils of farming lands. Such examples have continued and have multiplied through the years, and we find that they are still in the making today.

We may look about us as we meet here in Florida and close at hand find fitting evidence of how man has altered his environment to improve his well-being. As an example, let us consider Florida's great livestock industry: Fifteen years ago Florida's farmers had little more than 700,000 head of cattle on their farm and range lands; today they have approximately twice that number.

44

Yet, the portions of Florida where the greatest increase has taken place are not unusually well endowed by nature for such enterprise. Earlier livestock growers constantly encountered unusual problems. They noted that their cattle sometimes had abnormal hungers for such substances as dirt, bones, or wood. They were disappointed that their livestock sometimes failed to thrive even in lush pastures. Evidently nature had left some gaps in Florida's livestock-production environment. Man had to fill these gaps before the industry could thrive. How was this done?

Fortunately, the farmers of Florida were so associated that they were able to define their needs and give voice to them. Rising out of this definition of need from private groups came investigations by public research institutions wherein it was determined that in some soils of Florida a pronounced lack of certain minerals, especially phosphorus and cobalt, contributed directly to dietary deficiencies among livestock grazing on such soils. As a result of this research, it was relatively easy to prescribe compensatory fertilizing and feeding practices.

Fortunately, also, an extension service existed, as well as other private and public means of communicating agricultural information, so that livestock growers soon knew what techniques they must employ to cure the dietary illnesses of their cattle.

Fortunately, again, agricultural credit was available so that progressive growers could adopt the new fertilizing and feeding practices and expand their operations.

And, finally and fortunately, these growers were residents of a state in which the incentives resulting from good conditions of land tenure are remarkably widespread, for 80 per cent of Florida's agricultural land is owned by the farmers who operate it.

Here in Florida, then, and in neighboring areas of the Caribbean, and even into the farthest reaches of the world, the "human factors" in land utilization can be of greater consequence than the physical and natural features which define our environment. Man can compensate for deficiencies in his environment; to some extent he can even change his environment.

II

The world stands today on the threshold of a new era in technological advancement. All of the free nations are participating in new efforts to exchange knowledge, to share techniques, and to cooperate for mutual advancement. This Second Annual Conference on the Caribbean is an example of voluntary association between people of similar interest and purpose. Similarly, though on a magnified scale, voluntary associations for mutual progress are taking place through the United Nations and its specialized agencies, and through such nation-to-nation arrangements as those growing out of the technical cooperation programs sponsored by the United States. These cooperative efforts are directed at an immediate objective of improving the well-being of people and the long-range objective of fostering greater harmony and peace. Agriculture occupies a dominant role in this effort. The world's concern with effective land utilization is in no sense academic—it is occasioned by the inescapable fact that the world's population is outdistancing its food supply, and the companion fact that a hungry world cannot be a pleasant or a peaceful world.

Since cooperative effort for mutual advancement does exist between nations today, and since that effort is increasing, it is essential that it be directed into those avenues whereby it can make a maximum and lasting contribution to human welfare. It is essential that land resources be put to the best possible use in the housing, clothing, and feeding of people. Is there any key, any primary guiding principle, that people and nations can call upon as they cooperate to improve their utilization of land resources? I believe that there is.

I believe that a nation can improve its land utilization to the degree that it improves its human resources to give leadership to that task. Since "human resources" is an admittedly intangible term, let me substitute another—"social institutions." In our increasingly complex systems of living, we must look more and more to actual institutions, both private and public, as the fountainheads of progressive action. To me it is increasingly apparent that nations must strive to establish or to increase the competence and degree of leadership of their private and public social institutions.

This is true in all fields affecting human welfare—in agriculture, in health, in education, and in others as well.

There is no absolute rule whereby we can measure progress. We can gain a strong impression, however, of the social or economic or political development of a people by observing the virility and development of their social institutions. Such institutions make it possible for individuals and communities and societies to analyze and understand their situations, to decide how they might desirably modify those situations, to develop programs in the form of specific projects aimed at altering those situations, and, lastly, to carry the projects forward in a coordinated manner.

Earlier I mentioned four "human factors" that affect land use and referred to their application in improving the agriculture of Florida. They are factors that function through private and public social institutions. I would like to review those principles again, this time more broadly.

III

The first of these "human factors" is degree of association. All people tend to seek out others of similar interests. In primitive societies the association may be merely for pleasure or for protection. In more advanced societies, the association takes on stronger aspects of mutual gain. In the United States, if I may use my own country as an example again, we have an extensive array of county, state, and national agricultural committees; professional agricultural societies; and local, state, and national levels of farm organizations. Groups such as these are quick to notice and to call public and political attention to agricultural needs or agricultural inequities. They are both a motivating and a stabilizing influence. They stimulate local initiative to take responsible action. They give vital direction to local and national agricultural planning in that they provide the so-called "grassroots" influences which today are recognized as essential to democratic action.

Most parts of the world have insufficient association between people of like interests and objectives. This is true of many European countries, of Asiatic countries, of other regions as well. It is true of the Caribbean area. I hope that my country's Point Four Program of technical cooperation can be an encouraging in-

fluence in this direction, using every opportunity to demonstrate
to other peoples the greater rewards that will come from individual
effort when paralleled by associative effort.

The coffee growers of Latin America are in a relatively sound
position, economically and technologically. The corn growers of
Latin America, by and large, are not. Why is there this disparity?
Because those who have a primary interest in the coffee industry
have long been working in association for their common interest.
The corn growers are not associated: they have no group voice,
they have no one to champion their cause.

The essential oils industry of Guatemala, in a period of about
ten years, has risen to a pre-eminent position in world trade. Lemon
oil and citronella from Guatemalan producers is in world demand
because of its standardized excellence. How has this happened?
Because Guatemala's essential oil producers, through association,
have called upon research to improve their product, have dis-
ciplined themselves to maintain quality standards, and have been
able to obtain credit from outside as well as within their organization to increase production to meet increased demand.

By contrast, a new industry in Cuba is not progressing so rapidly
as it might because of insufficient association between those primarily interested. I am referring now to the kenaf fiber industry.
Kenaf is a jute-like fiber whose development in the Western Hemisphere is a credit to technical cooperation between agricultural
technicians of the United States and of Latin America. Kenaf is
a crop of good promise to the Caribbean area. Its fiber will be a
useful supplement to the huge quantities of jute that must be
imported annually from the Far East. It will be a valuable source
of new agricultural income. But the development of this new
crop—its production, its processing, and its utilization—is highly
dependent on governmental initiative. Increased impetus would
come to this important development if individuals and business
groups who stand to benefit from it were strongly associated, working in unison toward a common objective.

IV

The second "human factor" affecting land use is access to
information. There must be a flow of the world's experience to

farmers, processors, and marketers, in a form that they can use, or the most productive utilization of land resources cannot possibly be achieved.

Recently a World Land Tenure Conference was held at the University of Wisconsin at which representatives of thirty-eight nations explored relationships between people and the land. In their report they called special attention to "the prime importance of education and communication in a land tenure program." In the opinion of the delegates, "creating an ideal economic farming unit and putting it in the hands of an illiterate farmer bound to the old ways of agriculture by superstition and custom does little to solve the basic problem."

In order to obtain effective use of lands, then, farmers must have at their disposal a variety of agricultural information coming through a variety of media from a variety of sources. Adjoining the northwest sector of the state of Florida is the state of Alabama. Not long ago a survey was made to determine the ways in which Alabama farmers obtain the information that has caused them to improve their farming methods. The survey indicated that 38 per cent of the information came from reading matter, including farm magazines, newspapers, bulletins, leaflets, and circular letters; 24 per cent came from personal contacts, especially with neighbors and friends; 20 per cent came from attending group meetings held for reasons of agricultural improvement; 10 per cent came from listening to farm programs over the radio; and 8 per cent came from such visual aids as colored slides and motion pictures. We know from the years of experience of our Extension Service in the United States that there is no short cut to getting farmers to adopt recommended agricultural practices. For, in the first place, the information to be given them must be accurate and practicable; and secondly, it must be presented through a number of avenues so that it will fall into the hands of the largest possible number of farm people.

We commonly take it for granted that our banking industry must have financial information, our manufacturers must have supply-and-demand information, our merchants must have marketing information. There is equal need for a free flow of information in the field of agriculture. El Salvador is one of our neighbor countries that is giving strong recognition to this need. With the advice and consultation of one of our Department of Agriculture economists, and as part of our Point Four cooperative work with El Salvador, its Ministry of Agriculture has recently inaugurated a market reporting system. Our economist, Mr. E. W. Ranck, has sent us the following interesting report:

For the first time in the history of El Salvador, a market report of farm crops is being published weekly.

The *Centro Nacional de Agronomía* has assisted the Ministry of Agriculture in setting up a system whereby the Ministry's Department of Economic Studies and Statistics collects crop price information weekly in the Republic's fourteen principal market centers.

Items reported include: corn, milo maize, rice, wheat, beans (white, red, and black), sesame, beef, pork, and lard. This information in table form is released to the press on Fridays and appears in the week-end papers.

Surplus and scarcity frequently exist simultaneously in different parts of El Salvador with wide variation in the prices farmers get for their crops. Lack of information as to where surplus and scarcity exist has contributed to poor distribution of these articles of prime necessity. The new market reporting service should be of practical benefit not only to producers but to distributors and consumers alike.

I have stressed here the actual communication services of a nation without saying enough, perhaps, about the research and educational institutions, both private and public, that must exist to make the free flow of information possible. Where there are weather reports there must be weather stations. Where there are pamphlets on crop production there must be research stations. Where there are progressive farmers there must be educational institutions that constantly strive to raise the literacy and understanding of people. Put all such elements together and they spell the enlightenment that is essential if farmers are to make effective use of their resources.

V

A third "human factor" affecting land utilization is availability of credit. By credit I mean more than an arrangement whereby a farmer can borrow money at reasonable rates of interest, important as that is. I refer to a rational system of economics based on trust in which all members of a nation can participate. I refer, in short, to the need for making farmers more complete partners in the system known as capitalism, which permits the accumulation of capital on the one hand and its investment into creative enterprise on the other.

The farmers of the world, and this includes those of the Caribbean area, too often are excluded or at least partially excluded from the rewards that can come from the availability of credit and the equitable management of fiscal resources. These lines from Kipling, describing the Far Eastern peasant of half a century ago, still remain singularly appropriate:

> *His speech is mortgaged bedding,*
> *On his kine he borrows yet,*
> *At his heart is his daughter's wedding,*
> *In his eye foreknowledge of debt.*
> *He eats and hath indigestion,*
> *He toils and he may not stop,*
> *His life is a long-drawn question,*
> *Between a crop and a crop.*

Too often that economic description of the 1890's still applies today—with some exceptions. Here and there we find evidence of change for the better. In India, where those lines were written, I have seen rural cooperatives, recently organized and full of vitality, offering new financial hope to their members. In Puerto Rico, many farm families are benefiting from governmental production loans and home-ownership loans, and are proving to be outstandingly good credit risks. In other areas, as well, we have spotty evidence of greater economic opportunity coming to rural people—but we can regret that the opportunity continues to be much greater for the large farmer who grows a crop for world markets than for the smaller farmer who supplies his own family and local markets.

Effective land use cannot be brought about, in the Caribbean area or elsewhere, in the face of static economic opportunity. Economic opportunity is, in reality, a chain reaction. As capital is made available to producers, they are able to improve and expand their operations. This creates new income which in turn strengthens a nation's tax structure. Additional public revenue makes possible the expansion of such public services as research, education, dissemination of information, and similar essential facilities that improve the use of capital resources. Which is the more important or which comes first cannot be said, for each is equally important to the other.

VI

The fourth, and last, "human factor" is security of tenure. Access to land and security in the use of land are among the major determinants of land utilization in the Caribbean area. Many of you are acquainted with the Caribbean Land Tenure Symposium, conducted since the last war by the Caribbean Commission. This Symposium effectively brought out the contrast between the producer who has security and the producer who does not. In the words of Mr. Marshall Harris, agricultural economist representing the United States Department of Agriculture:

The farmer who occupies the land with a high degree of security will be encouraged to improve and conserve the land, to build it up, to farm in a husbandman-like manner, and to take pride in that which he expects to use over the years.... But what about the farmer who holds his land insecurely, who may move next year or at most the year after, whose expected occupancy is short? He cannot plan and carry out crop rotations and develop herds and flocks. He will invariably engage in the production of an annual cash crop. He does not have a reasonable incentive to follow soil-building and soil-conserving practices. He cannot afford to increase production through drainage or clearing; he will not take chances on liming or using fertilizers that will last for more than a year or two, for he does not know that he will enjoy the fruits of his labor.... The tenure system must provide a reasonable degree of security for every farm family. Not deadening security, not complete assurance, not an irrevocable occupancy, but enough confidence in the future to bring forth maximum effort to follow through on sensible long time plans....

We can be glad that recognition is being given in every part of the Caribbean area to this all-important problem of land tenure.

There is no unanimous opinion as to man's ideal relationship with the land he tills, but there is growing recognition that efficient utilization of natural resources, and community prosperity and stability, cannot come except as conditions of land tenure are significantly improved. Perhaps individual ownership may not always be the ultimate goal in the more populous Caribbean area, as it is here in the United States. Nevertheless, greater access to land and greater security in the use of that land must come to the Caribbean area if its farm people are to make their maximum contribution.

VII

We find, then, four principal human factors influencing man's effective use of land: the degree to which he associates himself with others of similar aspirations; his access to helpful information; the availability of credit needed to enhance his productivity; and, finally, his access to land and security of tenure in using that land.

Leadership in bringing these factors into play springs largely from social institutions, private and public, whose reason for being is to promote the greater welfare. It seems particularly pertinent at this time, with national and international programs for technical assistance bringing new hope to nations, that the essentiality of a people's own private and public institutions capable of exerting this leadership be kept in the forefront. In every country, however primitive, either the beginnings of these necessary social institutions exist or the seeds of their being are present. It should be a major aim of all technical cooperation programs, whether the Point Four Program of the United States or the international programs of the United Nations, to encourage these national institutions and let them assume positions of leadership. Solutions for land utilization problems, or any other national problems, must in the final analysis come from within a country, whether it is in the Caribbean area or elsewhere. This means, then, that people will find their answers within the institutions of their own making. Our assistance can be permanently effective only insofar as it fosters the development of such institutions so that they, in turn, can care for those four basic human needs—freedom of association, freedom of information, equality of opportunity, and security of tenure.

Rafael Picó:* SURVEYING LAND USE IN PUERTO RICO

PUERTO RICO has just finished the field work of a survey of which the scope and extent have not been matched elsewhere. The whole area of the island, 3,423 square miles of tropical plains and subtropical hills, has been thoroughly mapped on a very large scale. A wide range of geographic and cultural conditions is portrayed in this work. Level and humid (except in the irrigated South) sugar-cane fields, tobacco covered hillsides, coffee farms on the rainy flanks of the west-central mountains, native food crops all over the hills of the interior, forests clothing the highest peaks, a belt of mangroves bordering the coast-line—they are all graphically illustrated in this survey of the physical resources and man's labor on the Puerto Rican land. The large scale (1:10,000) and thoroughness of the survey and the diversity of the geographic regions make Puerto Rico's land-use survey unique.

The Rural Land Classification Program, as it is being carried out in Puerto Rico, is a geographic survey of the use of the land and its physical characteristics. The present land utilization indicates the enterprises that the farmer has found to be economically advantageous, but they might not correspond to the optimum use of the land from the social standpoint. Undoubtedly, much land

* Grateful acknowledgment for aid received in the preparation of this paper is hereby extended to Mrs. Zayda Buitrago Santiago, Geographic Researcher Assistant, Puerto Rico Planning Board, and to Mr. Héctor Berríos, Chief, Land Economic Division, Department of Agriculture, and other personnel of the Insular Department of Agriculture and Commerce.

could be used to better advantage. In land-hungry Puerto Rico, it is imperative for us to make the maximum use of our land resources. Consequently, this land-use survey is considered essential in the formulation of plans for the readjustment of the present agricultural pattern. Furthermore, an inventory of the potentialities of the land also should help to guide programs of public services and other expenditures of resources in any region of Puerto Rico.

With this goal in mind, the author of this paper invited, in 1949, Dr. Clarence F. Jones, of the Department of Geography of Northwestern University, to direct such a survey in Puerto Rico. As a result of this invitation, Professor Jones came to the island together with Dr. G. Donald Hudson, then head of the Geography Department of Northwestern, to discuss the feasibility of this program. Both men had wide experience in similar surveys. After several conferences with all the agencies interested in the program, Drs. Jones and Hudson prepared a statement on the objectives of the field mapping which would not only include the mapping of the land use, but which would also record, in one single operation, the physical characteristics of the land.

It was agreed that Northwestern University would furnish advanced students in geography who would do the field work for their doctoral dissertations in Puerto Rico, in connection with the mapping survey. A Puerto Rican technician, acting as interpreter and interviewer, was to be added to each team. The travel and subsistence expenses of the graduate students were covered by the insular agencies.

At the beginning, the Planning Board and the Social Science Research Center of the University of Puerto Rico were the local sponsors of the survey. Shortly thereafter, the Insular Department of Agriculture and Commerce joined the above-mentioned agencies in the direction of the program, as the department saw the value of the land-use survey in its plans for the betterment of agricultural conditions in the island.

The survey started with a modest appropriation of $16,000, to which was added $25,000 from funds of the Department of Agriculture. As the work progressed and it was necessary to accelerate the program, more funds were appropriated. In 1950 the Legislature of Puerto Rico appropriated the sum of $105,000 to the Department of Agriculture and Commerce to conclude the field work and compile a land use map with the material obtained. The total estimated cost up to and including the preparation of the final land use maps will be approximately $150,000. On July 1, 1950, the department took over entirely the administration and direction of the program. The original sponsors, that is, the Planning Board and the University of Puerto Rico, remained in an advisory capacity to the department.

The program was originally planned for four years, but owing to the urgency of collecting the data at the earliest practicable time, it was decided to reduce the mapping period to two years, from July, 1949 to September, 1951. That change required another adjustment as to the source of the graduate students. Northwestern provided the majority, but the program was expanded to encompass other universities in the continental United States. All applicants submitted their credentials to the Geography Department of Northwestern for their approval. In the end, ten universities were represented in the survey, as follows: eight students from Northwestern, two from Syracuse, two from Wisconsin and one each from the Universities of Chicago, Clark, Michigan, Washington, Illinois, Maryland, and Nebraska. I am happy to say that the first student who worked in the survey is now Professor Donald R. Dyer, of the Department of Geography at the University of Florida.

I. Mapping Procedure

The land use and the physical characteristics of the land were surveyed, on the basis of the unit-area method, using a fractional code system of notation of the field data. This method was first used by the Tennessee Valley Authority and it included the mapping of the land use, degree of slope, soil classes, condition of drainage, amount of erosion, degree of stoniness, and amount of rock exposure. In Puerto Rico the size of the unit area ranges from many acres on level land along the coast, to areas of one acre in the central part of the island. All buildings and other structures were mapped with standard or conventional symbols. Aerial vertical photographs and topographic sheets at a scale of 1:10,000 were used to plot the field information.

The identification of soil types was accomplished through the use of a soil map at a scale of 1:50,000, published in 1942 by the Division of Soil Survey of the United States Department of Agriculture.

A réconnaissance and a general field study of the present land use and the physical characteristics were made prior to the beginning of the field work. The mapping keys and the definitions of land use terms and physical conditions were prepared with the able assistance of the following insular and federal agencies in Puerto Rico: Soil Conservation Service, Planning Board, Forest Service, Insular Department of Agriculture and Commerce, Scientific Assessment Division of the Treasury Department, and Insular Agricultural Experiment Station.

The island was divided into eighteen mapping regions, each to be completed by one field team. These teams outlined the mapping areas, using municipal boundaries but trying to secure the maximum geographical homogeneity within them. Mapping regions ranged from 125 to 289 square miles in area.

Each field team was composed of a chief, who had had experience in this type of field work, another student receiving on-the-job training for a six-week period, and a Puerto Rican interviewer well acquainted with the area to be mapped. Each field team was equipped with a "jeep" to facilitate its work.

The interviewer, with his knowledge of crops, farming methods, and other agricultural problems of the island, helped the chief of the party and also interviewed farmers on a systematic and random sampling basis while mapping was going on. The additional information obtained on the Rural Property Interview Schedules provided abundant data which could not be recorded on field maps.

The farmers were interviewed on a sample basis. The sampling was done on the basis of the number of rural houses. The ratio to be interviewed was arrived at in the following manner: (1) one for every eight farmer houses, (2) one for every sixteen parcels less than three acres in size, (3) one for every thirty-two sharecropper or squatters' shacks, and (4) one for any other sixty-four rural dwellers. This ratio was increased or decreased daily according to the number of houses in the area being worked at. Those selected to be interviewed supplied information on all agricultural production during the past twelve months and other socio-economic problems. About six thousand interviews were taken throughout the island.

The first field team, under the direction of Donald Dyer, came to Puerto Rico in July, 1949, and did the detailed mapping of a cross-section traverse from the northern coast near Vega Baja to the southern coast near Ponce, in addition to fifteen small selected areas scattered all over the island, to try out the keys and to anticipate problems that might arise in the field.

II. Field Work

The area to be mapped was chosen when its main crop was still on the land. The students selected their areas on the basis of the themes that they had chosen for their individual dissertations. The team-chief selected his headquarters in the center of his area, so that he could become better acquainted with the people and the type of agriculture in the area. Each student, before starting work on his given area, made a reconnaissance trip around the island to become acquainted with its geographical features.

As an aid to speed up the work in the field, the soil series, selected land use features, and other land characteristics were added to the aerial photographs. All of this basic data speeded the field work tremendously.

A supervisor, John Lounsbury, was selected from among the first students, who finished mapping their areas, and was appointed assistant director of the project. He advised and checked the work of the other teams.

The land use and the physical conditions were recorded on the photographs by a fractional notation, for example $\frac{172}{1\text{-}5151}$. The numerator of the fractional notation indicates the use of the land. The denominator indicates the characteristics of the land. The notation 172 refers to cultivated land. The first digit (1) of the fraction stands for crop land, the second digit (7) for bananas, and the third digit (2) for average quality. In general, the major category is represented by the first digit, the kind or type of land use by the second digit, and the quality by the third digit, respectively.

The denominator recorded in our sample, 1-5151, would read as follows: The first digit (1) refers to the soil unit, followed by the degree of slope (5), condition of drainage (1), amount of erosion (5), and degree of stoniness (1). Any change within part of the notation means a change in the piece of land plotted. The numbers used to designate the items represented in the notation were selected from the keys of land use and land characteristics. Buildings and other structures were mapped with symbols.

III. Land Use

In Puerto Rico, land use is classified into the following eight major categories: cropped land, pasture and harvested forage grass, forest and brush land, non-productive land, rural public and community service land, urban and manufacturing land, quarrying and mining land, and miscellaneous land.

These categories are described briefly as follows:

Cropped Land.—Land in which produce is harvested for human consumption. This category is broken down into forty-three crops or combinations of crops.

Pasture and Harvested Forage Grass.—Land devoted to the growth of grasses for animal consumption. This includes natural pasture, improved pasture, harvested forage grass, and others. This category is divided into eight classes.

Forest and Brush Land.—All areas in trees, whether planted or part of the natural vegetation. This land also includes brush, which consists of trees below ten feet in height. Land considered as woodland pasture was mapped within class eight under the category of pasture and harvested forage grass.

Non-Productive Land.—Land without any agricultural productive value. This land may or may not be suitable for some productive use, but at present it has no productive value. This category is divided into three classes.

Rural Public and Community Service Land.—Indicates plots used for public and community services. Usually this land comprises small tracts or plots that fall into seven classes.

Quarrying and Mining Land.—Includes rock and mineral resources which are being removed from the land. Abandoned quarries and mines are included in non-productive land (category number four).

Urban and Manufacturing Land.—Land in which cities and towns are located. It also includes tracts outside the urban area devoted to any manufacturing activities. This category is divided into seven classes.

Miscellaneous Land.—Features of land use which do not fall into any of the above-mentioned categories. They are recorded on the field map by means of letters, and in some cases by numbers in addition to letters.

IV. Physical Characteristics

The physical characteristics mapped include the soil type, slope, drainage, erosion, stoniness, and rock exposure. They do not encompass all elements of the natural or physical environment. The main interest was mapping all important characteristics that affect the agricultural phase and that could be readily observed and mapped. The characteristics discussed appear in the order indicated in the denominator of the fractional code system.

Soils.—In Puerto Rico there are 367 types of soils as mapped by the United States Division of Soil Survey. These soil types were grouped in 53 categories based on soil similarities.

Slope.—The degree of slope was associated with the accessibility to the land of agricultural machinery to be used and with characteristics of drainage and erosion. On this basis the land was divided into six classes, ranging from class one, which does not show any erosion and can make extensive use of farm machinery, to class six that eliminates all cultivation except by terracing. This latter class is characterized by a severe erosion.

Drainage.—The drainage condition indicates both surface run-off and interior drainage. It ranges from class one (well drained), to class five (excessively drained).

Erosion.—The erosion classification depends on how much of the soil has been removed. In general the classification shows how much soil remains in the land. The erosion is classified into seven groups, from recent alluvial or colluvial deposits to very severe sheet erosion.

Stoniness and Rock Exposure.—Condition of rocks in the land, like the other characteristics mentioned, is somewhat associated with type of soil. The classification of stoniness and rock exposure takes into consideration the problem of how well the land could be cultivated without interference by rock exposure. The condition of rock exposure is subdivided into eight classes, ranging from no stone or rock outcrop which would interfere with cultivation, to severe rock exposure, which prevents cultivation. In the classification of rock exposure, after the digit identifying the amount of rock exposure, two additional numbers, one placed above the other, appear occasionally. The upper number indicates the class of stoniness and the lower number the class of rock exposure.

In general, the physical conditions mapped are closely related to the type of soil, but within those types of soil there are substantial variations that can be mapped. These variations suggest potential differences within soil types that are basic to a recommended land use program for the island.

V. Using the Data Collected

The data gathered in the field constitute one of the most complete inventories on land use ever done in Puerto Rico or elsewhere. It gives a clear picture of the land use and the potentialities of our soils as suited for cultivation. There is no doubt that this inventory is an essential basis for any agricultural or public service program, and for all types of rural planning throughout the island. It strikingly indicates problem areas in need of specific attention.

Since the field work started, a land use map, at a scale of 1:10,000, has been in preparation. This map is being prepared on dyrite paper, which is transparent and suited for oxalic copies. It shows, besides the land use, all buildings and structures, rivers and roads. Professor Edward B. Espenshade, an expert cartographer, also from Northwestern University, was very helpful with suggestions to improve the presentation of the final land use maps.

To obtain the appropriate statistical data, one out of every twenty-five acres of land has been intensively studied in the office. The information has been tabulated on IBM cards. The questionnaires filled out in the fields are also being tabulated on IBM cards. This information, together with the land use map, will help to portray the rural problems of the island as a whole, as well as by regions.

At present, a recommended land use program is being worked out. Specific land use recommendations will be made, based on the potentialities of the land. All soil types are going to be grouped according to their productivity and farm management. This will show certain management classes for which farm management plans will be made so that they will serve as models for the rest of the farms in each class. There is the possibility of working out a rural zoning map, once the recommended use is determined. This zoning map, likewise, may serve as the basis for the location of public services and industrial developments.

The list of the participants and their thesis subjects is given in the appendix with a note as to the status of their academic work. They certainly are a valuable set of reference material on the conditions and possibilities of agriculture in Puerto Rico. As many of the students' dissertations as possible will be published and all feasible recommendations will be taken into account in the proposed land use program.

A very important by-product of this survey was the spirit of cooperation it generated among continental students, Puerto Rican interviewers, public officials, professors who supervised the work, farmers, and the public at large who cooperated with the field teams, cheerfully supplying information. Each contributor to the survey supplied his knowledge or experience, often obtained in places very far from Puerto Rico; all contributed to a worthy cause with good will and a cooperative spirit. The graduate students had the opportunity to do field work with all expenses paid, in a tropical island with a rich geographical environment. As a result of their labor, the island has a very accurate land use survey that would have cost much more if done with regular employees. This cooperative procedure, which can facilitate mapping of underdeveloped areas, merits study and application in other lands.

APPENDIX

STATUS OF DOCTORAL DISSERTATIONS
AND SPECIAL STUDIES

I. Ph.D. Theses Completed:

Donald R. Dyer, "The Development of Geographic Survey Techniques for the Rural Land Classification Program of Puerto Rico," Northwestern University, 1950.

Vernon W. Brockmann, "Physical Land Types and Land Utilization in the Caguas-San Lorenzo Regions of Puerto Rico," Northwestern University, 1950.

Robert B. Batchelder, "Subhumid Plain of Northwestern Puerto Rico: A Study in Rural Land Utilization," Northwestern University, 1951.

Harold R. Imus, "The Mayaguez Area (Puerto Rico): A Study in Farm Economy Analysis," Northwestern University, 1951.

John F. Lounsbury, "Rural Settlement Features and their Association to Agricultural Economies in Aguas Buenas, Comerío, Corozal, and Naranjito," Northwestern University, 1951.

Arthur H. Doerr, "The Relationship of Human Activities in Southwestern Puerto Rico to the Semi-Arid Climate," Northwestern University, 1951.

II. Ph.D. Theses in Preparation:

David Naley, "Land Utilization in the Municipalities of Yauco, Guayanilla, Guánica, and Peñuelas of Puerto Rico," Syracuse, 1953.

Wallace E. Akin, "The Dairy Industry of the North Coast of Puerto Rico: A Study in Tropical Dairying," Northwestern University, 1952.

Bernt L. Wills, "An Analysis of the Physical Land Types and of the Rural Land Use on those Land Types of the Seven Municipalities of Cataño, Bayamón, Toa Alta, Toa Baja, Dorado, Vega Alta, and Vega Baja, in Puerto Rico," Northwestern University, 1952.

Robert N. Young, "A New Classification of Land Forms in Puerto Rico," University of Wisconsin, 1952.

Joseph A. Tosi, Jr., "Land Utilization of the Forest and Potential Forest Lands of Western Puerto Rico," Clark University, 1952.

Luther H. Gulick, Jr., "A Socio-Geographic Study of the Rural Population of the Western Highlands of Puerto Rico," University of Chicago, 1952.

Donald D. MacPhail, "The Cattle Industry of the South Coast of Puerto Rico," University of Michigan, 1952.

Dale E. Courtney, "The Geography of the Fruit Industry of Puerto Rico," University of Washington, 1952.

Donald L. Netzer, "A Climatic Study of Puerto Rico," University of Illinois, 1952.

George A. Beishlag, "The Influence of American Capital in Changing Land Use Patterns in Southern Puerto Rico," University of Maryland, 1952.

Richard L. Lawton, "Area Study in Northeastern Puerto Rico: A Study in Historical Development," Syracuse University, 1952.

Kermit M. Laidig, "The Problem of the Small Subsistence Farmer in Southeastern Puerto Rico," University of Nebraska, 1952.

III. Special Studies:

Dieter H. Brunnschweiler, "Land Use in the *municipios* of Ciales, Morovis and Orocovis in Central Puerto Rico," University of Zurich, 1952.

William W. Burchfiel, "The Geography of the Pineapple Industry of Puerto Rico," University of Maryland, 1952.

Part III

TRADE

Francisco Aguirre: THE CARIBBEAN: HEART OF THE AMERICAS AND CENTER OF WORLD TRANSPORTATION

I SHOULD LIKE to precede my brief exposition on transportation in the Caribbean with a tribute to the magnificent contribution which the University of Florida is making to inter-American understanding by sponsoring these discussions on the Caribbean area. The exchange of ideas which is taking place here cannot but strengthen the spiritual union of all Americans through the dispassionate and continuing study of the complex factors which influence the development of the Caribbean—an area which, in many respects, may be regarded as the heart of the Americas.

I am honored and gratified beyond words to find myself in this mansion of learning, which so successfully fulfills the mission of the modern university by stimulating the study, without limitation, of all that lies within the scope of human intelligence. In touching upon the problems of the Caribbean area, this famed University is playing a very important part in bringing the peoples of the Caribbean and of the United States closer together. By the same token, it is playing a very important part in bringing about that singleminded and supreme identification of all Americans which some day will be the greatest glory of our hemisphere.

There could be no more appropriate place than this University for a discussion of the problems of the Caribbean and their relation to the rest of the world. Faithful to the traditions of Florida, this University nurtures the memories of a far-off yesterday by carefully cultivating friendship with Latin America through specialized studies, such as those which the learned Professor A. Curtis Wilgus directs with such skill. History binds Florida to Spanish America, and geography makes her sister to the nations of the Caribbean.

In the days when the sea was the only medium of international transit, Ponce de León and other illustrious figures converted Florida into a rampart of defense for Spanish conquests of the New World. Today, in the miraculous air age of the twentieth century, it falls to this uniquely beautiful peninsula to be a keystone of transoceanic air travel.

There is still much room for progress in air transportation between the United States and the Caribbean countries, if we consider that the unlimited sympathy which exists between the peoples of those countries and the people of Florida has not as yet been exploited to the fullest. A common heritage and common ancestry must, for the present, constitute the best bridge of union among all the American peoples. But the University of Florida, with all its academic prestige and progressive tradition, is speeding the day when all Americans will be bound by a common present destiny, as well as by the rich heritage of the past; and little by little, trade in a more material sense will bring about a definite alliance of Florida and the Latin American countries through the Caribbean.

I

The Caribbean area embraces the American republics extending along the mainland from Mexico to Venezuela and the group of republics and dependencies which constitute the Antilles. Its geographical position gives it an extraordinary and immeasurable importance in inter-American transportation and world transportation.

I would prefer, within the limits of this brief discussion, to touch but lightly on the role of the airplane in Caribbean transportation. Air transportation is an established part of Caribbean communications and frequently, because of its ability to surmount topographical obstacles which impede land routes, is the only means of transportation between one region and another. But the establishment of air routes, once international agreements have been reached and official approvals extended, is a comparatively simple matter from the physical and economic standpoints. Within the brief time allotted to me, I would prefer to stress land and sea transportation in the Caribbean and, in particular, the Pan American Highway and Panama Canal as all-important factors in the present and future evolution of Caribbean transportation.

These are topics which have a singular personal and professional interest for me. Personal, because I am a native of one of the Central American republics which may be considered to lie within the Caribbean area. Professional, because as secretary of the Pan American Division of the American Road Builders' Association it has been my task, and the task of our many colleagues and supporters, to encourage and stimulate the construction of a hemisphere network of highways which would serve as a positive and undeniably valuable factor in the unification of the Americas, with the Pan American Highway as a nucleus. For twenty-five years our Pan American Division has labored toward this objective under the slogan of *La Unidad del Continente por el esfuerzo constructivo de los ingenieros*—"Hemisphere Unity through the Constructive Efforts of Engineers."

The Pan American Highway contains a segment, running from the southern border of Mexico to the Isthmus of Panama, which is called the Inter-American Highway. The chief difference between this segment and others which form part of the Pan American Highway lies in the method of financing. The keen interest of the United States in an overland link with the Panama Canal and the limited financial resources of the Central American republics and Panama led, in 1942, to an agreement between this country and Guatemala, Honduras, Nicaragua, Costa Rica, El Salvador, and Panama whereby construction of the Inter-American Highway would be financed by a two-thirds contribution by the United States and a one-third contribution by each of the other countries in connection with its respective section of the highway. At the present time, except for a few short segments which await completion, an overland route exists in the mainland Caribbean countries and countries bordering on the Caribbean area, as follows:

	Total Distance in Miles	Impassable Mileage
Mexico	1625	—
Guatemala	317	25
El Salvador	191	—
Honduras	94	—
Nicaragua	238	—
Costa Rica	413	241
Panama	316	—14
Colombia	1947	—
Venezuela	736	—

The Congress of the United States has already authorized a new appropriation of $7,000,000 which is being employed in renewed construction of the highway in the Central American countries and Panama, under the cooperative arrangement with the United States to which I have referred. It is estimated that another $85,000,000 will be necessary to complete the connection between the Panama Canal and the southern border of Mexico. Thereafter, it will be necessary to complete approximately 300 miles of highway across Darien, lying between Panama and Colombia, before a union of the highways of North America and South America can become a reality. Because of topography and dense jungle obstacles, the Darien highway project will be one of the most difficult engineering ventures in the history of the Western Hemisphere.

Besides linking the great cities of America, it will be the role of the Pan American Highway, as has been pointed out, to serve as the nucleus for transportation systems in the various American countries. To it falls the gigantic task of opening up new areas for development in our hemisphere, of serving as a vital link in the network of international land, sea, and air transportation which binds the American peoples with one another and with the rest of the world, and of serving the cause of New World unification. To neglect the Pan American Highway is to ignore a concept of supreme importance to the political, spiritual, and material well-being of our entire Continent, and of particular importance to the Caribbean area.

II

This concept of the Pan American Highway is matched by but one other—that of the Panama Canal—in the development of

Caribbean and Western Hemisphere transportation. It was the Panama Canal which converted the Caribbean, heart of the American continent, into a center of world transportation. There have been few endeavors in the history of mankind which have been so productive of good for all men. The opening of the Panama Canal gave a mighty forward thrust to the commerce of the whole world, as distances were slashed and the farthest extremes of the earth were brought closer together. With the broadening and strengthening of commercial ties, men of many lands and civilizations came to know one another, and the Panama Canal became a mighty weapon of understanding.

The impact of the Panama Canal upon the civilization of America and of the entire world was even more tremendous than that experienced from the Suez Canal. It would be foolish to minimize the importance of the latter, which joined the Mediterranean with the Red Sea and brought Europe nearer to Asia, Africa, and Australia. But the growing destiny of the New World as a potent influence in the trade and culture and international relationships of the earth invested the Panama Canal with a significance which the Suez Canal possessed, inevitably, in lesser degree.

The Panama Canal, pride of the Caribbean area, has fulfilled a complex mission of universal importance. For the Americas, it meant swift and easy communication between the Atlantic and the Pacific. For Europe, it meant direct communication with the Pacific coast of our hemisphere, without need to transit the long and perilous course which led through the turbulent Straits of Magellan. For the world, it meant a shortening of the distances between the Old World and the New World, between Occident and Orient.

A ship sailing from Europe saves at least 2,000 miles by using the Panama Canal to reach the West Coast of America. The Far East is closer to the Atlantic seaboard of the United States via the Panama Canal, than to Europe via the Suez Canal. Sidney, Australia, is 11,200 miles from Plymouth, England, via the Suez Canal, but it is only 9,851 miles from New York via the Panama Canal. The latter has brought Wellington, New Zealand, 2,000 miles nearer to New York than to any European seaport, while Yokohama, Japan, lies 900 miles closer to the great American

metropolis than to Europe. In a like manner, the Panama Canal
has brought a thousand points in East and West closer together.

A century and more ago, when the discovery of gold in California
beckoned to thousands of hardy adventurers in the western world,
their journey was long and filled with discomfort. Their choice
lay between the interminable sea passage around Cape Horn, and
a briefer sea journey leading to an arduous land crossing of the
continent at its narrowest point, across Nicaragua and the Isthmus
of Panama. Seven thousand miles of water and the turbulent,
hazardous Straits of Magellan lay ahead of the traveler before
he emerged into the Pacific. Today, a mere 2,000 miles carries
him through the Canal to the western ocean. In the twenty-five
years between the opening of the Canal and 1937, some 93,000
vessels with a combined tonnage of 449,000,000 made the transit
of the Panama Canal from one ocean to the other. Many tens
of thousands of ships, on missions of peace or war, have passed
through the Canal since then, to make it one of the greatest, if
not the greatest, of world waterways.

III

In these critical hours of world history, it would be rash and
imprudent of us were we to ignore the proposal recently made
by Premier Nehru, of India, that the Panama Canal be interna-
tionalized. Premier Nehru draws a most erroneous parallel between
the status of the Suez Canal in the Anglo-Egyptian controversy,
and the status of the Panama Canal *vis-a-vis* the United States and
Panama. This parallel and its unfortunate implications are of such
potential danger to the good relations between the United States
and Panama and to the welfare of the entire Caribbean area that
they will merit attention and refutation here. I should like to
delve briefly into this matter, with the conviction that it is
intimately linked to the future destiny of the Caribbean.

It is impossible to compare, on an equal and similar basis, the
public treaties between the United States and Panama on the
one hand, and England and Egypt on the other, even though
these treaties deal with a kindred subject matter involving the
control and use of the world's two great international canals.
Fundamentally, there are differences between the two which do not

lend themselves to comparison, and outstanding among these differences are the following:

1. The Suez Canal was conceived and constructed in its entirety as a *commercial enterprise,* without a basis in public treaty. Negotiations took place between Viceroy Mohammed Said, Egypt's highest authority at the time, and Count Fernando de Lesseps, who organized the *Compagnie Universelle du Canal Maritime de Suez* in France in 1858, as the sole concessionaire.

2. From its inauguration in 1869, the Suez Canal has been operated as a commercial enterprise, and Egypt participated in its earnings only to the extent that she held shares in the French company.

3. About 1875 England began to acquire working control of the Suez Canal through the purchase of shares, constituting about half of the total shares, then held by Egypt. This acquisition was a purely commercial transaction and was not the subject of a public treaty. England's participation at that time was limited to administrative activities and its property rights to the Suez Canal as a business enterprise.

4. Basically, Egypt has not ceded its jurisdiction over the civilian population of the Suez Canal Zone.

5. Despite its commercial aspects, the Suez Canal subsequently presented problems of an international nature which were reflected in public treaties concerned with the neutrality of the canal, and the maintenance and defense of that neutrality. The general intent was to prevent any single power from gaining control over the canal, to the detriment of other seafaring nations. The play of international events led to a number of treaties, but all of these had one characteristic in common: they confined themselves to the neutrality and defense of the canal, and to that alone. From the time of Turkish domination of Egypt, in force when the concession was granted to de Lesseps, to the eclipse of Turkey in the Treaty of Versailles, the great powers engaged in many negotiations dealing with the Suez Canal. Yet not one of these altered the status or structure of the *Compagnie Universelle.*

6. England emerged almost alone in its control over the Suez Canal by virtue of Article 152 of the Treaty of Versailles, by which it inherited all the rights over Egypt formerly held by the Sultan of Turkey. In short, Egypt, which had been a semi-

sovereign vassal state within the Turkish Empire, continued to occupy that status with respect to England. The Treaty of Versailles, in granting England a protectorate over Egypt, merely gave sanction to England's military occupation of Egypt in 1914, with the outbreak of war between that country and Germany and Turkey.

7. In theory, at least, England terminated her protectorate over Egypt in 1922, and a public treaty was signed between the two states. Nevertheless, this treaty imposed certain obligations on Egypt, in her relationship with England, in connection with the political and military status of the Suez Canal, which continued to be the property of the *Compagnie Universelle*. The Treaty of 1922 established that subsequent agreements would be drawn up between the contracting parties with respect to the definitive status of the Suez Canal. These agreements would also deal with the defense and security of the canal, and would contain guarantees that England would always enjoy free access to the canal and free transit of that waterway.

8. Undoubtedly, as a consequence of the Treaty of 1922, another treaty was signed in 1936. The latter instrument is still in effect, and is the bone of contention in the present tension between the two countries. It was directly motivated by the threat of Mussolini's imperialism in the Mediterranean area, which persuaded England that a new treaty was essential if its control of the Suez Canal was to remain secure. The Treaty of 1936 recognized Egypt's full sovereignty and called upon England to withdraw its military forces from Egypt, with the exception of 10,000 troops and 400 military aircraft *in the Suez Canal Zone*. England was also granted the use of Alexandria and Port Said as naval bases, and the right to move troops across Egyptian territory in case of war or the threat of war. In turn, England bound herself to defend Egypt against aggression and support her admission to the League of Nations. The Treaty of 1936, in short, had the semblance of a treaty of alliance and contained specific contractual provisions concerning the Suez Canal in time of war.

9. The concession granted to the *Compagnie Universelle du Canal Maritime de Suez* had a life of ninety-nine years. It was provided that, upon its expiration in 1968, the company would become the property of the Egyptian Government, although this

provision had nothing to do with the Anglo-Egyptian treaty concerning the alliance between the two countries and the defense of the canal. Obviously, Egypt alone would be unable to guarantee the neutrality of the canal agreed upon by the world powers following its construction. Possibly, however, the maintenance of the Suez Canal's neutrality might be the subject of revisions within the United Nations which could lead to another treaty or the establishment of a new status for the Suez Canal.

IV

The position of the Panama Canal, dream of European monarchs who envisioned a waterway across Nicaragua which would bring them untold power and riches, evolved along somewhat different lines:

1. Following a number of explorations and attempts by France and England to construct a canal across Central America, the celebrated French engineer and naval officer, Captain Napoleon Bonaparte Wyse, obtained a concession from the government of Colombia in 1876 for the construction and operation of a canal across the Isthmus of Panama. Wyse transferred his concession to the *Compañía Universal del Canal Interoceánico,* headed by that same Fernando de Lesseps who had covered himself with such glory in the miracle of the Suez Canal. Work on the Panama Canal was begun in 1882. Up to this point, there were many similarities between the Suez Canal and the proposed Panama Canal. To cite the most outstanding, the concessionaire in each case was a private, commercial enterprise, without need or justification for a public treaty.

2. For a number of reasons, including the mismanagement of funds, the *Compañía Universal del Canal Interoceánico* met with disaster—disaster with which the aging De Lesseps was unable to cope. Its concession rights were sold to a new enterprise, *La Compañía Nueva del Canal,* which met with no greater success, even though its efforts brought the reality of the Panama Canal appreciably nearer.

3. In the course of time the independence of Panama was declared, and in 1903 a public treaty was signed between that republic and the United States. That treaty had as its objective the

construction of the Panama Canal, an objective which previously had been the subject of negotiations between Colombia and the United States leading to a treaty which was rejected by the Colombian Congress. It was this action of the Colombian Congress which precipitated the independence of Panama.

4. The United States Government bought the *Compañía Nueva del Canal's* concession rights for $40,000,000, together with the company's properties. Panama assumed the prerogatives formerly held by Colombia and the situation abruptly changed. Now, two governments were engaged in negotiation, instead of a government and a private commercial enterprise.

5. The Treaty of 1903 was revised by a subsequent treaty, signed in 1936, which modified certain factors which had unfavorably affected Panama's status as a sovereign and independent state. Among these, for example, was the right of intervention in Panamanian affairs, which had been conferred upon the United States by the Treaty of 1903.

6. The Treaty of 1903 was of vital importance in making the interoceanic canal a reality instead of a dream. And let it be noted that this was one of the basic differences between the Suez Canal and the Panama Canal. Suez was built without benefit of public treaty.

7. In accordance with the Treaty of 1903, the United States acquired certain rights for "the construction, use, occupation, and control by the United States of the Canal Zone for the purposes of the efficient maintenance, functioning, sanitation, and protection of the Canal and auxiliary works."

8. The basic concessions of this treaty were perpetual in character, and were so characterized by Article 1, which read, in part, as follows: "The United States of America shall continue to maintain the Panama Canal for the development and use of interoceanic commerce, and the two Governments manifest their desire to cooperate in every way possible for the purpose of ensuring the *full and perpetual* enjoyment of the benefits of every kind which the Canal should offer *to the two nations which have made its construction possible,* as well as to all nations interested in world trade." *(Italics mine.)*

9. Needless to say, the treaty in force between Panama and the United States had its basis in the Canal itself, which became a

dramatic and magnificent part of the civilization of mankind upon its completion in 1914, even though six more years were to intervene before President Belisario Porras, of Panama, and President Woodrow Wilson, of the United States, met to dedicate it in 1920.

10. The Treaty granted to the United States certain jurisdictional rights over the Canal Zone which were to be "as though sovereign." This involved certain new norms in international law. Panama retained the maximum attributes of sovereignty, but jurisdiction within the Canal Zone, a strip forty-five miles long by ten miles wide, fell to United States authorities. This jurisdiction, needless to say, extended over the territorial waters of the Canal Zone to the three-mile limit, and included air space over the Canal Zone.

11. Likewise established was the pattern for the defense of the Canal and for measures to be taken in case of an aggression prejudicial to the interests of the two contracting parties in the interoceanic waterway.

12. The revenues derived from the Panama Canal do not imply a direct source of income for the Republic of Panama. The United States makes an annual payment of $430,000 to Panama for reasons which are unrelated to the revenues from tolls and other charges levied on vessels using the Canal. Here, too, is to be found another basic difference between the Panama Canal and the Suez Caanl, which is a direct source of dividends for shareholders in the *Compagnie Universelle du Canal Maritime de Suez*.

In short, the differences between the Anglo-Egyptian Treaty on the Suez Canal, and the United States-Panamanian Treaty on the Panama Canal, are as fundamental as they are manifest. The first was a consequence of the Suez Canal. The second *had* as a consequence the Panama Canal.

V

It would be impossible to treat fully all the complex aspects of this matter, or to predict what the future holds in store for the Panama Canal and the Pan American Highway. But of one thing we can be sure: The Caribbean will continue to be an area of incalculable importance, across which will course the great routes of the world in the service of America and of humanity.

Frank K. Bell: THE CARIBBEAN:
AMERICA'S SECOND BEST CUSTOMER

MY COMPANY is complimented, and I am honored, with this opportunity to address a gathering which, in the main, according to my impression, is more concerned with academic views than with those which we in commerce would normally consider of a more practical nature. I should not say that I am in strange company, but certainly the circumstances are unusual. I will therefore take the liberty of telling a little of my background and that of the Alcoa Steamship Company in relation to the Caribbean.

My first knowledge of the Caribbean came in the years 1915 to 1919 in Trinidad when, as an enforced World War I refugee, I was unofficially adopted by local friends. My experience in those impressionable years left with me a knowledge of Caribbean life which few are privileged to have. After twenty-one years in the United States, I returned to Trinidad for six years as District Manager for Alcoa, a position which brought me in close contact with officialdom from all parts of the world and most of the leading people of the eastern Caribbean. During the fateful years of 1942-1945, Trinidad was the center of shipping's strenuous war effort in the South Atlantic; the meeting place of convoys, and the transfer point of millions of tons of bauxite, which contributed so much to America's success in the war.

The Alcoa Steamship Company was born from the need to transport bauxite ore, discovered in Dutch and British Guiana over thirty years ago, to the United States. From small sample shipments, the traffic has grown to a movement of nearly four million

tons of ore annually. Alcoa is now responsible for the traffic from
Dutch Guiana, the British Guiana traffic being handled by a
Canadian company.

Sending ships in ballast on long voyages to load bulk ore cargoes
is not usually economical, so it was not long before Alcoa sought
paying cargoes to decrease the cost of getting ships to the mines.
The result is that Alcoa ships now serve fifty-nine ports in the
Caribbean, carrying general cargo and passengers, all vessels with
some few exceptions returning with full cargoes of bauxite ore.
Alcoa's effort to obtain a major share of southbound traffic has
developed an organization working continually to improve trade
and tourism in the Caribbean. The area covered does not include
Central America, which is properly of the Caribbean, but is composed of all the islands of the Greater and Lesser Antilles, excepting only Cuba and including the South American continent
from Venezuela through the Guianas.

I

I have used the title, "The Caribbean: America's Second Best
Customer," not necessarily to draw attention to a statistical position,
but as an expression of my belief that, in spite of the varied
national and racial backgrounds found in the Caribbean, more
American influence is present in that area than in any other
like area in the world. Trade figures are sometimes misleading in
that they are usually based on units subject to variable factors.
The Caribbean is one of America's top customers and will, I
believe, constantly hold this position because, apart from its increasing commercial demands, American products and the American
way of life meet enthusiastic support in the area.

The lifeline of revenue of this Caribbean region is kept flowing
by its two types of trade: commodity and tourist. It is an area
of great contrast: on the one hand a powerful, affluent economy
such as Venezuela's, capable of purchasing, through the development of its natural resources, an unceasing supply of United
States goods and services; and on the other hand, islands and
countries which seem consigned to an inexorable future of struggle
and want. And there are, at the same time, a few countries mid-
way between these extremes; and as they emerge with greater

progress with each passing year, they become fine examples of what can and has happened through wise planning and enterprise. It does not contribute to an easy solution that the largely under-developed area we call the Caribbean is logically a geographical entity, but one which in actuality is an eclectic potpourri of widely differing political units.

With but one or two exceptions, it is not in the tradition of these islands and countries to show a favorable trade balance. And so in effect there is a constant scrambling to get and stay ahead of the game, a sort of perpetual deficit financing. For most of the units of this territory, it can be said that there is no security in the one-crop agricultural economy they have cultivated—or inherited. In a day of complete absentee ownership and no labor costs, the system worked after a fashion, but now with so many wagons hitched to one star, we have the anomaly of a seventeenth- and eighteenth-century economy beset with twentieth-century com-plexities and desires. Each year the population of this area swells, and at the same time its great potential as a consumer market increases.

I have often heard the casual visitor to the Caribbean comment, on his return to this country, on the poverty and low standard of living found in the Caribbean. Comments of this kind are always relative and certainly may be justified when American standards are used, but anyone who has known the Caribbean for the last forty years, as I have, is constantly amazed at the rise in standards during these decades, and particularly in the last ten years. Where shacks made of kerosene oil boxes were an accepted type of residence years ago—and I am sorry to say there are still a few left—neat, attractive houses have appeared by the tens of thousands throughout the area, the families of oil-box shacks and flour-bag clothes being replaced by modestly but smartly dressed men, women, and children, living in modern dwellings, expressing the results of better education and a growing pride in a more dignified civilization. In many places, government has been active in housing plans, but I feel, in the main, that government activity has been supplemental to a normal desire for better living.

It is interesting to look at recent figures for exports from the United States to the area served by Alcoa. In 1939, exports from the United States amounted to about one quarter of a million dollars; in 1949, the figure had risen to over a billion dollars. The purchase of American goods in practically every category rose nearly 300 per cent during that period. It is particularly interesting to find that in machinery and vehicles, if one accepts these commodities as basic factors in the American way of life, the exports from the United States to the area increased over 500 per cent during the last decade. It is true that a fair percentage of increase in imports may be assigned to oil development in Venezuela, and that a number of islands are suffering from overpopulation and limited means for producing wealth. Yet, in spite of pessimism expressed by some economists, I have little doubt that, given unrestricted trade unbeset by exchange controls and limited world supply of goods, the Caribbean would have shown even greater progress since my earlier days there; and certainly there is ample promise of a golden era as the future unfolds.

Of course no Caribbean unit is going to progress very much if it depends entirely on an outside influence to help it along. It must have the willingness, and the spirit and the fire, to work within, and to use what outside opportunity is offered. And here is where I see real hope for the Caribbean. For on my recent trips there, it seems to me that there is an emergence of a consciousness of the necessity of enterprise, of a local business aptitude, and of an increasing appreciation of the hard goods identified with a high standard of living. This consciousness is being visibly expressed by numerous industrial plants springing up in all parts of the Caribbean—some to meet local needs, others to compete in world markets. Recent industrial developments include cement, beer, paper, bottles, time recorder machines, flour processing, and textiles. Many of the countries are engaged in publicity campaigns extolling their low cost virtues and pleasant environments in an effort to attract industrial plants from the United States and Canada.

II

The background of the present peoples of the Caribbean has been the subject of many studies, because in that area, in contrast

to most world areas, it is difficult to find amongst the population what would truly be a "native." Every race and every na-
tionality have contributed to the population from all over Europe,
Africa, India, the Near and Far East. The peoples who could be
considered as natives, the Caribs and the Arawaks, have long since
become a memory, destroyed by an invasion over the past few
centuries of more numerous and sturdy immigrants.

The national strains which up to now appear to have held on to
their original dominance are the French, the British, and to some
extent the Dutch, with some Spanish strongholds in Cuba and
Puerto Rico and particularly on the mainland of South America.
The most dominant strain of all, however, is that which originated
with the involuntary immigrants from Africa. The British and the
Spanish kept more or less to the lands taken over by their mother
countries, but the French families moved and spread as opportunity
and circumstances permitted; throughout the Caribbean, French
surnames are found, many of the families being traced back to
emigration from Martinique and Guadeloupe because of volcanic
and hurricane disasters. Throughout the Leeward and Windward
Islands is found the only language which bypasses the national
language of the island concerned—patois, basically French, but
with a smattering of Spanish, English, and words of local origin.
The only indication, except perhaps for color of skin, of African
influence is the sound and rhythm of the local music. This music
is commonly referred to as "Calypso," and I do not think any
authority would disagree with my belief that it stems from the old-
time singing fireside reports given the tribes by messengers and
nomads in various parts of Africa.

From all this national and racial vortex is slowly arising what
could be accepted as a new race of people, their skins an indication of their African and Eastern origin, their outlook an expression of the shrewd, enterprising, and freedom-loving nature
of many of their forebears who were responsible for their present
environment.

Several illustrations will indicate something of the racial mixtures
in the Caribbean which I think are of pertinent interest.

Of Surinam, or Dutch Guiana, it is said that the Dutch received
it in exchange for Manhattan Island. I do not know how the
Dutch feel about the exchange now, but at least we can be glad

that Surinam went to friendly hands in view of the contribution that country makes to our aluminum industry through supplies of bauxite ore. It is interesting, too, that only in Surinam were the Negro slaves brought from Africa able to establish their own freedom. Even today they live as their forebears did in Africa and still collect a bounty from the Dutch for keeping the peace.

Saba, and part of St. Martin's island, in the Leewards, with practically no change, have always been under the Dutch flag, and yet the population there speaks English. Saba is apparently an extinct volcano, the only habitations being on the top within the old crater, seven hundred feet above sea level. The name of the town is The Bottom.

Napoleon is reported to have once said of Tobago that with this island he could control the Caribbean, and probably the Americas.

In Trinidad many Portuguese are found. One story about their origin is that some converts of a Church of Scotland missionary in Portugal many years ago, suffering from religious persecution, found their way to Trinidad and formed a branch of the church there; the oldest Presbyterian church in Trinidad is said to be their original structure. It is known as St. Ann's Church of Scotland.

III

No comments on the Caribbean would be complete without mention of politics. Except for communistic and monarchic states, I doubt if one could find anywhere else in the world such good examples, with varying degrees of excellence, of every type of government the world has to offer. Although there are some signs here and there of extremist tendencies, there appears to be no indication of communism, even in the French islands which are represented in Paris as departments of France by so-called communist electives. The colonial crown-colony system is definitely of the past, with all the colonies emerging with self-determined constitutions; and there is much talk of confederation, particularly among the British. The older political systems found in Haiti, the Dominican Republic, and Venezuela appear to be leaving their growing pains behind as commercial and cultural conditions improve.

IV

I have been associated with some of the activities of the Caribbean Commission, which was initiated as the Anglo-American Caribbean Commission but which now embraces all national interests in the Caribbean. Although mainly advisory, the studies and recommendations produced by the commission have been and still are of enormous value to the area. To anyone interested in the Caribbean, the commission's reports will be found to include studies on practically every phase of life in the area.

As a result of one of the Caribbean Commission's recommendations, the Caribbean Interim Tourism Committee was founded two years ago. Although all countries in the Caribbean have not yet joined this committee, there are at present twelve individual members working through an Executive Committee and Advisory Board in New York to bring about more development of tourism in the area.

The Caribbean is fast becoming the Mediterranean of the Americas as a tourist attraction. To tourism the region can look as one of the outstanding possibilities of development. There are no exact statistics available, but some idea can be gained from the figures published by the Department of Commerce for the West Indies and Central America: In 1949, there were 271,000 visitors, with expenditures estimated at $57,000,000; and in 1950, some 323,000 visitors spent $60,000,000, an increase of 20 per cent in one year.

I know of no area in the world where one can find the variety of living to be found in the Caribbean, from modern luxurious hotels to the quiet seclusion of a cottage on a palm-fringed beach. Blue skies and comforting temperatures are the rule; even the very occasional storms which make the headlines in America at certain times of the year are seldom as severe as the weather we sometimes experience in this country. The people are friendly, hospitable, and eager to meet visitors, so I hope that all of you will include in your future plans a lengthy visit to the Caribbean.

George Wythe: INTERNATIONAL TRADE
IN THE CARIBBEAN AREA

To STUDENTS of international commerce the very mention of the Caribbean evokes long vistas of history, since the American middle sea, like its prototype in the Old World, has been one of the chief paths of trade for centuries. Not only was it the chief artery of commerce for the Spanish colonial empire, but this region was likewise of pivotal importance in the trade of the developing North American colonies. After a temporary eclipse during the nineteenth century, the last half-century has witnessed a vigorous renaissance throughout the Caribbean area.

It is a striking fact that the Caribbean region today occupies relatively just about the same position in our foreign trade as in the early years of our history, that is, it provides about one-fifth of the total value of United States imports and takes the same proportion of our exports. Of course, the volume has increased enormously as population and productivity have expanded.

The composition of the trade reveals impressive similarities as well as important changes. Historically the area has been famous for tropical produce and precious metals. For more than four centuries sugar cane has been the principal crop; sugar, molasses, and rum are still major articles of export, although they no longer have the political and strategic significance they enjoyed during the seventeenth and eighteenth centuries. Gold and silver are still important items but they have yielded the stellar role to a *parvenu* among commodities, the black gold of petroleum. Last year the Caribbean area produced 671 million barrels of crude petroleum, or 18 per cent of the world output. Although the larger part of this quantity is exported as crude or as products, local consumption is growing by leaps and bounds.

The cacao plant is indigenous to this area, and first Mexico and then Venezuela were long the chief sources of its nutritious and flavorsome bean. Although other regions of the world now produce larger quantities, the Caribbean area is still an important source, especially of the finer grades. During the last decade, the Dominican Republic, Colombia, Mexico, and some of the Central American republics have expanded production.

Coffee, although not a native, is grown throughout most of the Caribbean, which was the chief source of supply throughout the eighteenth century and well into the nineteenth. It is now the chief article of export from five or six of the republics and an important item in several others.

I. Specialization versus Diversification

In most of the republics or colonies one or two items comprise the bulk of the export movement, but it would be a mistake to draw hasty conclusions from this fact. For one thing, there are exceptions to this rule. Mexico, for example, has long had a diversified export trade, including metal bars and concentrates, crude and refined petroleum, raw fibers and their manufactures, manufactured and crude foodstuffs, handicrafts and some finished manufactures. Furthermore, in some of the countries where the exports are highly concentrated, as in Colombia, the internal economy is by no means lacking in diversity, and this shows up in an analysis of the import statistics. It is true, of course, that in the Caribbean area, as in other regions of the world, there is ample opportunity for diversification and improvement of agricultural and livestock production and for the establishment of industries supplying local needs or producing specialties for export, but the constructive approach to this problem indicates the desirability of adding new sources of wealth rather than a policy of restricting existing productive activities.

The larger countries have long had substantial manufacturing industries, and there has been rapid growth in this field during the last decade. Some idea of what is taking place is shown by the expansion of electricity production. In Mexico, the largest and industrially most important of the countries, the monthly average production rose from 207 million kilowatt-hours in 1937 to 368 million in 1950. Colombia and Venezuela, starting from a lower base, showed larger relative increases: from 15.5 million to 58.7 million in Colombia, and from 8.8 million to 43.4 million in Venezuela. In some of the smaller countries the increase has been equally impressive.

The principal industries of the area involve the grinding and refining of sugar, petroleum refining, and the smelting or reduction of metallic ores. Some of the world's largest and most efficient plants are located in this area. There is also a wide variety of activities embraced within the foodstuffs group of industries, most of which (other than sugar and rum) cater exclusively to national markets but some of which are on an export basis, such as canned vegetables, fruit, and fish, and also hard candies. Also important are the textile industries, working with cotton, wool, rayon, jute, and hard fibers. Cotton is grown in most of this area and has been an article of export since early colonial times. The climate is less propitious for wool, but some local fleece as well as imported yarns are used. Four of the countries now produce some rayon filament or staple fiber. Jute is not produced, but cordage and sacks are made from native fibers. Furthermore, experiments with kenaf in Cuba and El Salvador give ground for expectation that this fiber may become an important jute substitute, provided mechanized decorticating processes are perfected. Since 1941 Central America has developed the production of abacá, for marine cordage, on an important scale.

II. Geographic and Political Influences

Obviously it is difficult to generalize about the trade of an area that includes many distinct political and geographic units which differ as greatly in size and resources as, say, Grenada and Mexico. Nevertheless, from a trade standpoint, their geographic location is a factor of outstanding importance, and the climate and geology of the area affect the nature of production, making it in many respects complementary to that of countries situated in the temperate zone. One geographic fact of importance is the proximity to the

United States, the world's leading economic powerhouse, and another is the location of the area in relation to the Isthmus of Panama. This latter point, coupled with the direction of the prevailing trade winds, was vital during colonial days, became less significant during the nineteenth century, and again came to the fore with the opening of the Panama Canal. Mexico is the only country under consideration that has a common land frontier with the United States; and trade between the two countries has expanded greatly since rail connections between Mexico City and the United States were completed in 1888.

The political factor also carries some weight in the trade picture, as is seen most clearly in the case of the French West Indies and French Guiana, which since the war have been made French departments and apply the metropolitan import duties. Most of their exports go to France or other French possessions, and likewise the bulk of the imports normally come from France, although they were provisioned during the war by the United States and other American states. The islands continue to obtain from the United States some machinery and parts as well as, at times, some foodstuffs, and petroleum products.

The Dutch territories (Surinam and the Netherlands West Indies), on the other hand, follow a liberal tariff policy and accord no preferences. The refining of Venezuelan crude petroleum is one of the major activities of the Netherlands Indies. The derivatives go to various European and Western Hemisphere countries. The United States has a large share of the trade of the Dutch possessions, but Canada, the United Kingdom, and the Netherlands are also important.

The British possessions are embraced in the Empire preference system, so that goods from British Commonwealth sources are subject to duties about 50 per cent lower than the general tariff. In addition to the normal tariff preferences, British Commonwealth exporters receive advantages from the operations of the exchange control systems. Foreign exchange operations in the various possessions are controlled by local boards which, in accordance with policy directives from London, normally only issue import licenses involving dollar remittances when the goods are not obtainable in the United Kingdom or other soft-currency areas. Both Canada and the United States are affected by these restrictions. Effective

January 1, 1951, additional dollar exchange was made available to permit limited imports, on a quota basis, of selected commodities formerly excluded. Both Canadian and United States exporters were helped by this trade liberalization plan proportionate to the ratio of their trade in these commodities during the base years. It is assumed that the plan will be continued and probably expanded during 1952.

Generally speaking, the exports of the British Caribbean territories receive preferences in the markets of Canada and the United Kingdom, and some products, notably sugar, are handled on the bulk purchase system. Although the United States does not take any sugar from these territories, it is a good market for such things as cacao beans, various spices, chicle, mahogany logs, and natural asphalt—all of which enter duty-free in the United States.

III. Reduction of Cuban Preferences on U. S. Goods

Excepting United States possessions, Cuba is the only Caribbean country or territory having preferential tariff relations with the United States, and these preferences have been reduced substantially since 1947. In that year, at the first negotiating session of the General Agreement on Tariffs and Trade, held at Geneva, a general agreement was reached that the existing preferential margins granted by the contracting parties would not be increased, and furthermore negotiations were undertaken to reduce or eliminate the preferential margins on specific tariff items by means of concessions on the most-favored-nation rates of duty. Negotiations within the framework of the General Agreement, at Geneva (1947), at Annecy (1949), and at Torquay (1950-1951) resulted in reduction (or elimination) of many preferences in the United States-Cuba trade agreement that previously had been operative only between the two countries. During the course of this year, Cuba has concluded agreements with the United Kingdom, Canada, and Western Germany which have further reduced or eliminated the preferential advantages previously enjoyed by United States products in the Cuban market. These agreements have not yet been in effect long enough to warrant any speculations as to their influences on the trade. There had been a substantial revival of German trade before this agreement was made, but for some time to come, at least, European suppliers will be handicapped by the shortage of some types of goods and non-competitive prices on others.

In any event, the close economic ties between Cuba and the United States existed before preferences and will doubtless survive the reduction or elimination thereof. Even before independence, Cuba sold an overwhelming proportion of its exports in the United States and also depended on the United States for breadstuffs, lard, and provisions, as well as hardware, railway equipment, and other supplies.

For many years the United States has absorbed from 72 to 82 per cent of Cuba's sugar exports. Since 1934 a succession of United States sugar acts has guaranteed Cuba 28.6 per cent of this country's consumption requirements. Other provisions of these acts have enabled Cuba to supply additional amounts over this base. The balance of Cuba's sugar, not consumed in that country or converted into molasses, industrial alcohol, or rum, has been sold on the so-called world market. A significant feature of the new agreements with Canada, the United Kingdom, and Western Germany is that each of these countries agrees to take specified amounts of Cuban sugar in return for the duty concessions granted by Cuba.

IV. Move Toward Freer Trade in Central America

Mention may be made of the revival of interest in Central America for closer economic and political association among the five states that once were united under a single administration. On October 14, 1951, after a week of negotiation, the Foreign Ministers of the five nations agreed upon a plan for an Organization of Central American States that has been submitted to the governments for ratification. It is also open to adherence by Panama. El Salvador, the smallest but most densely populated of the countries, has been active in promoting bilateral "free-trade" treaties with its neighbors and would like to find a broader market for its growing industries, such as henequen bags and cordage, cotton textiles, and cement. Since 1918 El Salvador has had a commercial treaty with Honduras providing for a large measure of free trade between the two countries, and recently a similar treaty was concluded with Nicaragua. The latter country is the only one of the Central American countries that is a party to the General Agreement on Tariffs and Trade. Consideration is now being given at Geneva as to whether the El Salvador-Nicaragua treaty conforms to Article 24 of the GATT agreement relating to the establishment of customs unions or free trade zones.

The Republic of Panama occupies a special position by virtue of its location at one of the world's great crossroads. The transit trade and tourist expenditures have long been major sources of income, although the development of subsistence and export crops and of small industries has progressed. In 1948 Panama created a free zone at the Port of Colón, on the Atlantic side of the Isthmus, to encourage the establishment in the Republic of distribution and processing facilities by large manufacturers supplying adjacent markets. Two large United States firms have already shifted a large part of their Middle and South American export business to Colón, and various other companies are investigating the possibilities. The operations of the Zone are still somewhat handicapped by lack of adequate docks and warehouses. An American engineering firm has been contracted to study this problem, and the United Nations Economic Commission for Latin America is also advising the Panama government.

V. Volume and Direction of Trade

The international trade of the Caribbean area has attained truly impressive proportions. During the three years 1948-1950, the average annual value of exports from the area (not including United States territories) was around 3.5 billion dollars and that of imports, 3.3 billion dollars. The larger part of this corresponded to the twelve republics of the area (Mexico, Central America, the three island republics, Colombia, and Venezuela), with annual average exports and imports in 1948-1950 of 2.8 billion dollars and 2.4 billion dollars respectively. As the area has a population of about 65,000,000, this results in a per capita foreign trade of slightly over $100.

Venezuela is now in first place in this area as regards the value of foreign trade, with Cuba second, and Mexico third. The growth of Venezuela's trade has been spectacular: exports rose from an annual average of $25,000,000 in 1911-1913 to $1,161,000,-

000 in 1950, while imports increased from $18,500,000 to $537,000,-000. The foreign trade of Colombia, now in fourth place, also has expanded manyfold.

The United States has long been the leading supplier of the imports of the Caribbean area and also regularly uses over half of the exports of all of the republics, except the Dominican Republic and Venezuela. The United States is the principal market for Dominican cacao, coffee, bananas, molasses, tapioca starch, and miscellaneous produce, but most of the sugar crop goes to the United Kingdom. In the case of Venezuela, the United States takes about 70 per cent of exports other than crude petroleum and its derivatives. Directly or indirectly (after refining in the Netherlands Indies), a large part of Venezuela's petroleum exports comes to the United States. In this connection, attention may be called to the fact that public hearings were held in Washington on October 9-12, 1951, by the Committee for Reciprocity Information, preparatory to the inauguration of negotiations with Venezuela to supplement and amend the trade agreement of 1939.

As compared to prewar years, the United States now takes approximately the same ratio of the total volume of exports from the Caribbean republics but supplies a substantially larger proportion of imports, as will be seen from the following table:

DIRECTION OF TRADE, TWELVE CARIBBEAN REPUBLICS
PER CENT OF TOTAL

Country or area	Exports		Imports	
	1938	1950	1938	1950
United States	54	56	58	74
Continental Europe	15	9	27	10
United Kingdom	8	5	4	4
Canada	2	1	1	3
Other Latin American Republics	1	3	2	4
Other areas	20	26	8	5
	100	100	100	100

Direct commercial relations and shipping services have been resumed with Germany and Japan. In 1950 German exports to the twelve Caribbean republics aggregated $52,000,000. Before the war about 3 per cent of the imports of these republics came from Asia, chiefly rice, burlap, and Japanese textiles. Exports to Japan were smaller than imports from Japan.

VI. Types of Products Exchanged

The statement is frequently made that the United States trade with the Caribbean area consists of an exchange of manufactured goods for foodstuffs and raw materials, but this statement needs some qualification. In 1950 about two-fifths of the imports consisted of manufactured foodstuffs or semi-manufactures. Sugar, for example, is a manufactured foodstuff that is produced in large and highly mechanized plants endowed with the latest resources of mechanical and chemical science. Most of the imports of metals are likewise smelter or mill products. Imports of finished manufactures were about 2 per cent of the total.

As regards United States exports, it is worth noting that breadstuffs and provisions were long the chief articles of export from the United States and that food products still constitute an important part of the trade. Exports of crude materials and semi-manufactures are also important. Furthermore, Canada is also an important supplier of flour and other food products that can only be produced at excessive cost, if at all, in most of this region. It is precisely because each region produces and sells the products in which it has great natural advantages that the trade is large and reciprocally advantageous.

In most of the smaller countries, United States manufactured exports are chiefly in the form of consumer goods, but for the area as a whole the major items are machinery, motor vehicles and other transport equipment, and basic ferrous and non-ferrous products. In 1950, United States exports to Middle America (ten republics plus European possessions) of machinery, vehicles, metals, and metal manufactures amounted to $600,000,000 or 42 per cent of the total value of United States exports to that area. In addition, purchases of these items by Colombia and Venezuela were about $309,000,000.

It is reasonable to expect that capital goods will continue to be a large item in the import trade of the Caribbean as existing transportation systems are rehabilitated and expanded, as existing industries are modernized and new ones established, as more power equipment is introduced to supplement manual labor in agriculture and construction, as new extractive industries are developed, and as electric power systems are consolidated and expanded. The trend toward urbanization and industrialization has created rapidly expanding demands for electricity. After years of relative neglect, more attention is being given to the vital transportation question. As the iron ore resources of Venezuela and the bauxite deposits of Jamaica and other islands are developed, the economic life of large areas will be quickened.

VII. Outlook

There is every reason to expect that for a considerable period there will be a strong demand for the leading products of the Caribbean area. Furthermore, the area derives large amounts of dollar purchasing power from tourist expenditures, from new investments, United States Government outlays, and loans from the Export-Import Bank and the International Bank. The immediate outlook for the major export products is favorable. Cuban sugar mills are beginning to grind the largest crop in the nation's history. The curve of Venezuelan petroleum flow is mounting steadily, and oil exports from Colombia and Mexico again show an upward trend. The development of new iron ore and bauxite deposits promises a big increase in shipments of these materials, and other mineral developments have been undertaken.

Although Mexico's historic exports, silver and gold, have declined, larger shipments of agricultural products, canned fruits and fish, handicrafts, and manufactures more than make up the difference. Cotton is now Mexico's leading export. Coffee production is exceeding all previous records. Sugar has shifted from the import to the export column. Mexico has become self-sufficient in corn and in various consumer manufactures, but is a large importer of capital goods, semi-manufactures, industrial raw materials, and high-quality consumer goods. As a market for the United States, Mexico is first among the Latin American nations and third in the world.

Despite scarcities in some items, United States foreign trade figures for the first nine months of 1951 indicate that exports to the southern republics are running at levels near the 1947 peak, while imports are at an all-time high point. Perhaps some easing off of both exports and imports may be anticipated during the next six months or so, but no serious decline is expected. Likewise, it is unlikely that there will be any appreciable shifts in the distribution of the Caribbean trade as regards suppliers or markets.

10

William L. Schurz: FOREIGN CAPITAL
INVESTMENT IN THE CARIBBEAN

I

THE CARIBBEAN investment field comprises twelve of the twenty Latin American republics. It includes Mexico, the six Central American countries, the three island republics, and Colombia and Venezuela. Its total population is about 60,000,000. The bases of its economy are still agriculture and mining. Its staple crops are those familiar to the tropics—sugar, coffee, cacao, cotton, rice, and fruits. At least five of the twelve republics have a food deficit. Of those which do not produce enough for their people to eat, the fault is the country's in two cases. As for minerals, three of the twelve are producers of petroleum. Imports of oil are a heavy drain on the foreign exchange of the other nine. Cost to their consumers is prohibitive, except to the very well-to-do and to manufacturing industries. The same three countries have deposits of coal of sorts, so that the fuel resources of the area are highly concentrated. In addition to gold and silver, the area also produces large quantities of the industrial metals, such as iron, copper, manganese, lead, and zinc. But only half the twelve republics have a mining industry of any size, and so far only one of them has been responsible for the bulk of the output of industrial metals. Only four of the twelve have more than a very rudimentary manufacturing industry. Of the four, one has an ambitious and elaborate industrial system already in operation. Only two of the twelve countries have a basic network of transportation lines covering the national territory.

The economic ties of this area with the United States are very close. With only one exception, at least two-thirds of the foreign trade of each country is with the United States. The total of United States private direct investments in the twelve republics in the middle of 1943 was approximately $2,048,000,000. Of this about $1,700,000,000 represented investments in American-controlled enterprises. Investments in Cuba, Mexico, and Venezuela accounted for about 70 per cent of the total. In the four years 1946-1949, additional capital to a total of $1,066,000,000 was invested in the same countries, over half of it in Venezuela. In the meantime, considerable American capital had been repatriated, particularly from Cuba. So much for the recent *movement* of private American capital in the Caribbean area. Reliable figures for the current total direct investment of private capital do not exist, but it is probably under $3,000,000,000. By comparison, the market value of American holdings of the famous dollar bonds of the twenties is less than $50,000,000. These figures do not include the Export-Import Bank loans made in the past ten years, or loans of the International Bank to four of the republics.

All twelve are what are called "underdeveloped" countries, that is, they have not realized the possibilities of economic development which their natural resources would appear to justify and which their national interests require. In other words, they have not caught up with the Industrial Revolution. By any standards, national and average individual incomes are low. To right things they all need money—much more than they can accumulate in the course of the natural evolution of their present economies. And they are in a hurry. For their populations are growing too fast for what there is to distribute among them. As exporting nations, usually of a very few products, their economies are at the mercy of the international demand for the things they have to sell. They call themselves "colonial" nations, that is, like colonies, they have to trade the raw materials they produce for the manufactured goods they need. They are troubled, not only by the normal vicissitudes of foreign markets, but by the prospects of extraordinary disturbances inherent in the world situation today. They have lived in the economic backwash of two world wars, and they are afraid that if there is another war, a tidal wave will engulf their economies.

So if they seem to be in a hurry to shore up their national houses
against the storm, it is understandable. For the economic storm-
signals are up again all around the circuit of the Caribbean. The
chance that this has been a good year for most of them does
not lull them to the danger. For they consider the profits of 1950
and 1951 as a lucky windfall that might not come again soon.
If civilian rationing of coffee and sugar, chocolate and bananas,
should come again in the United States, they know that no amount
of increased buying of the so-called strategic minerals could compensate for the damage to their basic agricultural industries. They
also know that each war increases their dependence on the United
States by destroying or weakening their alternative markets and
sources of supply. Finally, they are afraid of the internal political
repercussions of economic stringencies on the mood of populations
whose margin of well-being is, at best, too small, and whose
emotional boiling point is correspondingly low.

As insurance against all the contingencies, economic and political,
their governments have plans to modernize the national economy,
or to increase the productive capacity of the country, or to raise
the standard of living of the people. Whatever the terms in which
the purpose is expressed, they all add up to much the same, that
is, to strengthen the national life against the potential impact of
outside forces. "Development," or *fomento,* has become a magic
word in the process, and development programs are the order of
the day. Some are quite elementary in their objectives and their
mechanics; others are very comprehensive and embrace practically
every segment of the national economy. They concern the direct
phases of production—agricultural, mining, and manufacturing—
as well as the various auxiliary functions or instrumentalities of
the economy, such as electric power, transportation, land reclamation, tourist business, and the machinery of credit. They also
concern the social or welfare functions, like housing, sanitation,
and education, that are necessary to improve the general conditions of living of the population. The ambitious development
program of Mexico covers virtually the whole range of interests
and activities, from native artifacts and the "Campaign against
Illiteracy" to irrigation dams and steel mills. At the other extreme,
a few countries like Honduras have scarcely given thought to their
future problems in terms of a concerted program of development.

II

Granted the need for development, the next question is: Where is the money to come from? What sources of investment capital are available? The logical pool of investment capital—that is, a national body of private savings and reserves from profits—exists in quantity only in Mexico. And even there it is far from adequate for financing development plans that have been speeded up beyond the normal tempo of industrial evolution. For example, in the past ten years Mexico has borrowed over $350,000,000 from the Export-Import Bank and the International Bank for Reconstruction and Development. Appropriations from the regular revenues of the state, generally channeled through the Ministries of Public Works or Agriculture, account for much of the public funds that are destined to development purposes. It is significant that in most of the twelve republics the budget for public works exceeds that for military purposes. Sometimes, the government becomes a borrowing agent and makes bond issues for specific development objectives, as in this country.

It has become customary for governments which have well-defined development programs to provide investment capital through the new administrative mechanisms. These tend to follow the general pattern of Chile's *Corporación del Fomento,* and the trend will doubtless be towards concentrating all official development activities in such an organization. This procedure would end the autonomy of the specialized credit institutions like the Venezuelan *Banco Agrario y Pecuario.* A somewhat similar centralizing function is performed in Mexico by the *Nacional Financiera.* This agency has obtained twenty separate credits from the Export-Import Bank—a total of over $278,000,000, to be applied to such diverse objectives as highway construction, the purchase of railway rolling stock, the building of dams and power plants, and the financing of heavy industry in manufacturing and mining.

In default of sufficient domestic capital from official and private sources, governments are forced to turn abroad for investment funds. In the search for money, they shun the New York brokerage houses, which floated the 8 per cent loans of the roaring twenties. The regular commercial banks are no more interested in the public investment field than are their counterparts in Latin America. On occasion, the United States Government has made direct grants which have had the effect of promoting the development of the republics, as in its financing of the Pan American Highway in Central America. The transfer of wartime airfields, for a token consideration, as in Cuba and Guatemala, the price support of silver, and purchases of strategic minerals for stockpiling have had similar results. But the United States Treasury does not pretend to serve as a general source of credit for the development plans of the Latin American republics.

By a change which extended its original jurisdiction in the field of foreign trade, that wide function now belongs to the Export-Import Bank. The Export-Import Bank opens credits for the account of foreign governments and enterprises at interest rates of from 3.5 to 4.5 per cent. It has made loans for a total of over $423,000,000 to ten of the twelve Caribbean countries, the only exceptions being Guatemala and Honduras. About 85 per cent of the total has gone to Mexico and Colombia. It has helped to finance the agricultural development of the Artibonite Valley in Haiti; the construction of hotels in Colombia, the Dominican Republic, Panama, and Venezuela; electric power plants in Mexico, Nicaragua, El Salvador, and Venezuela; the purchase of equipment for the railroads of Colombia, Cuba, and Mexico; the building of highways in Colombia and Mexico; and the equipment of a variety of industrial enterprises, chiefly in Mexico.

An alternative source of investment capital is the International Bank for Reconstruction and Development. Since it is not a dependency of the United States Government, and as fewer strings are likely to be attached to the utilization of its credit facilities, there is a growing disposition on the part of some of the republics to appeal to it for assistance in their development projects. However, its limited capital stock and loaning capacity and the worldwide demands made on its resources have restricted its activities in the Latin American field. In the past two years, the International Bank has granted eleven credits to four of the Caribbean countries— Colombia, Mexico, Nicaragua, and El Salvador—for a total of a little over $115,000,000. The bulk of these funds have been destined for power development, but other fields of investment have been road building and repair, the purchase of agricultural machinery for resale to farmers, and the erection of a plant for the drying and storage of grain.

An interesting innovation in its operations has been the grant of a $10,000,000 credit to a consortium of eight Mexican banks and *Nacional Financiera* for the making of loans to small industrial concerns. This element in the Mexican economy largely consists of the rising class of enterprising industrialists associated with the *Cámara Nacional de la Industria de Transformación,* whom Sanford Mosk calls "The New Group" in distinction from the older and more conservative capitalist class, whose financial roots go back to the pre-Revolutionary regime. In view of this belligerent nationalism, it is natural that they should have recourse to the International Bank rather than to the Export-Import Bank for assistance in expanding their business enterprises.

A special feature of the services performed by the International Bank for potential borrowers is the comprehensive survey of the nation's economy which it is prepared to undertake as a preliminary to making a sizable development loan. It has already made detailed studies of this kind for the governments of Colombia and Guatemala. Panama has requested a similar survey of its economic resources and needs, and a Bank mission of limited scope visited Cuba last year. The Bank is also helping the government of Nicaragua to draw up an over-all development program for the country. These detailed appraisals of a country's economic problems and potentials by disinterested outsiders are of great value to the government in formulating its development plans on a more realistic basis than would otherwise be possible.

III

Closely related to the question of investment capital is the provision of technical assistance or "know-how." Sometimes this is as important as the actual allocation of investment funds. The process of making available to the Latin Americans the benefits of our technological and operating experience has been going on for many years and through a wide variety of channels, both official and private. Without the knowledge gained in this way, the execution of some of the development programs would be very seriously handicapped.

Through its various cooperative programs, the Institute of Inter-American Affairs has made valuable contributions to the technical capacity of the countries in which it has operated. As the agency responsible for carrying out the Point Four Program in Latin America, its usefulness in this respect can be expected to increase greatly in the next few years. In addition to the capital invested in its special projects, the Venezuelan Basic Economy Corporation is adding to the store of technical knowledge in that country.

The various training and interne programs provided for Latin Americans by the member agencies of the famous Interdepartmental Committee of the federal government have been responsible for creating a large body of skilled personnel in such fields as agriculture, mining and geology, fisheries, commercial aviation, meteorology, rural electrification, and fiscal administration. And long before Point Four was ever heard of, many experts in specialized lines were detailed to governments in the area under the provisions of Public Law 63 of the 76th Congress. This program, which was a particular interest of President Roosevelt, has since been brought within the scope of Public Law 402 of the 80th Congress, passed in 1948, which now regulates the government's activities in the general field of educational and scientific interchange. Another official source of technical advice is the International Bank, which is in the habit of assigning advisers to the governments to which it has loaned development funds.

Private organizations which have contributed to the pool of scientific and technical knowledge in the area under our consideration include the Rockefeller Foundation, which, in addition to its work in medicine and public health, is now carrying on a project for the improvement of corn production in Mexico. Also, several American companies which operate in the Caribbean region, like Creole Oil, International Harvester, and Westinghouse Electric, are doing much, by their training programs, to raise the level of technical and managerial skills in these republics. In the same general connection, the agricultural school at Zamorano in Honduras, which was founded by the United Fruit Company, can be counted on to show a general improvement in farming methods throughout Central America as its graduates gain in experience and position.

IV

So much for the economics and mechanics of investment. What about the conditions affecting investment—the "climate" of investment? This is a composite of many factors, the most decisive of which are liable to be political rather than economic, and, therefore, more unpredictable than the normal risks of business enterprises. The investor must consider not only the basic factors of the extent and quality of the resources to be developed, the quantity and efficiency of the labor force, and the probable trends of the country's foreign trade; he must also consider the policies and attitudes of government, and the interests and emotions of groups behind the government. He must be willing to accept the hazards of an atmosphere in which subjective terms like "revolution" and "imperialism" and "exploitation" may be part of the customary parlance of politics. Even though they may be used primarily for local effect, they are nevertheless reminders of explosive possibilities. He must accept the fact of the new nationalism, with all its implications—its militant assertion of national sovereignty, its latent xenophobia, its tendency to exaggerate the national potential and readiness for economic independence.

One of the most important elements in the investment "climate" is the influence of domestic politics. This is particularly true of the pressure of labor as a special interest. In their bid for power the new politicos who lean towards the left naturally make an appeal for the support of the working class. This has been the recent pattern in Guatemala, as it is in Argentina, and as it would have been in Colombia if the Gaetán wing of the Liberal Party had triumphed. Candidates may arouse expectations in this group which they are unable or reluctant to satisfy once they are in office. Meanwhile, popular emotions are aroused to the point where the government is no longer able to control the temper of its supporters, and business negotiations with investors on a reasonable basis become impossible. Whatever the particular merits of the current controversy between the Guatemalan Government and the United Fruit Company, the fact remains that an impasse like that between the Government of Iran and the Anglo-Iranian Oil Company is fast developing in Guatemala. And so long as this situation persists, private capital cannot be expected to look upon Guatemala as a favorable field for investment, unless on highly speculative terms. The tendency of labor to ignore economic realities in its demands is illustrated by the experience of Mexico, where, as Frank Tannenbaum points out, the industrial workers obtained benefits whose cost is out of line with the needs for the accumulation of investment capital in Mexican industry. Another device for paying off the debt of a political party to its labor backers is to turn over the bill to the foreign companies in the form of requirements for increased welfare benefits and support of union demands for higher wages and other advantages. Recourse to this device in Venezuela has resulted in one of the highest ratios of labor costs to productivity of any country on earth.

Among other psychological factors in this general problem is a basic distrust of private initiative or enterprise, either national or foreign, in favor of dependence on government action. This attitude might be understandable in old and battered nations like Britain, whose people decided for a time in favor of state socialism, because they believed that the country could no longer afford the competitive effects of unrestrained free enterprise. In young countries like those around the Caribbean, it is a sign of premature national senility, if not a confession of the individual's distrust of his own economic capacity. For organized labor, the elimination of the profit motive from industry strengthens its own power, as a political pressure group, to obtain its demands. For it, the issue then becomes one of whether the return in investment capital should take the form of social dividends or of dividends in money.

V

As everywhere, the conditions of capital investment in the Caribbean republics are increasingly at the mercy of the international situation. With the mounting costs of defense preparations, less capital will be available for investment in normal industrial development abroad. Increasing pressure is being put on lending agencies like the Export-Import Bank and the International Bank to subsidize the establishment of strategic enterprises that bear little relation to long-term peacetime needs. An example is the Export-Import Bank's credit, granted this year, for the financing of a sulphur plant in Mexico. Continued international tensions, whether or not they end in open war, are certain to have an even greater disturbing effect on the normal course of foreign trade and on the exchange value and buying power of currencies. The investment "climate" for sound development projects will be progressively rendered that much less favorable. In other words, no country can expect to progress in the way and at the rate it has a right to expect so long as the world carries this monstrous burden of war or preparation for war. That is as true of Haiti or Honduras as it is of the United States. In such an atmosphere, no nation can be blamed if it dreams of finding relief in efforts at autarchy or economic self-sufficiency, however ill-prepared it may be for that form of economic escapism.

VI

On their merits, disassociated from the alarums of war and the incidence of emotional and political factors, an excellent case can be made for the development programs of the Caribbean countries. Naturally, the pattern must vary greatly from one to another. More plain business sense is needed in the planning and application of these programs. They should be strictly tailored to the capacities of the country, and their sponsors should recognize that most of these republics can no more be sufficient unto themselves than can Florida or my state of Arizona. We both may be economic "colonies" of New York, but in the meantime we manage to do rather well in our colonial vassalage. The governments of the republics must not try to make their development programs the occasion for a "Revolution" with a capital "R." They should not make a fetish of industrialization, as in their plans for agricultural development they tend to worship the cult of the tractor before they have given the plow a trial. And in their need for capital it will be to their advantage in the long run to rely more on private sources and on the contributions which American direct investments can make to their welfare. Their bogy of American "economic imperialism" has no substance, and the social record of American private enterprise in these times is a better guarantee of their national interests than can be provided by any amount of restrictive laws.

BIBLIOGRAPHY

The Brookings Institution. *Major Problems of United States Foreign Policy 1951-1952* (Washington, 1951), Chapter XVI.

Business Week. "Business Week Reports to Executives on South America." New York, August 25, 1951.

The Chase National Bank. "Latin-American Business Highlights" (New York, November, 1950; February and September, 1951).

Export-Import Bank of Washington. "Twelfth Semi-Annual Report to Congress for the Period January-June, 1951" (Washington, 1951).

Feuerlein, Willy, and Elizabeth Hannan. *Dollars in Latin America* (New York, 1941).

Fitzgibbon, Russell H. (ed). *The Constitutions of the Americas (as of January 1, 1948),* (Chicago, 1948).

Gordon, Wendell C. *The Economy of Latin America* (New York, 1950), Part III.

Guatemala. "Speech of the Lt. Colonel Jacobo Arbenz Guzmán, March 15th, 1951" (Guatemala, 1951).

.... "Exposición del Presidente de la República, Ciudadano Jacobo Arbenz ante la opinión pública nacional y el Consejo Nacional de Economía sobre su programa de gobierno." (Guatemala, 1951).

Hanson, Simon G. *Economic Development in Latin America* (Washington, 1951).

Horn, Paul V., and Hubert E. Bice. *Latin-American Trade and Economics* (New York, 1949), Part IV.

International Bank for Reconstruction and Development. "Sixth Annual Report 1950-1951" (Washington, 1951).

International Development Advisory Board. "Partners in Progress: a Report to the President" (Washington, 1951).

Mosk, Sanford A. *Industrial Revolution in Mexico* (Berkeley and Los Angeles, 1950).

Olson, Paul R., and C. Addison Hickman. *Pan American Economics* (New York, 1943), Chapters 4-8.

Tannenbaum, Frank. *Mexico: The Struggle for Peace and Bread* (New York, 1950), Chapters 11-14.

United Nations. "Economic Development in Selected Countries: Plans, Programmes and Agencies" (New York, 1947), pp. 132-148.

United States Department of Commerce. "Private United States Direct Investments Abroad," Report by Samuel Pizer and Fred Cutler, in *Survey of Current Business* (Washington, January, 1951).

United States Department of State. "U. S. Bilateral Technical Assistance: Principal Activities in Underdeveloped Areas under the Direction of U. S. Governmental Agencies Fiscal Year 1950" (Washington, 1950).

United States Treasury Department. "Census of American-Owned Assets in Foreign Countries" (Washington, 1947).

Winkler, Max. *Investments of United States Capital in Latin America.* (Boston, 1929).

Wythe, George. *Industry in Latin America.* (2nd ed., New York, 1949).

APPENDIX A

United States Holdings of Latin-American Dollar Bonds
(At end of 1950)

	Total market value	Par value	National	Provincial	Municipal	Government guaranteed	Private corporate
	(Millions of Dollars)						
Colombia	28.3	54.1	23.6	22.8	5.4	1.1	1.2
Costa Rica	.5	2.9	2.9				
Cuba	12.8	13.1	10.7				2.4
El Salvador	2.2	3.5	3.5				
Guatemala (redeemed)	.2	.4	.4				
Mexico	3.9	27.8	7.0			20.8	
Panama (new issue)	10.1	10.1	10.1				
Total:	58.0	111.9	58.2	22.8	5.4	21.9	3.6

Source: United States Department of Commerce.

APPENDIX B

International Bank for Reconstruction and Development
Loans to the Caribbean Republics
(1949-1951)

COLOMBIA
  $ 5,000,000.00 (7 years)
      Caja de Crédito Agrario, Industrial y Minero.
      Purchase of agricultural machinery.
  3,500,000.00 (20 years)
      Central Hidroeléctrica del Río Anchicayá.
      Power development in the Cauca Valley.
  2,600,000.00 (20 years)
      Central Hidroeléctrica de Caldas.
      Power development in Manizales area.
  16,500,000.00 (10 years)
      Government of Colombia.
      Highway construction and rehabilitation.

  Total: $27,600,000.00

EL SALVADOR
      $12,500,000.00 (25 years)
         Government of El Salvador.
         Power Development of Río Lempa.
MEXICO
      $24,100,000.00 (25 years)
         Comisión Federal de Electricidad and Nacional Financiera.
         Power development.
      10,000,000.00 (1 year; refunded)
         Same.
         Power development.
      26,000,000.00 (25 years)
         Mexican Light and Power Co., Ltd.
         Power development.
      10,000,000.00
         Consortium of eight banks and Nacional Financiera.
         Financial assistance to small companies.

         Total: $70,100,000.00

NICARAGUA
      $ 3,500,000.00 (10 years)
         Government of Nicaragua.
         Highway construction.
      1,200,000.00 (7 years)
         Banco Nacional.
         Purchase of agricultural machinery.

         Total: $4,700,000.00
GRAND TOTAL: $114,900,000.00
Adapted from *Sixth Annual Report, 1950-1951*.

APPENDIX C

EXPORT-IMPORT BANK OF WASHINGTON
Credits granted to the Caribbean Republics
COLOMBIA
   (1) $20,000,000.00 (2 loans)
         Government of Colombia.
         Materials, equipment and services.
   (2)   10,000,000.00
         Caja de Crédito Agrario, Industrial y Minero.
         Materials and equipment.
   (3)   8,500,000.00
         Banco de la República, for Empresa de Energía Eléctrica, S.A.
         Materials and equipment.
   (4)   6,503,389.00
         Government of Colombia for National Railway Administration.
            (a) 5,000,000.00
                   Railway equipment.
            (b) 1,503,389.00
                   Diesel locomotives.

(5) 3,057,600.00
     Banco de la República, for Hotel San Diego, S.A.
     Goods and services for construction.
(6) 13,678,609.44 (7 credits)
     Government of Colombia.
     Seagoing dredge, highway construction, busses, railroad materials,
     construction of grain storage facilities, etc.
(7) 20,000,000.00 (Nov., 1951, 15 months)
     Government of Colombia.
     To finance imports of cotton.

     Total: $81,739,598.44 (Principal repaid $17,493,432.65)

COSTA RICA
     $ 7,000,000.00
          Government of Costa Rica.
          Construction materials and service.
CUBA
     $12,000,000.00
          Cuban Electric Company.
          Equipment, materials, and services.
DOMINICAN REPUBLIC
     $ 3,000,000.00
          Dominican Government.
          Materials, equipment, and services for hotel construction.
HAITI
     $ 5,000,000.00
          Sié. Haitiano-Américaine de Développement Agricole.
          Agricultural development of Artibonite Valley.
     14,000,000.00
          Government of Haiti
          Construction materials, equipment, and services.

     Total: $19,000,000.00

MEXICO
(1) $278,472,767.17 (20 credits)
     Nacional Financiera.
     (a) $ 30,972,767.17
              Highway construction, equipment, and services.
     (b)   8,000,000.00
              Steel mill equipment: Altos Hornos de México.
     (c)   19,000,000.00
              Railroad equipment: National Railways.
     (d)   20,000,000.00
              Materials and supplies.
     (e)   344,250.00
              Equipment, facilities, and services.
     (f)   3,500,000.00
              Electrical equipment: Nueva Cía. Eléctrica. Chapala.
     (g)   5,000,000.00
              Agricultural equipment.

(h)   7,000,000.00
       Railway equipment.
(i)   5,000,000.00
       Sugar mill equipment.
(j)   6,000,000.00
       Ammonium sulphate plant.
(k)   1,515,750.00
       Tampico-Ciudad Madero water works.
(l)   12,900,000.00
       Railway equipment: National Railways.
(m)   5,000,000.00
       Railway equipment: Southern Pacific Railway of
       Mexico.
(n)   2,740,000.00
       Coal mine development.
(o)   1,500,000.00
       Raw materials.
(p)   114,000,000.00 (1950)
       Development of agriculture, transportation, communi-
       cations, and electric power.
(q)   12,500,000.00
       Falcón Dam and power plant.
(r)   1,000,000.00
       Anzalduas Dam.
(s)   17,500,000.00
       Yaqui Alto Canal.
(t)   5,000,000.00
       Expansion of steel mill.
(2) 1,079,570.87
     Fred Leighton, Inc.
     Development of handicrafts industries.
(3)   800,000.00
       Cía. Fundidora de Fierro y Acero de Monterrey, S.A.
       Steel mill and electrical equipment.
(4) 1,875,000.00
     Mexican Gulf Sulphur and Mexican Sulphur Co.
     Erection of sulphur plant.
     _____
     Total: $282,227,338.04 (Repaid $40,862,729.89)

NICARAGUA
(1) 2,000,000.00
     Government of Nicaragua.
     Construction materials, equipment, and services.
(2)   600,000.00
       Government of Nicaragua, for Empresa de Luz y Fuerza Eléc-
       trica, S.A.
       Equipment for power plant.
       _____
       Total: $2,600,000.00

PANAMA
    $ 2,500,000.00
        Government of Panama for Hoteles Interamericanos.
        Construction materials, equipment, and services.
EL SALVADOR
    $ 1,726,000.00
        Government of El Salvador.
        Construction materials, equipment, and services.
VENEZUELA
  (1) $ 6,000,000.00
        Government of Venezuela for Banco Obrero.
        Construction materials and equipment.
  (2)   2,337,697.00
        Government of Venezuela for Banco Obrero.
        Goods and services for construction (Hotel Tamanaco, C.A.)
  (3)   600,000.00
        S. & S. Construction Co. de Venezuela (C.A. de Seguros La
          Nacional & St. Paul Mercury Indemnity Co.)
        (U. S. goods and services)
  (4)   500,000.00
        S. & S. Construction Co. de Venezuela, C.A. (C. W. Smith,
          W. L. Stevens, and Raymond A. Jones)
        U. S. goods and services.
  (5)   7,108,000.00
        Corp. Venezolana de Fomento, C.A. de Electricidad de Caracas.
          (a) $1,950,000.00
              Diesel electric generator units.
          (b)   5,158,000.00
              Electrical equipment (International G.E. Co.)

Total: $16,545,697.00

GRAND TOTAL FOR TEN REPUBLICS: $397,112,633.48

Source: Export-Import Bank of Washington, *Thirteenth Semiannual Report to Congress.* Washington, Government Printing Office, 1952.

APPENDIX D

VALUE OF AMERICAN-OWNED FOREIGN ASSETS IN THE

CARIBBEAN REPUBLICS

AS OF MAY 31, 1943

(In millions of dollars)

	Interests in controlled enterprises	Securities	Bullion, currency and deposits	Real property	Estates and trusts	Various	Total
Colombia	117.6	31.4	1.0	3.0	.1	25.8	178.9
Costa Rica	30.9	1.1	.6	.4	(x)	3.7	36.7
Cuba	529.0	24.1	2.3	11.8	1.7	21.5	590.5
Dominican Republic	71.5	3.2	.3	1.8	.5	3.2	80.5
Guatemala	87.3	1.4	.3	1.6	(x)	2.4	93.0
Haiti	14.2	2.1	.2	.5		.8	17.7
Honduras	37.2	.9	.4	.4			42.2
Mexico	287.3	21.4	13.0	21.7	2.7	76.1	422.2
Nicaragua	4.2	1.0		5.9		2.4	13.5
Panama	110.8	20.1	2.9	3.6	.9	16.1	154.4
El Salvador	15.1	1.7	.2	1.0	(x)	(x)	20.4
Venezuela	372.9	7.8	.8	6.4	.3	10.4	398.6
Total:	1,678.0	116.2	22.0	58.1	7.5	166.7	2,048.5

Source: United States Treasury Department, *Census of American-Owned Assets in Foreign Countries.* Washington: Government Printing Office, 1947.

Note: (x) *included in total*

APPENDIX E

MOVEMENT OF PRIVATE DIRECT INVESTMENT CAPITAL
(1946-1949)
(A-1946-47: B-1948-49)
(In millions of dollars)

	Manufacturing		Distribution		Agriculture		Mining		Petroleum		Utilities		Misc.		Total	
	A	B	A	B	A	B	A	B	A	B	A	B	A	B	A	B
Colombia	2	1	3	1	5	3	3/	3/	15	8	3	2	1	1	21	14
Costa Rica			3/	3/	10	2	3/	3/	3/	3/	2	1	2	4/	14	3
Cuba, Haiti, D. R.	12	4	4	2	16	9	3/	3/	5	1	3	7	4	3	2	4
Guatemala	3/	3/	4/	1	4	4	3/	3/	3/	3/	1	1	1	4/	4	6
Honduras	3/	3/	4/	4/	9	8	3/	3/	3/	3/	3/	3/	12	13	21	21
Mexico	5	5	10	4/	3/	3/	3	3	2	2	6	3	2	5	20	12
Panama	1	1	1	4/	4	3			102	162	9	3	31	4	146	165
Venezuela	3	6	6	7	4/	8	3/	3/	171	370	4/	4/	11	35	191	426

Total: 1946-47, $415,000,000.00, 1948-49, $651,000,000.00.

Source: United States Department of Commerce.
(3/-included in "Miscellaneous."
4/-less than $500,000:
1/-"inflow" or repatriated capital.)

Part IV

CULTURE

Muna Lee: SOME EARLY CULTURAL RELATIONS IN THE CARIBBEAN

THIS HAS BEEN a year rich in anniversaries having special significance for the Caribbean. Five hundred years ago, in 1451, both Isabel of Spain and Columbus, her Great Admiral, were born. Four hundred years ago, in 1551, the University of Mexico was founded, as was the sister institution of San Marcos at Lima. Three hundred years ago, in 1651, was the birth of the incomparably gifted Sor Juana Inés de la Cruz, whose poetry is still to many critics the best ever written in any language by any woman in this hemisphere. Two hundred years ago, in 1751, George Washington, still in his teens, was on the visit to Barbados which gave him a lifelong affection for and understanding of the Caribbean area. One hundred years ago, in 1851, Narciso López made his second attempt to free Cuba, failed, was captured, and declared as he was executed, "My death will not change Cuba's fate!"

These anniversaries, so diverse in character and significance, have one important characteristic in common. Each, directly or indirectly, started a chain reaction that has to some extent modified the way of life or the manner of thought, or both, in the region of the Caribbean and in ever widening areas, with consequences that could not have been foreseen at the time. Let Isabel and Columbus stand for Discovery and Colonization; the University of Mexico for Education, in a world so new that a European-parented generation had scarcely had time to grow to maturity in it; Sor Juana, the lovely Tenth Muse, for Arts and Letters; George Washington (whose diary for the stay in Barbados shows a farmer's interest in

117

planting and plantations) for Agriculture; and Narciso López—
Venezuelan-born, landing at Bahía Honda a force collected in the
United States and in Latin America—for the hemisphere determina-
tion for Freedom: and it is not too fanciful to say that 1951's
centenaries and multi-centenaries embrace most of the primary
interests of the Caribbean peoples throughout the years. For the
sake of completeness, we may bring the record quite down to the
present, and add an instance of Industrialization, since in January
of this year the Insular Government of Puerto Rico celebrated the
establishment of the one-hundredth industry on that once wholly
agricultural island.

There are four and one-half centuries of recorded relations and
interchanges in this area, which before the airplane and before the
steamship had the islands for stepping stones and the trade winds
for motive power. The very earliest reports are among the most
fascinating: what Columbus himself wrote, and Dr. Chanca, Acosta
and Oviedo and Vesputius and Peter Martyr, Castellanos and
Bernal Díaz del Castillo, are of perennial interest. To recall how
meaningful to us today those early relations were, let us glance
back for a moment to the Europe of 1492, when Isabel and
Columbus alike had passed their fortieth year, and so, in the view
of those days, were aging fast.

The year 1492 was beyond question a year of movement and
projects in Europe. The printing press was already functioning
enthusiastically, and costly parchment was giving way to cheap
Egyptian paper. Trade had increased along with exploration. There
was an abundance of great art, great architecture, much discussion
of Aristotle. Spain had expelled the Jews and dreamed of Christian-
izing the world. In Germany the international money-lenders were
becoming powerful. English merchants at Bristol organized trading
expeditions, which were usually risky and very minor enterprises of
a single ship. Obviously there was much to interest and excite the
imagination.

But ordinary living was chilly, miry, evil-smelling, badly lit,
harassed, and verminous. Life was short, and many diseases pan-
demic. Furniture was massive, richly carved, and uncomfortable.
Beautiful tapestries attempted unavailingly to keep out draughts.
Huge fireplaces smoked, and could not warm the great clammy
rooms anyway. Candlelight was lovely, but wax was expensive.

That did not matter so much as regards reading because, while books were few and also expensive, they were printed in black letters that did not require strong light. The food was dull, dim, and tasteless, except when it was meat that had been hung too long. Either way—tasteless or rancid—it needed to be highly spiced to make it palatable; and hence the incessant demand for more, and more pungent, spices. It was a dreadful age in which to be ill, a dreadful age in which to be homeless and hungry, and a dreadful age in which to be at home and fed. And then the entrancing islands and the lands beyond suddenly loomed on Europe's vision, rising from the blue Caribbean at the end of the world. And there were pineapples and wild strawberries, and grapes running over the trees, and potatoes and tomatoes, and fresh soft air in a climate that needed no fireplaces, and hammocks, and birds with colors which European eyes until then had seen only on flowers, and fireflies as softly bright as their candles.

The earliest chroniclers in their several languages describe the fruits and vegetables of the Indies with a zestful relish, a smacking-of-the-lips satisfaction, which publicity agents for fruit and vegetable products today try manfully to emulate. But the combined resources of skilled ad-writers and shiny colored pictures in the higher priced magazines are not enough to give that original thrill. "Quinetas are red inside," Peter Martyr wrote to the Pope. "The turma is purplish, the hobas yellowish, and the atibuniex has a violet skin and a white pulp.... I am aware," he added defensively, "that in enumerating these species I shall provoke envious people, who will laugh ... at my sending such minute particulars to Your Holiness, who is charged with such weighty interests and on whose shoulders rests the burden of the whole Christian world ... [but] Pliny and the other sages famous for their science ... mingled together obscure reports and positive knowledge, great things and small, generalities and details; to the end that posterity might ... learn everything together."

Sir Henry Colt said of the pineapple, it is "most like unto a great white ripe strawberrye ... sweet, sharp, moyste...." "The cochos nut and plantans are very pleasant fruites," averred Thomas Cates in 1585. "The said cochos hath a hard shell and a greene huske over it, as hath our walnut, but it farre exceedith it in greatness.... Next within the hard shell is a white rine, resembling ...

the white of an egg when it is hard boyled. And within the white of the nut lyeth a water of a very cool fresh taste, and as pleasing as anything may be. . . . The plantan," he continued, "groweth in cods, somewhat like to beanes, but is bigger and longer, and much more thicke together on the stalke, and when it waxeth ripe, the meate which filleth the rine of the cod becometh yellow, and is exceedingly sweet and pleasant."

In that description of the plantain—which was, of course, our banana—Cates was recording, though he did not know it, one of the earliest and most important of the cultural interchanges in the Caribbean. It is no news, however, to the guests at this table, that it was Columbus who had brought the banana to the New World, where it was to spread from island to island to mainland, and to create an economy of its own. So with coffee. So with sugar cane. So with orange and in lesser degree with mango. The breadfruit introduced by Captain Bligh in the eighteenth century was an attempt at a cultural relationship—or, shall we say, was a Point Four experiment—of the same pattern, but has never come to be much more than a haphazard, though useful, visitor from region to region.

It was likewise from the Caribbean—specifically, in the first instance, from Puerto Rico and Santo Domingo—that the barnyard fowls and the livestock of Europe were to find a new home and a new development in this hemisphere. Undoubtedly the Spaniards who brought the livestock had their own agricultural and commercial ends in view. But according to Father Cobo, an even more important consequence of the importation of Spanish cattle was the fact that it put an end to cannibalism among the Caribs; while horse and mule and wheeled cart carried many a hundredweight that theretofore had weighed in this hemisphere upon aching human shoulders.

And if—led on, perhaps, by the fact that this is a luncheon meeting—I seem to be giving a disproportionate amount of attention to food as a cultural factor, let me point to the work in the Caribbean and elsewhere in Latin America of the *Sociedades Económicas de Amigos del País;* for example, to that of Cuba, still active and still productive. It may be said that the first official cultural relations program of Cuba with other countries was initiated on January 9, 1793 with the inaugural session at Habana of the

Real Sociedad Económica de Amigos del País. The Society from its foundation was dedicated to the advancement of agriculture and education on the island, the translation of publications to that end, the creation of a school of chemistry and the establishment of libraries, and the maintenance of cultural contact with other countries. While most of its work—which has been increasingly fruitful over a period of more than a century and a half—has been within the insular boundaries, the Society has also some notable international services in its cultural history. When consulted officially in 1844 with respect to the carrying out of the treaty between France and England regarding slave immigration, the Society stood firm for free immigration and for some years suffered for its stand. In 1847, responding to the stimulus of the Universal Expositions of Industry initiated by France, the *Sociedad Económica de Amigos del País* sponsored the first Cuban public exhibition and in 1862 was responsible for the excellent Cuban exhibit at the London Exposition of that year, a service for which it was thanked officially by the Cuban government. Its present activities are for the most part in the field of education. It maintains a number of schools, and has a magnificent library.

As often has been said, the Caribbean Sea was the gateway, and its islands were the milestones, from Europe to the Americas, both North and South. Through the sixteenth and seventeenth centuries, in the European mind these islands far outweighed in importance the lands north of the Rio Grande. France, as you know, decided that Martinique was of more value, strategically and economically, than Canada; Spain refused to consider exchanging Puerto Rico for the Louisiana Territory. Then, with the invention of the steamboat and the advent of the industrial age, islands for a hundred years or more ceased to dominate the hemisphere's trade routes. Now, with the coming of the air age, the wheel of circumstance has made another great revolution, and islands are once more of major importance in world affairs. That is true in all seas and all oceans. It is especially true in the Caribbean, where again the Greater and the Lesser Antilles, the Leeward and the Windward Isles, are outposts, sentries, and bastions of the Americas.

For the first generation or so after the Discovery, Santo Domingo remained the active center from which went out conquistadors, civil authorities, missionaries, teachers, soldiers and colonizers:

Ponce de León and Juan de la Cosa, Pizarro, Cortés, De Soto, Las Casas, Coronado. Again, in the Period of Independence, the Caribbean was to be a dominating center. Haiti would become the second republic of the hemisphere, with Venezuela and Mexico to follow. And after discovery and colonization and independence, it was in the Caribbean area that an international consultation of states, planned and expounded by Bolívar, upheld by Henry Clay, was to take form in the Conference at Panama, forerunner of all Pan American Conferences, precursor of the League of Nations, of the United Nations. It is more than a century and a quarter since Bolívar called that first of the many inter-American meetings that have advocated and helped bring about the solidarity of the American states in their collective will for freedom, through arbitration of differences, mutual aid against aggression, and equality at the common council table. José Cecilio del Valle of Honduras, drawing up Central America's declaration of political independence in 1821, declared that "the proper study of the man of America is America." Do not the historic past and the predictable future authorize us to add, "and especially the Caribbean?"

Harriet de Onís: THE SHORT STORY
IN THE CARIBBEAN TODAY

THE SHORT STORY is one of the literary forms most cultivated in Spanish America today. As we cannot consider any phase
of the literature of the area under study at this conference without
bearing in mind its relationship to the larger framework of which it
forms a part, it has seemed to me that an attempt to analyze certain
of the dominant tendencies displayed in the work of representative
short-story writers of the Caribbean might be revealing. It will, I
hope, assist in an understanding of the Caribbean world, and also
show the intrinsic value of this production and its importance in
the Spanish-American creative field.

It is unnecessary to point out to a gathering of this sort that,
although there is an undeniable justification for the use of the term
"Caribbean," it is a loose denomination, and slightly in the nature
of a Procrustean bed. It brings together countries that are geographically related, but that differ greatly from one another and
within themselves. Behind the sea they share lies the interior, the
backland of these countries, which are so much larger than they look
on the map, each with its own national characteristics, the product
in many cases of a totally different cultural origin. And these inland regions have remained strangely aloof from the influence of
the teeming, restless coast. It might not be too farfetched to suggest that the sea has been the route of invasion, the land the
path of evasion. It is as though there were two centers of gravity
in these areas: the coast, which has been the polarization point of

movement, change, foreign influence of many sorts; and the inland, nucleus of the permanent, the timeless, the autochthonous.

The ethnic composition of the area, so determining a factor in its culture, is disparate, too. A large part of it—Yucatan, Guatemala—gravitates toward its Mayan past; even the present is, in a sense, a continuation of the past. In certain regions the African element has been of decisive importance; in others a racial blend of Negro, Indian, and Spaniard, in varying proportions, has become fixed. The Spanish-speaking countries, to which I have limited myself, share, in addition to the sea that links them, the fact that they all belong within the general Spanish-American cultural pattern, and, specifically, they constitute Middle America. The basic characteristics of the general culture are present in them, but with a typical, local accent.

Rather than weary you with a list of names, which would be unavoidable if I were to try to do justice to the contemporary short-story writers of the Caribbean—so many and so good—I have preferred to select four who seem to me to exemplify the two main tendencies, which at many points fuse into one, I have noted in this literature of the region. In them are to be found, in great intensity and perfection, the themes, the sensibility, the techniques shared by the majority of the others. By and large, it is a proletarian literature that deals with both the rural and urban proletariat, and a literature of implicit protest. But as Jorge Mañach of Cuba pointed out at your last conference, Spanish-American literature " . . . exhibits in a more marked way that 'aesthetic accent' which has been recognized as the distinguishing characteristic of the Latin American mind."[1] And so in the short story of today the aesthetic sense triumphs over the social attitude, giving this writing a permanence, and what, for lack of a better term, I must describe as a kind of innocence, an affirmation of the simple virtues and an underlying, if tacit, belief in the perfectibility of life on the basis of the brotherhood of man. It is a kind of a posteriori justification for the location of Utopia in America.

[1] "Literary Homogeneity in the Caribbean," in *The Caribbean at Mid-Century* (Gainesville: University of Florida Press, 1951), p. 215.

I

The first author I have chosen to deal with brings me dangerously close to a paradox. He is not, in the strict sense of the word, of the Caribbean. Salvador Salazar Arrué—Salarrué, as he signs himself, is from the republic of El Salvador, which is cut off from the inter-American sea by Nicaragua. But it is comprehended within the Middle American culture, and as Salarrué represents to a high degree the tendencies dominant in so many of the inland writers of the Caribbean area, he has seemed to me of singular importance in himself, and as a link between the literatures of the various Caribbean lands, and between them and that of the rest of Spanish America.

Salarrué, who was born in San Salvador in 1899, is another of the many Hispanic writers whose fame rests on a single book, *Cuentos de barro,* published in 1943. He received part of his education in this country, and has held diplomatic posts both in the United States and abroad. But it is as though his absence from his native land and his contact with foreign cultures had only sharpened his awareness of and love for his own. His work is impregnated with infinite tenderness toward the people, the land, the poor monotonous life with its rudimentary, but moving incidents. It is colored with irony, but an irony close to tears. The language he employs is that of his people of Salvador, with its archaisms, its incorrections and deformations, its Indian infiltration; not as a student of philological curiosities might use it, or seeking effects of local color, but as the only adequate medium of expression for the material he writes of.

There is little or no plot to his stories; they are episodes in the day-by-day living of the peasants of Salvador—the capsized fishing boat, the daughter who is dishonored, the haunted house where a restless spirit must be exorcised, the dream of finding buried treasure —and the traditional virtues: family loyalty, fidelity in friendship, charity, and compassion. There is no sentimentalizing in Salarrué's writing, but it is informed with a poetry, a rustic fragrance, a spirit of resignation under the juggernaut of circumstance that makes it incredibly moving. Perhaps the most powerful protagonist in his work is nature, so untamed, so treacherous, so unpredictable—

the sudden storm that can sweep away home and crops, the river that can be the source of a man's livelihood as of his death. Life is a game in which the elemental forces hold the trump cards.

In addition to being a writer, Salarrué is also a painter, and this reveals itself in his literature. He sees his people as they are—ugly, dirty, ignorant, superstitious—making no attempt to beautify them superficially, but, like Velázquez, discovering their essential human quality by the depth of his penetration. With Fray Luis de León he knows "that this is the true beauty, that everything should act according to its nature."

The perfection of his technique is very great, and this may explain the paucity of his production. His seeming artlessness is the result of great art. He never employs a superfluous word, there are no explanations; the characters live and move and have their being in an atmosphere where reality has been transmuted into poetry by the author's lyric power. With disarming modesty he writes in the foreword to his book: "My poor little stories of clay. . . . They are as nothing compared with the thousands of beautiful stories that flower day after day; as they have not been turned they have come out crooked, rough, flawed. . . . But it is clay of the soul that went into them, and where this has been removed a little hole remains that the winters of the heart have filled with melancholy. . . . " Enveloping all is an atmosphere of magic evoked by the persistence of the elements of folklore that flow like a subterranean current through so much of the work of Spanish-American writers. Lionel Trilling has given a definition of this attitude which I think very good: a sense of piety toward the past. And the strength of our response is probably due to the fact that it reaches us in "our secret and primitive minds." When Coleridge uses as an epigraph to *The Rime of the Ancient Mariner* the lines "a judicious belief in the existence of demons has the effect of keeping the mind from becoming narrow and lapsed entirely into mean thoughts," the point he is making, says Professor Trilling, is "that the world is a complex and unexpected and terrible place which is not always to be understood by the mind as we use it in our everyday tasks."[2]

2 Lionel Trilling, "The Meaning of a Literary Idea" in *The Liberal Imagination,* (New York: Viking, 1950).

II

There can be no question as to the rightful place in the Caribbean of the other exponent of this same tendency followed by Salarrué. Juan Bosch of the Dominican Republic has found his inspiration in the countryside of his native island, and with equally felicitous results. Less lyric than Salarrué, he brings very great power, insight, and a somewhat more impersonal, though equally compassionate, irony to the treatment of his material. He deals not only with the country folk of Santo Domingo, but also with the poor Haitians who cross the border in search of work, and whose life is tragedy amidst the hostile, alien corn.

Bosch, born in 1909, is an exile from his island. He is an active member of the *Partido Revolucionario Dominicano*, working for the overthrow of President Trujillo. But despite the fact that the sea plays so active a part in his life, with the comings and goings connected with his political activities, it is not a motif in his writing. His stories deal with the life of the interior, perhaps in a nostalgic effort to recapture that from which he has been cut off.

His production in the field of the short story is limited to two small books, *Dos pesos de agua* (1941) and *Ocho Cuentos* (1947), and several of his stories have received distinguished literary awards. He is a master in the use of a sober, restrained, yet vivid language, and he achieves strikingly dramatic effects, often by understatement. He has a masculine forthrightness that recalls Ricardo Güiraldes. Like him, he can take a threadbare theme, as though to show how unimportant plot is, and give it new, pulsating life. Bosch has a social conscience closer to the surface than Salarrué, and occasionally in the course of his writing it jogs his elbow. When this happens he throws in a fiery phrase to remind the reader and himself that he is an angry man. But this happens only rarely, and when it does it really defeats its own ends, for the effect is almost humorous. It recalls the formula: "We now pause briefly for a word from our sponsor."

In Bosch, too, the elements of folklore and tradition are very strong, giving his work a deep sense of continuity. As José Luis Martínez, the able Mexican critic, has said: " ... our writers became more and more aware of the zones in which their authentic originality resided. The notes that truly defined them were forms and shades of emotion, spiritual rhythms, persistent concepts and beliefs. And the letters of Spanish America continue to seek these out . . . ever more certain of their route."[3]

It is in this preservation of its tradition as a perennial and vital source of inspiration that Spanish-American literature shows its true greatness, in its capacity for assimilating the new without losing touch with the old. And nowhere in all the continent did the varied strains of folklore, Spanish, African, Indian, leave a heavier precipitate than in the Caribbean area. It was here they first met and fused, setting their imprint on all they touched. And, although this is not the place to enter upon a discussion of the matter, it would not seem too far afield to suggest that it was from here that they radiated to the rest of the continent, carried by the earliest of the discoverers and conquerors, who possessed among their other attributes the gift of ubiquity. Otherwise it is difficult to account for the presence of the same or similar legends, beliefs and vital attitudes from one end of the continent to the other.

III

The majority of the short-story writers of the Caribbean fall definitely within the tendency exemplified in Salarrué and Bosch. The native, the Creole, climate, in which the form was born, has been growing steadily in intensity. Nearly all of them would seem to have taken as their artistic criterion the advice Sarmiento gave the writers of Chile a century ago when he was carrying on his famous polemic with Andrés Bello: ". . . cast your observing eye upon your own land, upon the people, the customs, the institutions, the problems that exist there, and then write of them lovingly, with your heart, what you feel, what occurs to you, and this will be good in content, even though the form may be faulty; it will be charged with emotion, even though at times it may be inaccurate . . . good or bad, it will be yours."

There is the vigorous group of young Panamanian writers, speci-

[3] José Luis Martínez, *Las corrientes literarias en la América hispana* (Mexico, 1949).

mens of whose work have been brought together in an excellent anthology published last year.⁴ In Venezuela, which is outstanding in the field of narrative literature, the short story has been cultivated with abundance and great skill. Arturo Uslar-Pietri and Julián Padrón, themselves among the most gifted in the field, have brought together in a two-volume anthology the work of recent Venezuelan short-story writers.⁵ One can hardly be grateful enough for these collections, for much of the work contained in them was published in magazines or newspapers, has not been collected in book form, and would otherwise be unavailable. Although there has been little direct influence of the Caribbean on the short story in Colombia, it has infiltrated into the interior through Cartagena and Barranquilla, and has left its traces on the literature of the region of Antioquia, as fecund in this activity as in so many others.

One point I should like to stress is that in the work of the writers we have been discussing the characters are almost never presented in racial terms. They may deal with whites, *mestizos*, Indians, Negroes, but basically as members of the community of which they form a part of life on an equal human footing. The basis of the distinctions and conflicts that exist are economic and social rather than racial. Uslar-Pietri's analysis of the influences that have brought about the flowering of the short story in Venezuela could with equal propriety be applied to the entire Caribbean as well as to the rest of America: "In its most recent forms the Venezuelan short story, which began as a vehicle of artistic prose, which at the crest of the wave of Creolism became a steady delving into and investigation of the popular, is becoming increasingly infused with the breath of poetry, with an ineffable and moving power that stems from the living source, without falsifying a single detail of reality or of subject matter or of the balance of the narration. The work of our most recent short-story writers falls into this category ... those who are seeking out the Venezuelan soul on Venezuelan soil."⁶

⁴ Rodrigo Miró, *El Cuento en Panamá* (1950).
⁵ Arturo Uslar-Pietri y Julián Padrón, *Antología del cuento moderno venezolano*, Biblioteca Venezolana de Cultura (1940).
⁶ *Ibid*, Introduction, Vol. II.

IV

I must confess that I have found myself baffled to account for the relative absence of the sea in the literature of the Caribbean. The bewilderment, however, is not mine alone. In his introduction to *El Cuento en Panamá* Rodrigo Miró raises the question: "How, then, can we explain that in a country where the sea is one of its permanent, ever-present dimensions, it should have been overlooked in the work of its writers?" Miró attributes it to social and economic reasons, having nothing to do with literature. I do not find this explanation convincing. To me it seems rather an unconscious effort to guard against the general and leveling influences, and to emphasize the peculiar, the individual.

Only two of the short-story writers of this area, as representative in their field as Salarrué and Bosch in theirs, have set their stories, in part at least, against a background of the sea. They are Lino Novás Calvo of Cuba and Guillermo Meneses of Venezuela, and they are urban writers. In Novás Calvo as much as the sea it is the things the sea carries in its wake: the foreign tourists that throng Havana, the picaresque, catch-as-catch-can life of the waterfront, the smuggling, the rum-running, the contact with the United States, mostly in the form of attempts to elude the Coast Guard, that make up the ambient of his writing. The human element is largely the Negro and the mulatto because they constitute a principal part of the urban proletariat.

In Novás Calvo, who was born in Spain in 1905, but who has spent his life since early childhood in Cuba, two strains have met. On the one hand there is the Creole, with its realistic presentation of atmosphere and persons, and on the other, the psychological approach, an attempt to discover the peculiar, the unique human essence in the realm of the subconscious, often the abnormal. His best short stories are contained in the volumes *La luna nona y otros cuentos* (1942) and *Cayo Canas* (1946). It may well be that foreign influences are stronger or at least more direct in Novás Calvo than in the other writers we have been discussing. His resemblance to Hemingway and Faulkner has often been pointed out. Perhaps this is more a question of approach and *Zeitgeist* than actual influence, for there can be no doubt of his originality. What Lionel Trilling has said of these two North American

writers could, it seems to me, fairly be applied to Novás Calvo:
"We feel that Hemingway and Faulkner are intensely at work on
the recalcitrant stuff of life . . . . And our pleasure in their activity
is made the more secure because we have the distinct impression
that they are not under any illusion that they have conquered
the material upon which they direct their activity." [7]

Under the sensuality, the harshness, and a violence that often
verges on the brutal, there is a rough tenderness in Novás Calvo,
a deep sense of comradeship with the lost and the lonely, an
affirmation of the essential humanness that knows no distinction
of race or color. He brings into his work the primitive rites and
superstitions of the Cuban Negroes, the spells, the incantations by
which they endeavor to control the forces that shape their lives
and lend interest and excitement and a sense of power to their
drab, poverty-stricken existence.

There is a vigorous school of Negro literature in Cuba, both in
prose and poetry. Lydia Cabrera and Alejo Charpentier, to mention only two, have used the myths and legends that were brought
to the island by the African slaves as the subject matter of their
narrations. Beautiful though they are, they are an exotic growth,
and give little sense of the reality of the Negro of Cuba, who is
no longer an African, but an integral part of the culture of Cuba,
and who cannot be studied out of his context if he is to reflect
his life today.

V

The work of Guillermo Meneses, born in 1911, the youngest of
the four I have chosen to discuss here, centers about the life of the
port of La Guayra, Venezuela. His production has not been
abundant, and he is perhaps better known as a novelist than as
a short story writer. In the latter field he has written a volume
entitled *Tres Cuentos Venezolanos* (1938), and a long short story,
or novelette, which is one of the most perfectly achieved examples
of the form, "La balandra Isabel llegó esta tarde." It is a tragedy
played on muted strings, a story of the rivalry between a woman
and the sea for a man's love, a rivalry at least as old as Jason
and Medea and the Argonaut. The setting could hardly be more

[7] Lionel Trilling, *op. cit.*

commonplace: a freighter, a ship's hand, and a prostitute. Such action as there is has to do with the girl's despairing effort to keep from losing him to her more powerful rival. But Meneses has so charged it with poetry, with pathos, with the eternal tragedy of frustration and loneliness that it has an application far beyond the immediate situation it deals with. It is a cross section of life along a Caribbean waterfront—which resembles that of any port— with its taverns, its sailors, its prostitutes, and all the human flotsam and jetsam the sea throws up on its beaches. Nothing really happens; the man sails away, the girl remains, her last hope of happiness shattered when a voodoo spell she has invoked to bind him to her side fails, and life goes on, indifferently, monotonously. Meneses' best novel, *Campeones,* is really a series of episodes in the life of a group of boys who have grown up around the waterfront, and whose goal of existence is to become professional players of baseball, that imported sport that has become as popular in Venezuela as in its place of origin.

Fabián Dobles of Costa Rica has approached the coastal areas of the Caribbean in certain of his stories dealing with the life of the workers on the banana plantations of the foreign fruit companies. But his best work is that which centers about the inland regions of Costa Rica, and the same thing is true of Emilio Belaval of Puerto Rico.

VI

I should be reluctant to conclude without mentioning certain Caribbean authors who have cultivated a special type of short story that does not come wholly under either of the above classifications. One is the excellent group of writers who have found their inspiration in the Mayan civilization: Ermilo Abreu Gómez and Antonio Médiz Bolio of Yucatan, and Miguel Angel Asturias and Carlos Samayoa Chinchilla of Guatemala. They are steeped in the mythology of the Popol Vuh and other Indian chronicles, and have both recreated the old legends and sought out their persistence among the present-day inhabitants of those lands.

And there are Carmen Lyra of Costa Rica and Antonio Arraiz of Venezuela, who have adapted to a local setting the animal fables that have acquired citizenship in every land since they set out so long ago on their travels from their native India. Arraiz is at times inclined to inject a moral lesson into his work, but Carmen Lyra relates the exploits of Brer Fox, Brer Rabbit, and their scampish or victimized associates with the same rollicking inconsequence as our own Joel Chandler Harris. Like him, she would probably have called herself a "cornfield writer," but she achieved the superlatively difficult task of giving new life to a twice-told tale, putting into it the suggestions conveyed by the landscape, the customs, the traditions of her native land.

One of the things that has given me the most food for thought in examining the literary production of the Caribbean today is the absence of so many of the themes that are the focal point of writers elsewhere: the world wars, the struggle between conflicting ideologies, the breakdown of modern civilization. It is as though the Spanish-American writers had turned their back on a world they never made, and in which they feel themselves pawns in a titanic chess game rather than active participants. They have preferred to withdraw and turn their eyes upon their own peculiar problems.

To be sure, there is not much that the sense of anxiety and insecurity which grips the world today could say to those who have never known security—torn as they have been by civil wars, political instability, economic depression, and underprivilege. It could only be the extension on a larger scale of a tragedy that is endemic among them. But perhaps this ignoring of the issues that convulse the world today, which at first glance might seem a limitation, may indicate a deep aesthetic intuition. Perhaps this steadfastness to the timeless quality of art, to that which survives through periods of interruption, diminishment, and transformation, is an act of faith and an offering in its defense. For in one way or another, to our satisfaction or our chagrin, these besetting problems will be resolved one day, and when this happens much of the writing that now seems so vital and pertinent will have become musty documentation. Paul Valery has put it very well in his prologue to the French translation of Gabriela Mistral's poems: "I have seen in Latin America . . . a laboratory where the essence of our creations and the crystallization of our ideals combine with the virgin principles and the natural energies of a land wholly dedicated to the poetic adventure and to the intellectual fruitfulness of the days to come."

The best summing-up of the guiding principles and objectives of the literature I have touched upon so briefly here, comes from a man who is the essence of the Caribbean, and whose name is a beacon in the literature of all the Spanish-speaking world, Rubén Darío:

> *Yo no, yo persisto. Pretéritas normas*
> *Confirman mi anhelo, mi ser, mi existir.*
> *Yo soy el amante de ensueños y formas*
> *Que viene de lejos y va al porvenir.*

13

Arturo Torres-Rioseco: SOCIAL EVOLUTION
AND THE MEXICAN NOVEL

I HAVE affirmed more than once that Latin American literature
has already reached its period of maturity. With this in mind we
shall be able to undertake a series of studies derived from this
statement and arrive at conclusions interesting not only to the literary critic but also to the sociologist, the historian, or the student
of political science.

In the present essay I wish to consider the social evolution of
Mexico as it is revealed in the most representative novels of this
geographical zone, since Mexico is the most important sociological
laboratory in Latin America. But first, and as introductory remarks,
I shall make some brief observations about certain political, social,
and economic changes that have taken place in Latin America
and that may be used as points of reference in this discussion.

I

The great industrial development in Latin America, which
begins in the second half of the nineteenth century, revolutionizes
the cultural panorama of the whole continent. Produced by the
influx of European immigration, its first consequence is the rapid
increase in wealth of the capitalistic class, the extraordinary growth
of cities, the creation of institutions of a democratic type, the
development of popular education, the weakening of oligarchical
and dictatorial governments, the formation of workers' federations,
and a progressive leveling of society. Some of these signs of progress

135

are permanent and others temporary, but at bottom a process of economic, political, and social evolution has been established, a process which reactionary forces may be able to retard but never to destroy.

Towards the end of the nineteenth century there appear as great cities Buenos Aires, Mexico, São Paulo, Rio de Janeiro, and Santiago de Chile; cattlemen, industrialists, miners, farmers, bankers, businessmen, and speculators begin to amass huge fortunes. A vigorous middle class arises which soon will dominate the political and intellectual horizon of our nations, founding its growth and power on solid democratic principles. The industrial life of the cities improves the economic level of the workers, and through the formation of unions creates in them a stronger social consciousness. At the same time, as the cities grow richer they feel the desire for a greater culture; hence, the advance in popular education.

The words Democracy and Liberty begin to acquire a very real significance, thus weakening Autocracy, which is the prevailing political system of the first half of the nineteenth century. One by one the *caudillos* begin to fall and they are replaced by the first constitutional and democratic presidents, such as Juárez, Balmaceda, and Sarmiento.

In our century this progress is more evident: immigration increases; mining is greatly developed; oil, nitrates, rubber, sugar, coffee, wheat, and even bananas and tourism become new sources of wealth. But coincident with this prodigious progress of industry, commerce, and exploitation of raw materials, we observe the disturbing lack of balance in the distribution of wealth. Economic inequality seems to be a fatal necessity in our societies, and the more the fortunes of the rich increase the more evident are the poverty and the misery of the peasant, the unskilled laborer, and the Indian. Political democracy has betrayed the people by creating new privileges for some and new injustices for others. One feels the need for the creation of a democratic structure that could be applied to the social and economic life of the people.

The great masses of exploited men, guided first by the democratic example of the United States and second by the golden promises of leftist propaganda, acquire a consciousness of their human rights; thus, we face the biggest problem of Latin America, that is, the struggle between capital and labor, between the exploiters and exploited, between misery and wealth. Democracy is the loser. When the masses demand decent living conditions and fair wages the so-called forces of law and order are mobilized, and the protest or strike is suppressed by the police or the army.

Thus we have here a fast anti-democratic process in which constitutional guarantees are violated, opening the way to dictatorship and despotism. With methods of this kind the abyss which separates the worker from the boss, the liberal from the reactionary, liberty from totalitarianism, is enlarged; and this is the reason why Latin American nations pass with incredible facility from demagogic democracy to absolute forms of dictatorships. Brutal dictatorship produces the formation of rebellious groups, or underground resistance; democratic activities become forces of violence, and the men who represent the progressive spirit find themselves all of a sudden among the most militant radicals. Liberal youth, always ready to sacrifice itself, joins these resistance groups and openly challenges the forces of reaction and absolutism. This is a common process in all the countries of Latin America.

For the purpose of this paper, however, I shall leave aside the progress of liberalism in South America; the struggle of 1918 against the Chilean oligarchy; the university reform in Argentina of the same year; the establishment of the popular universities in Peru; the founding of the *Aprista* party of Haya de la Torre and the fostering of its principles throughout the continent; and I shall limit myself to studying the case of Mexico.

II

In the year 1910 the revolution against the dictatorship of Porfirio Díaz broke out. The tyrant had ruled his country for thirty years with an iron hand. With the murder of the humanitarian Francisco Madero, a period of anarchy began which lasted nearly twenty years. Ambitious generals and immoral political chieftains betrayed the most elementary principles of the Madero movement. When it appeared that the revolution had been a complete failure, the government of Lázaro Cárdenas succeeded in giving a higher meaning to the revolutionary ideal, and Mexico entered into an era of peace and democratic reconstruction, the results of which are evident today. Cárdenas' regime marks the highest moment of the revolution.

The Mexican writers who, during the time of Porfirio Díaz, had escaped reality, cultivating almost exclusively lyric poetry and the romantic novel, entered with the revolution into a world of bitter and stark realism. It was as if all of a sudden artists and writers had made a discovery of the fatherland. The same year of the fall of the tyrant, Justo Sierra founded the National University of Mexico; at that time also the *Ateneo de la Juventud* was formed by young thinkers, men of letters, and artists full of an intense faith in the culture and the destiny of their country. Among the founders of this institution we find some of those men that soon were to be the leaders of new cultural movements: Antonio Caso and José Vasconcelos in philosophy, Pedro Henríquez Ureña and Alfonso Reyes in literature, Diego Rivera in painting, and Manuel Ponce in music.

The *Ateneo* forgets the Olympian attitude of the writers of the Porfirio Díaz epoch, and tries to get closer to the people; thus it creates a society for public lectures and organizes the first popular university of the nation. We are witnessing a revolutionary cultural movement. All these intellectual leaders are men of social ideals; therefore, they are innovators in sociology and literature, and soon they will discover the formula which characterizes this last half-century of Mexican art: art for the people.

Since 1911 there has also existed in Mexico a social phenomenon called the Indianist movement. The interest in the Indian goes beyond the desire to incorporate him into the civic life of the nation, to make him a civilized being. One has to study his prehistory; hence the development of archeology (Alfonso Caso, Gamio); one must interpret him in painting (Orozco, Rivera, Alfaro Siqueiros); in music (Chávez, Revueltas); and in literature (Heriberto Frías, Médiz Bolio, Azuela).

One of the founders of the *Ateneo de la Juventud*, D. José Vasconcelos, who had become Secretary of Education in 1921, began a series of radical reforms. He is the great popularizer of art in Mexico; he took the statues from the museums and scattered them about plazas and public parks; he brought about the publication of a series of world classics (The Bible, Aeschylus, Dante) to be distributed gratis among the people; he sent hundreds of teachers to remote Indian villages; he called the great muralists to decorate government buildings; he encouraged young composers and writers. In short, Vasconcelos is the soul of the educational, intellectual, and artistic life of his generation.

In the meantime, literature goes through a process of change. Two great poets transform and give new vigor to poetry. Enrique González Martínez gives to it new depth and thought; Ramón López Velarde enriches it with provincial themes, and finally, in his definitive poem, *Suave Patria,* gives us a masterful interpretation of the greatness and beauty of his homeland. The revolutionary novel becomes a mirror where one can see that complex and chaotic world which is contemporary Mexican society. Plastic and literary forms become symbols and to the brutal scenes of a fatal reality correspond the tragic scenes of Rivera's and Orozco's pictures and the dramatic novels of M. Azuela, Martín Luis Guzmán and Gregorio López y Fuentes.

The whole process of the revolution is portrayed in the novel. In *Los de abajo* (1916) we find the failure of those ideals of reform and justice which were the core of Madero's philosophy. Azuela sees the revolution without a partisan attitude, such as it is in its bitter reality, and this is why many of his critics say that he is not an authentic revolutionary writer. Nevertheless, the hero of *Los de abajo,* Demetrio Macías, is the most exact replica of that general of the revolution that appears after Madero's death: a general without ideals, without culture, fighting for personal ambition; a general who dies without leaving a trace in the history or in the soul of his country.

The long gallery of popular types which parades through this novel reflects the ignorance, the cruelty, the ambitions of many army men, who by a whim of fortune, became political leaders.

The Mexican sociologist Jesús Silva Herzog makes the following comments on *Los de abajo,* recognizing its documentary and realistic value:

The Mexican revolution, outside of a few political ideas, did not have a previous ideology, an economic and social program. The ideology of the revolution developed slowly, along with the heat of battles, the fire of civic struggle, and the unleashing of popular passions. Here we have the novel of Mariano Azuela which paints with exactitude the revolutionary landscape, a novel which is at the same time a work of art and a real and convincing historical document. Azuela did not mean to write a revolutionary novel; this genre was not in vogue then. Its merit consists in the fact that Azuela wrote what he saw and as he saw it, and relates the impressions left in his spirit by the war.[1]

The evolution of the revolutionary movement is so well defined in *Los de abajo* that I cannot resist the temptation of quoting again a few lines of Señor Silva Herzog's article which explain the process of the revolution and which can be applied to Azuela's novel:

> ... The war assumed the form of a class struggle and became radical and bloody. At bottom it was the struggle of the poor against the rich, of the "haves and the havenots," of the proletariat against the bourgeoisie, the church and the landowners. The socializing philosophy of the revolution, nebulous at the beginning, did not have its origin in the minds of the leaders but in the suffering of the hungry and abandoned masses. Perhaps we should make an exception of the Zapata rebellion, since from its very beginning this movement had a perfectly clear ideal, an ideal which its leaders summed up in two words: land and liberty.[2]

This class struggle gives meaning and color to *The Underdogs*, and the theory that the socializing thought did not have its origin in the minds of the leaders is conclusively proved in the comparison that Macías, hero of *The Underdogs*, makes between the revolution and a stone thrown from the top of a mountain: the human hand gave the impulse, but soon the stone keeps on rolling by its own momentum.

The crisis of the Mexican Revolution studied by Silva Herzog in his essay (lack of ideological orientation, lack of honesty of the leaders, too much politics) can be observed in the moral turpitude of the first leaders of the revolution as they appear in the novel of Martín Luis Guzmán entitled *The Eagle and the Serpent* (1928), which is a living document of the early years of the revolt. The novel consists of a series of brutal deeds and a description of historical characters, among whom the most prominent are Carranza, Villa, Angeles, and Obregón. It would be useless to try to find in this novel a definite ideal of moral conduct or a serious belief in

---

[1] *Cuadernos americanos*, 5 (Sept.-Oct., 1943).
[2] *Ibid.*

social reform. On the contrary, we find in every chapter the brutality of the generals, the utter ignorance of the soldiers, bossism, arbitrary actions, disrespect for the most elementary laws. There is a moment, just before 1915, in which all the leaders are hopelessly inadequate. Guzmán describes this situation in the following words:

Under the leadership of Carranza the Revolution went straight toward dictatorship. Carranza dreamt of the fantastic possibility of being a second Porfirio Díaz. . . . Nobody could imagine Villa as the leader of a reform movement, since even considered as a "brutal force," he had so many defects that his contact implied more dangers than the most inflammable explosive. Obregón, that great winner of battles, also was threatening to become a "caudillo." (*Villismo y Carrancismo.*)

These are the supreme chieftains of the revolution, and Guzmán sees them such as they are. Therefore, his attitude is frankly pessimistic. In his novel *The Shadow of the Caudillo* (1929) Guzmán accuses Obregón and Calles of electoral intervention and points them out as the real murderers of Gómez and Serrano, the two rebellious generals. Guzmán is one of those intellectuals for whom the revolution should have been something different: a morally articulated structure, a patriotic undertaking. He has faith in the salvation of an oppressed and hungry people. Guzmán, like Vasconcelos, represents the evolution of that political thinking of Mexico which finds its final expression in the government of Lázaro Cárdenas.

Of all the novelists of the revolution the one who knows best the rural people, their habits, language, and psychology is Gregorio López y Fuentes. In his most famous books, *Campamento* (1931), *Land* (1932), and *The Indian* (1935), he presents vivid pictures of the revolution and philosophizes about its meaning. The themes of his novels are the basic points of the revolutionary movement, namely: (a) distribution of land, called in Mexico the *ejido* question, and the nationalization of the subsoil; (b) separation of the Church from politics; (c) dignifying of the Indian through liberty and education; and (d) limitation of the power and influence of foreigners.

The Indian is his masterpiece. The book consists of a succession of scenes of Indian life in a mountain village. The rural school-

teacher appears for the first time as the hero of a novel. He
is a modern teacher with new ideas on educational reform, agricultural improvement, the building of roads, and laws fair to the
Indian. Here we witness an obvious evolution in the process of
dealing with social, racial, and political matters. The schoolteacher
is more interested in economic and social changes than in cold
classroom discipline. Here is a picture of the master in front of
his class:

The teacher, upon preparing his lessons, thought rather about
planning his social program. The Indians had told him that the
custom of forced labor was still in use, although it had been
legally abolished; it was necessary, then, to denounce this abuse,
even at the risk of antagonizing the village authorities. The Indians
told him that the lands they had received had not improved their
economic situation, because they had no tools with which to
cultivate them, and because, being forced to work for the bosses,
they had no time to work their own land. The teacher felt that
he had to obtain loans and subsidies, so that the Indian farmers
would not fall into the clutches of speculators accustomed to buying the crops before they are harvested. They needed tools and
instructors to teach them new agricultural methods.

The Indians told him that often they had to give away their
products, which they could not sell because of the lack of means
of transportation. The teacher thought it necessary to have a
road—not like the one the authorities had built in the valley,
to connect God knows what remote places, along which the Indian
travels on foot, swallowing the dust raised by the car—but a road
that would serve the tribes, isolated now by their old racial fear.[3]

As we see, we are dealing with a question in which it is indis-
pensable to have economic reform to satisfy a revolutionary code.
The authorities must protect the native farmer, and all forms of
duress and exploitation must end. Only thus will dignified work
regenerate the Indian. Work is then the solution of the great
agrarian problem of Mexico; work and not chance or good luck,
as many farmers believe. To prove this point López y Fuentes
wrote his novel, *Huasteca,* in which he tells us of the rise and fall
of a rural family on whose lands oil was found. Determining factors in the sad adventure of this family are chance, the lack of

3 *El Indio* (Norton & Co.), pp. 154-155.

foresight of the Mexican, his spirit of ostentation, his lack of character in the face of economic failure, and last but not least, the influence of foreign companies.

In his novel, *Land (Tierra)*, dealing with the uprising of Zapata and with the assassination of this hero, we find, along with the dramatic thread of the story, many opinions on agrarian policies. Zapata is not only the great general who beats the federal armies, but also the apostle who fights for the division of the land among the Indians. The social zeal of López y Fuentes is so intense that at times he forgets he is writing a novel, as when he quotes, for example, "the law of the sixth of January," a legal document that establishes the division of the land. We often find in this novel paragraphs like the following:

How about the lands? Shall they continue in the hands of the rich? Shall we continue being slaves of the landholders? We shall continue to fight until we recover the lands they have taken from us.[4]

The moral and didactic purpose of these novels is sometimes so obvious that we think we are listening to a schoolteacher, or to a preacher addressing his neophytes to show them how to avoid falling into vice and error. Such is the case of *My General* (1934) and *Huasteca*. Nevertheless, there are some literary critics who see in other works of López y Fuentes the most successful approach to the theme of the regeneration of the Indian in America. Thus Fernando Alegría writes:

It is possible that the novel which synthesizes in epic and artistic form the complex drama of the American Indian has not been written. However, I like to think that López y Fuentes and Icaza are the best authors of an Indianist novel which tries to go beyond the concrete details of reality to embrace in vigorous symbols the universal meaning of the drama of the American Indian. López y Fuentes seeks in his novel, *The Immovable Pilgrims (Los peregrinos inmóviles)*, the metaphysical roots of the conflict which divides the Mexican people; he seeks the religious and magic origin of a race with two heads that insists, nevertheless, in remaining united, wounding itself, bleeding and exploited, but wonderfully insistent and dynamic.

4 *Tierra,* ed. Mexico, 85.

Rubén Romero, another novelist of this period, has occasionally a mystic conception of the revolution. One of his characters says:

The Revolution is a noble desire to rise, and I shall rise; it is the hope of a fairer life, and I believe in it. Today more than yesterday I feel that I belong to the Revolution, because I became poor again all of a sudden. The Revolution, like God, destroys and creates, and we seek it, as we seek God, only when sorrow afflicts us.

But, in spite of this desire to rise, there is an excess of violence, brutality, and injustice in his revolutionary world. Often, after having shown the courage and nobility of the people, Romero ends his story with an episode in which it is evident that all has been lost, and that bossism appears again, fed by the blood of the heroes.

The Mexican critic Rafael Múñoz, writing on Romero's work, asks this question:

Where is the great novel of the writers of the Revolution? Where is the work of art which presents with clearness, good style and good taste, the origins, development, failures, and successes of the Revolution? Where is, in short, the novel which contains a synthesis, the soul of the Revolution?[5]

He himself gives the answer:

In reality there isn't such a novel, among other reasons because nobody has tried to write it. The Revolution has covered such an extensive area, is so deep in its origin, so varied in its appearances, so long in duration, so complex in its problems, that it is not possible, within the modern technique of the novel, to write a work of art which might contain all that can be said of the Revolution.[6]

It is only right to think like Rafael Múñoz on reading the novels of José Rubén Romero: *Desertion* (*Desbandada,* 1934), *The Innocent Town* (1934), *My Horse, My Dog and My Rifle* (1936); it is right to think this way, for it seems that Romero should have been the author of the interpretative novel of the revolution. Romero masters a genuinely popular style derived from the spoken language; he has a rich repertoire of anecdotes about people and events; he knows well provincial customs and the psychology of the

---

[5] *Homenaje a Rubén Romero* (Lear, Mexico, 1937), p. 18.
[6] *Ibid.*

people; and finally, he himself took part in the revolution. And yet, Romero has not written the representative work of this cycle. Why? According to my way of thinking, Romero lacks conviction. He is too skeptical and flighty; his constant humor usually is only indifference and cynicism.

Perhaps we should make an exception in the case of his novel, *The Useless Life of Pito Pérez* (1938). Here, the central character, Pito Pérez, is a synthesis of the tormented soul of the Mexican people. It is interesting to notice that, at a distance of one hundred years, Rubén Romero coincides in his aesthetic manner and psychological interpretation with Fernández de Lizardi, on creating the hero of a picaresque novel who expresses in sensibility and actions both the best and worst of the Mexican. In *The Useless Life of Pito Pérez* we find what we may call the tragedy of the revolution. The life of Pito Pérez is the symbol of a nation which has not fulfilled its destiny and which drifts without ideals or ambitions, oppressed by the bosses, haunted by the police, until one day, like Pito, it falls dead on a heap of rubbish and its ashes are scattered by the wind. One cannot help thinking that Romero had the Mexican people in mind when he wrote Pito's testament:

To the poor I leave my contempt because of their cowardice, because they do not rise and take possession of everything in an impulse of supreme justice. Miserable slaves of a church which preaches resignation and of a government which demands submission, without giving them a thing in exchange.[7]

The Mexican people are not bad, but nobody has ever recognized their courage and their dignity. Pito Pérez knows this: "I never had faith in anybody; I never respected anybody. Why? Because nobody had faith in me, because nobody respected me."

The people of Mexico, like those of all the countries of Latin America, lived for a whole century under the spell of that Messianic formula imported from France: "Liberty, Equality, Fraternity." But one day these people awoke and realized their mistake. Let us listen again to Pito Pérez:

[7] *La vida inútil de Pito Pérez* (Mexico, 1938), p. 225.

Liberty, Equality, Fraternity! What a ridiculous farce! Liberty is killed by all those who have some authority; equality is destroyed by money, and fraternity dies at the hands of our egoism.[8]

I do not know if the Mexicans heed this novelist who has so much intuition, but they ought to listen to him, because he knows the town life of his nation better than any other writer, and we must remember that the misery and poverty of urban and provincial life in Mexico are one of its main sources of unhappiness. The modern politician thinks that Mexico City is the nation and that the country has been saved because the Federal capital has magnificent hotels, prosperous banks, skyscrapers, monuments, thousands of motorcars, a population of three million. In Mexico we observe a characteristic Spanish American phenomenon: The nation has a huge head on a dwarfish body. If we transpose this lack of equilibrium to the economic field we are sure that Mexico City is ruining the rest of the country. Must we remind the "políticos" that Mexico City was not the initial center of the revolution? *The Useless Life of Pito Pérez* is a document of the moral and material misery of his country. After reading this novel, we are sure that the social and economic evolution of Mexico can be shown more convincingly in the legislation, the political theories, and the speeches of the senators than in a trip of observation and study throughout its towns and rural districts.

There are still other novelists of this period to whom the revolution has been a great disappointment. Rafael Múñoz, in his novel *Let's Go Along with Pancho Villa* (1931), shows an intimate knowledge of the psychology and heroic deeds of this general. We find in this work the same platitudes in the mouths of the peasants: justice, land, liberty, bread; but what impels these men to fight is the worship of Pancho Villa and a desire to avenge individual humiliations and suffering. There are two outstanding characteristics in this novel: first, a strong anti-American feeling, shown in the assault on the American border town of Columbus and the punitive expedition of General Pershing; and second, an exaltation of Mexicanism, expressed in a feeling of loyalty to the leader, personal courage, and strength of character. There is a symbolic type in this book, Tiburcio Maya, a fanatical follower of Villa. The brutal general kills Maya's

8 *Ibid.*, p. 225.

wife and his only daughter, but the old man still follows him like a faithful dog. Finally he is taken prisoner by the Americans, who try to make him reveal Villa's hiding place. He suffers all kinds of tortures, he rejects an offer of fifty thousand dollars, and finally he is hanged from a tree, but he remains silent, without betraying his idol.

III

I have mentioned the names of the outstanding novelists of the revolutionary period. Now I shall deal with the writers of the post-revolutionary generation. In this group an interest in social problems is of paramount importance, while the picturesque and dramatic sense of the struggle loses ground.

A few of these writers are political theorists for whom literature is only a propaganda tool. They use the novel as a loudspeaker to reach the masses and preach social revolution. Their ultimate purpose is to create a system of socialist government in Mexico.

The best known writer of this group is José Mancisidor, author of *Riotous Crowd* (*La Asonada*, 1931), *The Red City* (*La ciudad roja*, 1932), *Traverse Board* (*La rosa de los vientos*, 1941). The most common episodes in these novels are labor troubles, strikes, police intervention, assassinations, brutality of the army, and injustice on the part of the "patrones."

Mancisidor sets down his ideals as a novelist when he writes in *Riotous Crowd:*

If the reader, judging by the name of this work, thinks that he will find in it scenes of shooting, blood, and fire, he is mistaken. In these pages pregnant with truth, the characters move about without a noble ideal, without a definite aim, without a worthy conception of their own ambitions. They are all military men, men tossed up to positions of power by the waves of our Revolution, which, like many other Revolutions, ends by devouring its own children.[9]

Mancisidor tries to write documentary novels with the object of giving his readers an idea of the tragedy of Mexico. He accuses the generals of having betrayed their people:

[9] *Riotous Crowd,* Introduction.

The generals of our army have been the greatest obstacle to the attainment of popular aspirations. The troops, the hungry soldiers, are the cannon fodder sacrificed so that the general may rise to power or fall in the swamp of his crooked ambitions.[10]

On this rotten social foundation Mancisidor wishes to build his golden city for crowds of people oppressed by the yoke of immemorial traditions. Mancisidor is, then, a national writer who follows a rather universal trend, combining in his novels the human experience of his land, with the broad political doctrines which are disturbing the world of today.

I shall only mention here the works of three novelists who must be taken into consideration in a more detailed study of this literary cycle. They are Mauricio Magdaleno, with his books *Campo Celis* (1935), *Splendor* (*El Resplandor,* 1937), *The Big Earth* (*La Tierra grande,* 1949), *Cornsilk* (*Cabello de elote,* 1949); Jorge Ferretis, with *Hot Land* (*Tierra caliente,* 1935), *The South Burns* (*El Sur quema,* 1937), *When D. Quijote Gets Fat* (*Cuando engorda el Quijote,* 1937), *Saint Automobile* (*San automóvil,* 1938), *Men in the Storm* (*Hombres en tempestad,* 1942), and Xavier Icaza, author of *Panchito Chapopote* (1928). I shall, however, study in a detailed manner two novels which to me represent the ripe product of the last literary crop of Mexico. They are *Nayar* (1941), by Miguel Angel Menéndez, and *El luto humano* (1943), by José Revueltas.

The action of *Nayar* takes place among the Cora Indians of Nayarit, in the high sierras near the Pacific. In spite of all efforts to conquer the Cora tribe since the early days of the colony, these brave Indians have maintained their independence; and there they are in the Sierra de Nayar, isolated, free from contact with Spaniards and halfbreeds, living with their superstitions and old customs. One day the author and his friend, the halfbreed Ramón Córdoba, arrive in the Sierra de Nayar. Ramón, a fugitive from justice, has killed the judge of San Blas who had a love affair with his wife; the author, a clerk in the custom house of San Blas, has decided to accompany his friend Ramón in his flight. They undertake a long trip along the Santiago River to the forest. The author is preoccupied with two important matters: the

10 *Ibid.*

world in which they move and the misery of the people who live in those places. It is March and the bean stalks are in bloom; by the month of May the crop will be ready to be harvested:

The Crop! A miracle of nature, sudden blooming of the Earth, which wants men to live. Miserable fallows, superficial scratchings of the wooden plough pulled by sickly mules, in which you drop any kind of seed and it blooms. Crop that the farmer sells even before he has cleared the forest, at whatever price they offer him; for if he does not accept the offer he does not sow, and if he does not sow he does not eat.[11]

The two friends travel by night in the black, wild forest. They pass through the land of the salt pits where the workers go blind from looking at the salt under the sun. They arrive at a little Indian island from which they are expelled by the Indians, who do not trust white men. They go through towns and villages. On their way to the "Tigre" they meet a group of Cora Indians, miners in trouble with the "gringos" who exploit the gold mines. The boss appears and a battle ensues in which four men lose their lives. Mr. Land, the foreign exploiter, is one of the victims. The author and Ramón become friends of the Cora chief, Pedro Gervasio, and together they continue their journey through Sinaloa, Durango, Zacatecas, and Jalisco. The author describes the life of the Coras, their patriarchal government, religious ceremonies, witchcraft, superstitions, and legends.

These are the people who refuse to accept the friendship of the Spaniards. The reason is obvious. Take, for example, the "pueblo" of Saint Teresa. It used to be a large "pueblo" but now it is deserted. After the arrival in the village of a halfbreed merchant, the Indians, who refused to deal with him, abandoned their homes. The merchant lost his customers, but the Indians needed money to buy or rent new lands. Then the merchant became a moneylender. If after a certain time the Indians could not pay their debts, the merchant would send his partner, Major Cometa, at the head of a group of army men, to collect. The Indians came to the conclusion that the only way to put an end to these abuses was to own bullets and rifles. The fight between the "cristeros" and the government troops reaches the Indian settle-

11 *Nayar,* p. 69.

ments. The Indians are caught between two enemy groups. One of them cries, Long live King Christ!; the other, Long live the Government!

Gervasio explains the Cora Indian situation this way:

It makes no difference. Both are halfbreeds. It is the same enemy. They are divided in order to fight, and they use us as bait. That's why we keep away from both. No matter who wins, we always lose.[12]

Precisely, that's what always happens. The "cristeros" take the village; they kill the men and rape the women; they cut the school-teacher's ears off and steal the food of the Indians. Then the government troops take the town; they destroy churches, they kill the men who are left and rape the women. So on this occasion, when the federal troops and the "cristeros" appear, Gervasio and his men decide to hide in the caves of the sierra. There they live, among spiders, scorpions, bats, red ants, waiting for the "redeemers of the country" to go away. Indian messengers bring Gervasio news of the atrocious brutality of both soldiers and "cristeros."

Finally, the "redeemers" leave. The Indians return and find the ruins of their homes. A messenger, sent by Gervasio to see what has happened to other farms and ranches, finds them all destroyed by floods, rains, and bullets. Seeing this picture of desolation, the Indians decide to migrate to the lowlands.

The only road open to them was to find work in the sugar plantations, in the tobacco fields, in the grazing lands where the masters are halfbreeds.[13]

But fate spoils the plans of the tribe. When Gervasio is ready to abandon his beloved sierra, an Indian delegation arrives to demand the death of the medicine man Uchuntu, whom they blame for their miseries. Ramón is opposed to this barbaric accusation, but Gervasio bows to the demands of the tribe, and Uchuntu is condemned to be burned alive. Ramón, wishing to save the life of a human being, runs in search of help to the federal soldiers, who unfortunately arrive when the body is on fire. The soldiers shoot from a distance, and Ramón is killed.

[12] *Nayar*, p. 189.
[13] *Ibid.*, p. 245.

Now Gervasio is in jail in Tepic. He could save himself by saying that he was following the desire of the tribe, but he remains silent. He turns his back on the halfbreed who questions him; the court clerk, knowing the psychology of the Indian so well, answers his own questions and smiles.

There is no more evident proof of the failure of the revolutionary principles than the one contained in this novel. The author deals here with the Cora Indians, but isn't this a question that can be applied to any group of Indians in Mexico? We face here the old problem of the struggle between civilization and barbarism, except that in this case the values have been switched: barbarism is represented by judges, army officers, priests, landlords, money lenders; civilization, by the innocent and pure Indians. The childish world of the Coras is trampled upon and destroyed by hordes of villains, who, thirsting for blood, disgrace the name of Christ, as well as by soldiers, who, instead of preserving order, are evil forces of disintegration and chaos.

We witness here the case of a liberty-loving tribe of Indians who, having been able to keep their independence during four centuries of colonial oppression, fall now before the onslaught of a government whose sacred duty it was to protect them. Menéndez makes in this novel one of the most serious accusations of our time; and if the Mexican politicians remain indifferent in the presence of these abuses, it means that they are not worthy of being considered the representatives of the people or the interpreters of a revolutionary philosophy.

The degree of intensity with which Menéndez attacks the Indian problem reveals in him a capacity for human understanding and tenderness rare among the writers of his generation.

The novel of José Revueltas is entitled *Human Mourning* (*El luto humano,* 1943), and might well be called the Novel of Death. It is the story of a group of workmen fleeing from a storm, one of them carrying the corpse of his little daughter. During the course of the tragic flight they die, one by one, until the last ones are devoured by the buzzards. But death, or rather, the proximity of death, is only a pretext for the author to relate to us the most intense episodes of his characters' lives. In a continuous psychological zigzag these people go from real experience to the zone of remembering and then from the latter to the former. It is as if, close to death, man should stop suddenly and begin to live backwards. Let us hear what the author says:

Their lives now had only one terminal dimension. From then on the minutes were going to be only a preparation. Their old past, rich or poor, would recommence in their remembrance: childhood, youth, love, suffering, eagerness, all that had been life would prepare itself from now on for death.[14]

From this process of remembering derive the disturbing scenes in the lives of the characters of this book, scenes which are terrible nightmares in the mind of Revueltas. He offers a guide of all the types created by the Mexican Revolution: the general, the governor, the judge, the schoolteacher, the priest, the labor leader, the assassin, the "cristero," the striker, and the strikebreaker. He also presents in *Human Mourning* the most fundamental problems of post-revolutionary Mexico: the violence of rural life; the rapacity and the poison symbolized in the Mexican emblem, the Eagle and the Serpent; the dispossession of Indian villages; the agrarian reform with its modern system of irrigation and farming; the syndical movement; the right to strike; the appearance of a new type of man in the labor movement; the religious schism with the establishment of a Mexican church; the reform of rural education; the development of a new generation of teachers with a revolutionary consciousness; the clash between teachers and "cristeros"; easy death, deep hatred, blind faith, and utter cynicism.

In *Human Mourning* everything ends in failure and death: the revolution, in the hands of ignoramuses and thieves; the strikes, in the desertion of the workers; the agrarian reform, in the spirit of exploitation of the banks; rural education, with the brutality of the peasants, who punish the liberal teacher by cutting off his tongue; pure Christian faith, in the deification of the criminal "cristeros," who sacrifice their lives to superstition and hatred.

Very rarely does an encouraging idea appear in the mind of this writer. He expresses admiration for a man only in passing, and immediately his pessimistic mood defeats his intent. He says the following about General Zapata:

[14] *El luto humano,* p. 66. There is an English version entitled *The Stone Knife.*

Zapata was a general from the people. He did not know where Verdun was situated. During the war of 1914, he believed that his enemies, the Carranza men, were attacking Verdun. Zapata was a man of the people, of the pure and eternal people, in the midst of a savage and just revolution. Those people who knew what Verdun was, did not know, on the other hand, anything else. They were absolutely ignorant of everything else. And life left them looking backwards, turning their backs on all that was the Revolution, on that dear, dark, high, noble, and sinister process of the revolution.[15]

Human Mourning reveals the most intimate fibers of the Mexican soul. Revueltas even speaks of "Mexican death," that death which is carried out by the professional criminal, and which gives him "that hard emotion, that voluptuous masculinity, that invigorating animal sensation." He also speaks of "Mexican love," defined thus:

You belong to me body and soul. Physically, morally, spiritually, you belong to me. As you are now and when you become ashes. Your bones are mine, your head, your teeth, your feet, your thoughts are mine. You belong to me. You will always belong to me.[16]

Essentially Mexican are all the characters of this novel. The new man, the pure and energetic worker, as well as the generous woman:

Natividad was expecting to transform the land, and his doctrine presupposed the existence of a new type of man, a free man in a free land. That's why Cecilia, who was the land of Mexico, loved him, even though she did not know the secret, deep forces underlying such a love.[17]

There are, however, other characters—those who have not found their way or their aims in life, perhaps 80 per cent of the Mexicans. They are also revealed in *Human Mourning*:

Calixto and Ursulo were something else. They were the bitter, blind, deaf, complex, contradictory transition toward something that is waiting in the future. They were the unexpressed desire, the confused hope which appears in a people trying to discover its destiny.[18]

---

15 *El luto humano,* p. 229.
16 *Ibid.,* p. 68.
17 *Ibid.,* p. 298.
18 *El luto humano,* p. 299.

Here is, then, all the political and social thought of Revueltas.
Land in itself, as it is in Mexico today, is useless. Land is a dark
goddess. Land demands the effort, the dignity, the hope of man.
Transformed by means of fertilizers, irrigation, cooperatives, it
would become free and new; and the Mexican woman, Cecilia,
loved Natividad because unconsciously she established that unity
without which the world would end: love and work, that is to
say, Woman and Earth. The others, Calixto and Ursulo, went
blindly through life. Although they also had illusions, their future
was more uncertain, their life less pure. Their existence was hope-
ful, but without direction. Thus with all the Mexican nation.
Some men die for an ideal; others kill for pleasure, need, or
lust; a few are creative men who affirm, have faith, love; others
doubt, deny, hate. And they all go around in the wheel of time
upon the same tragic land, until one day they remain quiet under
that land, so as to leave a place to oncoming generations.

All the people in this novel die. The feast of the vultures
tragically underlines the last page of this book, but it would not
be just to think that all hope has died in the heart of the author.
When the defeated peasants ask Ursulo: "Why must we remain
here, to eat earth?" he answers, putting a handful of earth into his
mouth, "And why not?" Thus, he is setting down a line of conduct, an ideal. The earth, the noble example, the idea, the revolution, all remain. The example of the new man does not die,
the love of the woman able to understand a man with those
ideals does not die.

The contemporary Mexican novel, as a product of life, also goes
revolving around in that indestructible unity of action, dreams,
illusions, hopes, in the wheel of time. It does not matter if it
affirms or denies the revolutionary movement; if it deals with rot,
ugliness, brutality, beauty, it does not matter. The novel is an
integral part of that unity which is the entire soul of a people in
movement, a people passing through cactus deserts, salt pits, ceme-
teries, and also through green forests and snow-capped sierras.
Not all is "human mourning" in Mexico!

Doris Stone: SCHOOLS THAT LIVE

A NATION has only one natural heritage: land. If the soil is abused, the nation is abused. Therefore man, the citizen, must know how to preserve that heritage, how to conserve the natural resources of the country. This is the fundamental key to all happiness.

And man is not born knowing. His adjustment, adaptability to life, is the result of an accumulation of experiences on his part and on that of a community. This is not a mere philosophy. It is a fact. It becomes very evident the more remote the individual or group is from the ordinary centers of national or international intercourse. The isolated, the ignorant, or, better said, those poorly trained in the fundamentals of living, are most responsible in ruining that which constitutes the backbone of a people: the land.

There is only one solution of this problem: education in a vital living sense. The country of Costa Rica in Central America has been fortunate in that the area apart from its urban or densely populated zones has lent itself to experiments in human living in accordance with the environment and the needs of particular and divers groups. Southern Costa Rica has served admirably in this case because of the mixtures of cultures and their corresponding necessities. This commingling is found in a relatively small territory with a physical environment similar to the Caribbean and Atlantic littoral of northern, southern, and eastern Central America.

I

The second largest plateau of Costa Rica is known as the General Valley. This is drained by the General River which joins the Platanares and Coto-Brus to form the Diquis or Río Grande de Térraba. In late pre-Columbian times all of this region appears to have been inhabited by Boruca Indians, a sedentary group whose cultural roots seem to point to western South America, in particular Ecuador and Peru.

The Talamancan Range, highest in Central America, forms the division between the Caribbean and the Pacific slopes of Costa Rica. The section known as Talamanca is in truth the area drained by the Sixaola River and its tributaries. Here, before the Spanish Conquest, dwelt a number of tribes each with a different tongue among which were included the Térrabas, Cabécares, and Bribris. All were of eastern South American stock with a manner of living showing great similarity to the rain-forest cultures of Venezuela and northern Colombia. Shortly before the Spanish arrival the Bribris had conquered the Cabécares, imposing their lay rule and much of their speech, but accepting the religion and greater knowledge of the other. All groups in this area, however, combined against the white invader, and the fact remains that the people of Talamanca were never really subdued or converted by colonial Spain. Franciscan fathers built missions, and Spanish men dwelt in new-formed towns. But around 1700 the Indians rebelled, and with decided and bitter resentment burned the white communities and momentarily again became masters of their own heritage. As a punishment for these offensives and brutal destructions, the colonial government transplanted some of the most rebellious groups to the Pacific side of the range, and founded the Indian colonies of Ujarras, Salitre, and Térraba in land belonging to the already subdued Boruca Indians.

Land was not scarce in southeastern Costa Rica. There were more forest and earth than people to inhabit it. In truth, not until 1945, when a line was cut for the proposed Pan-American Highway, did men from the Central Plateau become interested in this area. The government of Costa Rica found itself faced with the problem of four groups, distinct in language and culture, who were utterly unprepared to protect themselves against the unscrupulous individual with designs to seize and exploit their land in the vicinity of the highway. The situation was further aggravated in that few of these tribes spoke the official tongue, Spanish, and each was in a different stage of economic and social development. There was need for action, and the action was education.

The government organized a "Junta," or committee of five, to carry out this project. It is composed of a lawyer, a representative of the National Geographic Institute, an engineer, an educator, and an anthropologist. The economic aid came at first from a liquor tax, but is now a regular subvention from Congress. Four schools were started under this plan. They are based on the idea of a grange, but one that takes into consideration the particular environment and needs of the community in which it is situated. The fundamental thought behind the project is the recognition that the Indian is a human being and can develop into a contributing and useful citizen of the republic instead of being a charge of the state.

Psychology lies at the roots of this experiment. For this reason emphasis is given to both languages, the Spanish and that of the particular group. This creates the greater importance of tribal legends and histories. One primer in the Cabécar tongue is in use and another in Bribri is being written. Indians trained in Spanish and their native speech employ this primer to teach the newly arrived student. The idea is to acquaint the pupil with the printed word as well as to offer a bridge from the old to the new language which surrounds him. The indigenous teachers are being further schooled to enable the opening of other granges deep in the heart of Bribri and Cabécar territory where a knowledge of Spanish is practically non-existent. Still, in connection with this plan, all aboriginal customs which can be incorporated in modern living or which do not hinder the nationalization of the individual are encouraged.

The education in itself is functional. Arithmetic, for example, is taught with numbers but also with objects of the environment such as *havas* or baskets of corn, pounds of meat or vegetables, or *kintals* of coffee or rice, and the measuring of a lot in the agricultural field. Finally, the more advanced students are taught the use of money by working in the school commissary. These commissaries are stocked only with essentials not obtainable in the area, such as salt, household medicines, soap, and matches. They sell with a minimum of profit just to the Indians, the gain being used as a token payment to the pupils who work behind the counter.

The basis of these schools is farming, and each community differs both in natural environment and in the degree of preparation for our way of life. Vacations vary slightly depending on the crops and the time of planting and harvesting. When this program started, the Bribris of Salitre were really not past rain-forest culture, and by tradition dedicated themselves to hunting, fishing, and as little planting as possible. Their principal domestic occupation was raising the wild *pecarí*. Matrilineal clans formed the basis for their social environment, each group inhabiting a given area but without an idea of individual ownership of this land. The Cabécares were similar to the Bribris, but were slightly more dedicated to cultivation and, at the time of the opening of the grange school in Ujarras, were living as separate families in distinct, not clan, houses. Nevertheless, the region where they dwelt was considered the property of the whole tribe for use as grazing land and, to a certain extent, agriculture. The Térrabas, who had been under the influence of Paulinist priests in the latter half of the past century, had their individual farms which were passed on within the family itself and abandoned only when the earth refused to yield. There was little problem with the Borucas. They had been under Spanish influence since the conquest, and in fact had at one time boasted a *cabildo* or town hall. Their farm lands were governed by a council which allotted given areas, and when the committee took over the direction of this group, they were accustomed to sell or exchange with one another, although no Indian had a title to his property.

It is obvious why the school had to mold itself to the local environment before it could exert its influence towards any change of custom. There are certain aspects which are common in all the granges, however. Both sexes work in the fields, and help in the making of compost or natural fertilizers, in irrigating, in terracing against erosion, in grafting, and in seed selection. Two methods of planting are used side by side: a small patch in the aboriginal manner, and a larger one in the scientific way with worked soil and natural fertilizers, for example. The result is that the school takes a vital place in the community. Even the older people living back in the forest-covered hills come to see the "magic" of corn resplendent with full ears instead of one or two poorly grained ears on a stalk. Little by little the wary villagers copy the new methods.

The fundamentals of animal husbandry are also taught to both boys and girls. This includes the proper feeding and care of pigs and chickens and the construction of pens or coops with materials taken from the surrounding forests. The girls learn sewing and cooking, particularly the preparation of the produce from the fields.

It is the emphasis in the instruction which changes according to the location. In Salitre, of the Bribris, cultivation is limited to such crops as yuccas, plantains, and rice. These can easily be grown in quantity on land that is not too good and can serve as food for human beings as well as for the pigs and chickens which form the chief elements of their economy. This is also true to a certain extent of the Térrabas. The Cabécares of Ujarras inhabit a fertile, beautiful valley. Here the school has developed truck gardening with the result that vegetables are frequently sent to augment the students' tables in Salitre, or sold in the neighboring non-Indian village of Buenos Aires. Nearly every house in the community of Ujarras has its own vegetable patch.

The Borucas, in contrast to the other tribes that live in houses scattered all over their territory, boast of having a town of the most picturesque nature. The Boruca school has cane, cotton, and vegetables, as well as a mill for making brown sugar. This has been a great stimulus for the local inhabitants. They have increased their own cane fields, use the mill, and in fact are beginning to feel that the school is a fundamental part of their life. The Borucas have an outstanding heritage in cotton weaving and were famous in colonial times for purple cloth decorated with patterns in the single weft weave. The Spaniards demanded kilos of this material as tribute to be sent to the king and the pope. Classes in dyeing the cotton and in weaving have consequently formed part of the curriculum. The best pieces made by the townsfolk, as well as the students, are bought by the school to be sold at a small profit in the capital of the republic.

Football, basketball, and baseball have been introduced in all the area, and also the custom of popular assemblies with songs, plays, and dances. This helps to take away the natural shyness

of the Indian and to prepare the individual to confront strange
or different situations.

II

Salitre, the headquarters of this educational work, has a boarding
school where the best students from all these communities are sent
for more advanced preparation with the idea of forming both
teachers and better developed citizens. This year, 1951, the day of
national independence, September 15, saw the first graduating class
and the initiation of a new and revolutionary custom. The Committee of Indian Education has control over the lands inhabited by
and surrounding all these peoples. No non-Indian can buy or
live within this territory. In order to incorporate these groups
even more into the national way of living, the school commenced
this year to give to the male graduates both a diploma and a
parcel of land in their own area which they and the committee's
administrator, an agronomist, choose. A legal title goes with this
land, but the owner cannot sell nor turn over his property for a
five-year period, and in any case he must consult and receive the
approbation of the committee. Economic aid is given for the construction of his house, which is made of materials taken from the
forest and his own surroundings, and for the first plantings. The
individual is expected to select and save his seed for the future,
and if he wants to enlarge or to start a new crop a small monetary
advance is permitted. The Indian has the right to sell his produce
to whomever he wishes, including the committee for use in the
schools.

Besides these gifts, every member of the graduating class receives
a subscription to one or more agricultural magazines. There are two
prizes for the corresponding best students. The first consists of a
pair of blooded hogs, and the second of a rooster and five fine
chickens. The committee's administrator assumes from there on
the role of tutor for all graduates, and presents a detailed report
of their agricultural development at the end of each fiscal year.

Annually, on graduation day, the Salitre school sponsors an
agricultural and animal husbandry fair at which all Indians can
participate. There are three divisions: swine, fowl, and agricultural products, with money for first prizes, and certificates of hon-

orary mention for the second place. Two consecutive certificates are equivalent to a first or money prize.

The committee has engineers measuring the farms of all the Indians within the Salitre reservation with a view of registering these properties and giving each owner his plan and title. A population census, as well as a census of domesticated animals, is being carried out in connection with this.

Little by little these once-forgotten people are coming forward to take their place in the daily life of their changing communities. The school is the focus, and even the older people gather there to learn to read, or sew, or take part in various festivities. It is hoped that eventually the need for a reservation will not exist, and that these people will be able to defend themselves and form a useful group within the Costa Rican republic. Meanwhile, the school carries on its normal educational functions and at the same time has taken a definite place within each indigenous center as "the house of the people," with the distinct task of, in truth, teaching the people how to live.

John P. Harrison: OPPORTUNITIES FOR
INTER-AMERICAN STUDIES IN THE
NATIONAL ARCHIVES

THE NATIONAL ARCHIVES would like the scholars of all disciplines to be more fully acquainted with the research possibilities offered by the records of the federal government. The object of this paper is to indicate to those interested in Latin America in general and in the Caribbean in particular, the scope of the materials available for research at the National Archives.

The archives of the United States are not part of the working consciousness of any large segment of scholars in fields other than diplomatic history. Perhaps the most important reason for this is the immensity of the volume of records in the National Archives—872,000 cubic feet at the latest estimate. The volume is so great that most scholars shy away from exploring it. The research methods followed in most of the disciplines in the social sciences, moreover, cannot be applied effectively to the exploitation of records in the quantity in which they are created by government agencies. The mountain of records is thus too overwhelming, and the ways by which to scale it are too unknown.

I

Perhaps a few words of explanation on how this volume of records is controlled and administered within the National Archives will make the way easier for those who wish to use the records. The first step taken in the National Archives in controlling this volume is to ascribe all records created by the federal government to particular record groups. These groups consist simply of all materials originating in specified governmental entities, which may vary in size and importance. Numbers have been assigned to the record groups in the order in which they were established within the National Archives. In a word, the voluminous mass of government records is first divided into smaller groups, which number 276 to date, and which are called record groups; and these record groups have their origins in various governmental entities, usually bureaus of departments, or independent agencies.

One other matter needs to be understood, namely, that all further work in arranging, describing, and servicing records in the National Archives proceeds on a record group basis. Within a record group the materials are arranged and analyzed and described in terms of their administrative and functional origins—not by the subjects to which they pertain. This is done in accordance with a basic principle of the archival profession, namely, the principle of provenance under which records of one source are kept together and handled as a unit. Thus the various parts of the record group are traced to the organizational subdivisions of the agency that created them, and are described in relation to the function that resulted in their creation.

If a scholar is to scale the mountain of modern documentation in the National Archives, he must have a working idea of the methods followed in the archival profession. If he understands that records are kept together by record groups, and that within such groups they are arranged and described in relation to organization and function, he will be in a better position to find the materials he is looking for. He will not look for information on the topic of his interest under subject headings in catalogs and indexes, for such cannot be created for the hundreds of millions of sheets of paper. Instead he will ascertain which agency, or subdivision of an agency, dealt with the topic that is of interest to him. Once he knows this, and archivists will be quick to help him to a knowledge of it, he will look into the inventories and lists of records of the agency, in which he will find identified and described the subgroups and series that may yield the information he desires.

For the investigator who has not worked in the National

Archives or whose acquaintance with the institution has been a
passing one, the most important thing is to appreciate the general
nature of the records to be found in the Archives: to learn the
types of material the scholar might expect to find there. I believe
this can be done more effectively by putting the emphasis on a
few groups of records than by a facile listing of all the record
groups containing Latin American materials. The danger is that
you may go away with the impression that you have heard about
the most important groups of Latin American papers in the National Archives, or, what would be worse, with the subconscious
impression that only the few record groups discussed contain
materials for research into Latin American problems.

The situation is just the opposite. Of the 276 existing record
groups over half have some papers relating to Latin America,
while about forty contain substantial amounts of important research materials. The following examples indicate the type of
government agency that created these records and offer a general
picture of Latin American materials in the Archives.

The records of the Supreme Court of the United States contain
the records of the Court of Appeals in Cases of Capture, 1776-1787
—the so-called Revolutionary War Prize Cases. These papers have
a great deal on the West Indies, where, it seems, every cove sheltered
a privateer or a pirate. The General Records of the Department
of Treasury include the "Letters Received" by the Secretary of the
Treasury from Collectors of Customs. The Treasury Department
maintained agents at Colón, Panama, and San Juan del Norte,
Nicaragua, during the 1850's. The collectors at United States ports
were concerned with vessels being outfitted for filibustering expeditions. The records of the Office of Indian Affairs include
letters and reports concerning the movement across the border
into Mexico of Kickapoos, Apaches, Comanches, and Pawnees, as
well as the more often described migration of the Seminoles. The
General Records of the Department of Interior contain the records
of the attempts at Negro colonization in Haiti during the years
1862-1869 and a similar venture in Belize, where southern whites
also were involved.

When you consider the history of the War Department, the
Marine Corps, and the Navy it is obvious that their records
must contain vast amounts of materials on all aspects of life in

the Caribbean. For example, the conditions on the Florida Keys are well described in the records relating to the service of the Navy and Marine Corps on the coast of Florida during the Florida-Indian War of 1835-1842. Similarly the records of the Panama Canal, the Bureau of Foreign and Domestic Commerce, the Provisional Government of Cuba, the Military Government of Cuba, the Petroleum Industry for War, the foreign claims section of the War Department, the Office of Foreign Agricultural Relations, the Military Government of Vera Cruz, the Office of Inter-American Affairs, the Division of Territories and Island Possessions, and the Boundary and Claims Commission Arbitration, all of which are separate record groups, offer substantial amounts of research material for the scholar interested in Latin America.

II

Within record groups there are easily identifiable subgroups and series of records relating to Latin America, and I shall now turn to a description of some of these smaller segments. The illustrations were chosen to show the variety rather than the amount of pertinent material in the records. Geographically the examples are confined largely to the Caribbean area.

Geographers and social and physical anthropologists will find a great deal of material in the reports and notes of field technicians of the Rubber Development Corporation, the records of which are a part of the records of the Reconstruction Finance Corporation (RG 234). The Rubber Development Corporation was, as you know, the wartime group that endeavored to locate and exploit all commercial stands of wild rubber in the Western Hemisphere. It made exploratory surveys in Mexico, the Central American republics, Panama, Colombia, Venezuela, Trinidad, Brazil, Paraguay, Bolivia, Peru, and Ecuador; and it made efforts to increase the amount of rubber that was being gathered in all of these countries except Paraguay. About half of the records are concerned with Brazil and more than three-quarters of them deal with the Amazon drainage.

The men who surveyed the continent in search of rubber recommended both the regions to be exploited and a program for doing the job efficiently. In reaching their decisions they considered not only the density and productivity of rubber trees in a given area but also the availability and cost of labor, the problem of food supply, transportation costs, the competing enterprises in the region, health and sanitation, the technical assistance required, and many other factors. The reports of the technicians are important for different reasons, depending on the area they were surveying. There is material pertinent to a description of rural society in the Caribbean side of Costa Rica and Nicaragua. In contrast to the emphasis on human problems in Central America the technicians who explored the drainage of the Apaporis River in southeastern Colombia discovered a new variety of non-commercial *hevea* in an area left uninhabited by both man and the *anopheles* mosquito. There is probably no better physical description of the Vaupes River drainage than the one found in the succinct reports of these technicians. The descriptions of the central *oriente* of Peru and Ecuador are most noteworthy for the information they contain on the customs and tribal boundaries of the local Indians. The description of the Auca Indians, a tribe not mentioned by name in the *Handbook of South American Indians,** comments on the loose social organization within the tribe, the extreme primitiveness of their weapons and other material culture, and especially the frequency of their murderous forays against neighboring peoples. The attitude of the technician who had to deal with this intransigent tribe was not original. He felt that the best Auca was a dead Auca.

The scope of a technician's activity is well indicated by the following title taken from a Venezuelan field report: "The federal territory of Amazonas: communications, forest products, climatic and sanitary conditions, and other factors of the Upper Orinoco, Casiquiare, and Río Negro; a report based upon observations made during April-May 1940, and December 1941 to July 1942."

These records do not contain the business correspondence of the Rubber Development Corporation, but production problems arising out of the intricate skein of relationships between rubber gatherer, small merchant, landowner, concessionaire, central banking institution, local and United States government agencies, and the corporation are discussed.

---

* There is evidence that Auca may be a generic term for wild Indians like *motilón* or *chichimec*.

Many maps and photos accompany these records. The maps give, in addition to the location and type of rubber trees, the location of Indian tribes (and note if they are hostile or friendly), the location of trails and what is carried over them, and the position of rapids and condition of portages on navigable rivers. Many of these maps give enough detail that the 1:1,000,000 map of the American Geographical Society should be checked against them. The photographs frequently are non-professional from a technical point of view but they usually manage to make the point intended by the author.

Of the General Records of the Department of State (RG 59), the series of diplomatic and consular dispatches are the most widely known. These papers have been used extensively for researches into diplomatic history but their possibilities for economic studies are just being realized. They have been little used as a source for local history, sociological studies, or historical geography. An example of this type of material that has been ignored is a dispatch from a missionary, who doubled as the United States commercial agent on the Colombian island of San Andrés, off the Mosquito Coast, in which he contemplates the social and economic changes effected on the island during the quarter-century 1850-1875 by the abolition of slavery and the gaining of a profitable export market for coconuts. An 1886 dispatch from Medellín, Colombia, offers another example of fresh material in these much used reports. The manager of extensive United States gold-mining interests in the Department of Antioquia points out with great emphasis that the revolution going on at the time was not detrimental to United States capital investments in Colombia. It was just the opposite, he indicated, explaining that the margin of profit was at an all time high. Labor was cheaper and less troublesome during periods of internal strife because it was well known that the military respected the rights of the company and did not molest its workers.

The largest and least-used group of papers originating in the State Department form a separate record group called Records of the Foreign Service Posts of the Department of State (RG 84). These records kept by foreign service personnel at the consular and diplomatic posts—as distinct from the dispatches sent to Washington—remain virtually untouched by scholars. A program was begun in 1930 to ship all of the older, non-current post records to Washington. The process has been accelerated until now most of the post records through 1935 are in the National Archives. The use of these records is subject to the restriction of a twenty-five-year time lag that applies to other State Department documents. The post records contain all interconsular correspondence, letters to and from local officials and commercial firms, a voluminous correspondence with individuals and business firms in the United States, personal record books, remarks on local conditions, and copies of all dispatches sent to the Department in Washington. The quality and amount of material, especially before 1912, depends wholly upon the individual stationed at the post.

Post records after 1906 are of great utility for area studies because in that year the State Department started a central filing system based on a subject classification so that the consular dispatches from, say, Havana or the diplomatic dispatches from Cuba are no longer bound in a separate series. Only in the post records can material be found grouped by place of origin and arranged chronologically by year. Starting in 1912, the materials within each year are arranged according to the same subject classification as has been used for the central file of the State Department since 1910. About 70 per cent of the material is classified under the headings of either commercial relations or internal affairs of the country in question.

Over the years, consulates have opened and closed, with the result that post records exist for a surprising number of places. Using the Caribbean coast of South America as an example and omitting the major commercial centers, the United States has at some time maintained consulates in Quibdó, Turbo on the Gulf of Urabá, Río Hacha, Bucaramanga, Cúcuta, San Cristóbal, Tovar, Valera, Coro, Valencia, Barcelona, Carúpano, Cumaná, and Caripito. The post records for Maracaibo contain excellent, if sporadic, reporting from the agents in the interior of the consular district for the last two decades of the nineteenth century. The consular agent at Valera emphasized the effect of the sharply dropping world price of coffee on landowners who had overextended their credit to open new lands in the expectation of better prices; the agent in San Cristóbal was most concerned with the contractual details of a new railroad and what this venture meant for exploiting nearby copper mines and lowering the cost of producing coffee; while the agent at Coro stressed the political situation. The Post Records for Santa Marta are a rich source of information on the production, labor, and political factors involved in the twentieth-century development of a tropical banana zone. The records for Colón offer excellent material on land speculation and colonization along the east coast of Panama during the 1920's.

Diplomatic post records differ from consular post records in that they are complete from the arrival of the first United States minister, and that the correspondence with local officials and United States consuls is more voluminous and of greater value. Diplomatic officers do not carry on commercial correspondence; but papers relating to claims cases in their records frequently contain important data on the economic activities of United States citizens in foreign lands. The following examples of diplomatic post record material indicate what is to be found there in addition to the series of letters received and sent, instructions from the department, copies of dispatches, and memorandum books.

Among the diplomatic post records of Colombia are three volumes of papers relating to the Panama Riots of 1856 and one concerned with the Colón fire of 1885. With the records from the Dominican Republic are four boxes of unbound papers relating to the case of the Santo Domingo Improvement Co. *v.* the Dominican government. The diplomatic post records for Mexico are especially full and well organized. In addition to the type of material mentioned earlier, there are several series of reports and correspondence files regarding agrarian expropriation and land problems; memoranda of conversations held at the Mexican foreign office from 1897 to 1904; and eight volumes of newspaper clippings starting in 1899 and ending, in 1910, with the headline that Madero was gravely wounded.

Two of the record groups in the National Archives composed entirely of Caribbean materials are the records of the Danish government of the Virgin Islands and the records of the Spanish governors of Puerto Rico.

When the United States bought the Virgin Islands from Denmark it acquired, in addition to the land, most of the local records kept by the Danes. These are now in the National Archives, where they make up Record Group 55. Some records were taken to Copenhagen but these dealt mainly with the Danish foreign policy and colonial administration. Except for political history, the records now in the custody of the United States are complete. The emphasis of these local records is on the ownership of real and personal property. They include estates account books, estates cases, inventory appraisals of plantations, auction sales accounts, church records, slave lists, His Majesty's slave importations, lists of freed slaves, livestock books, lists of tradesmen and merchants, labor contracts, customs records, the veterinary livestock book, and a record of rats caught—practically everything needed to describe the economic and social pattern of the islands. An understanding of local government may be gained from the official compilations of royal letters and resolutions, 1660-1812 (28 volumes); the forty-six volumes of the official gazette, 1798-1840; notes to and from the consular representatives of other countries; and military records.

In so far as I have been able to ascertain, these records include the most complete file of Virgin Islands newspapers in the United States. The two most important items are the semi-weekly *St. Thomas Tidende* for the years 1831-1917, and the *St. Croix Dansk Vestindisk Regierings Ans* from 1827 to 1917. Other more recent newspapers in the collection include the *Emancipator,* 1921-1935; the *Bulletin,* 1905-1935; and the *St. Croix Herald,* 1918-1935. During the Danish period English was more used in the news section of the newspapers than the official language. In addition to Danish and English, advertisements appear in both French and Spanish.

Another record group composed entirely of materials originating on a single Caribbean island, Record Group 186, consists of approximately two hundred *legajos* of the former archive of the Captaincy-General of Puerto Rico, 1750-1898. Like the Virgin Islands archives, this body of records came into United States custody by reason of a treaty provision. Before these papers arrived in jumbled disorder at the National Archives in 1945, their peregrinations were complicated and obscure. Certain fact is that the records were shipped from Puerto Rico to the Library of Congress in 1898. A few Puerto Rican writers succeeded in turning myth into reality for a large number of Puerto Ricans who now believe that a major part of the manuscript record of their island's heritage was shipped back by careless United States officials, not to San Juan but to Havana, where the records were left on the docks to rot until a hurricane completed their destruction. The documented fact is that the records not kept in Washington were returned to Puerto Rico in 1901. The present collection in the National Archives is less than a tenth of the records that left Puerto Rico for the Library of Congress in 1898. The Archives' staff, with assistance from the University of Puerto Rico, is now preparing them for public use by trying to reconstruct their original arrangement. When this job is completed the plan is to microfilm the more important series of these records. There are few papers dated before 1810, but there is a quantity of material on interisland trade and the activities of freebooters and pirates during the period 1810-1830. For the years after this the records are most voluminous from 1850-1875, at which time problems of municipal government, land tenure, slavery, and the cost of living were emphasized. There is scattered documentation for foreign relations and colonial government, but the dominant theme is local history.

III

In order to emphasize the record group concept, each example that I have used up to now was taken from a different record group. It is necessary to cut across this arrangement to point out the existence in the National Archives of a variety of private journals and diaries. As these manuscripts were not created as federal records the scholar may be surprised at finding them in a government record repository. All of these journals, however, had become part of some agency's records before they were transferred to the Archives. Most of them were written by federal employees, although some continue after the author left government service.

In the last category belongs the journal of Lewis Seegar, who describes himself as a "rambler at large." The account begins in 1817, and from 1819 until the journal ends in 1823 Seegar is occupied in the Caribbean. He landed at most of the important Caribbean islands and some that were uninhabited, as well as visiting the larger ports of northern South America. Seegar was attached to a United States naval vessel until 1823, when he accepted a commission as lieutenant in the Mexican Navy and, as commander of the ship *Chalco*, swore allegiance to General Santa Anna. While in Mexican pay he was active in the region of Alvarado and Vera Cruz.

The Seegar journal, along with a few other manuscript diaries and descriptive accounts, is part of the State Department Records. By far the largest single group of journals is in the Naval Records Collection of the Office of Naval Records and Library, which contains over three hundred volumes of logs, diaries, journals, and collected correspondence. Approximately half of these manuscripts are concerned, at least in part, with Latin America. Typical journals in this collection include the one kept by Lieutenant Charles Gauntt aboard the ship *Macedonian* on a voyage from Boston to Cap Haitien, March 21 to June 20, 1822; and that kept by Captain James Biddle, commander of the *Ontario,* on a cruise from New York to the Columbia River and back to Norfolk, 1817-1819. Captain Biddle describes conditions in the Chilean port of Valparaíso at the time of the battle of Maipó. His particular concern was the fleet of United States merchant vessels that were prevented from going out to sea by the blockading Spanish squadron while their crews were deserting for the better wages offered by patriot sympathizers. Biddle gives a firsthand account of the negotiations that resulted in a United States merchant ship's making a substantial profit carrying a cargo of wheat from patriot-occupied Valparaíso to royalist-held Lima, an operation not calculated to aid the republican cause.

Of interest to ecologists and regional geographers would be the 250-page diary kept during 1818-1819 by John Landreth, a timber cruiser who made surveys extending nearly a hundred miles inland along the Gulf Coast from the western boundary of Louisiana to West Florida, looking for stands of red cedar and live oak suitable for naval construction. Landreth describes the soils, natural cover, cultivated crops, water supply, wildlife, commercial activity, transportation problems, and the customs of the inhabitants. His descriptions of the islands and bayous of Louisiana are accompanied by a series of water-color detail-maps. Along with such diaries and journals in the Naval Record Library are a considerable number of log books, some taken from captured foreign vessels. There you will find the two volumes of *cuadernos* kept aboard the Spanish battleship *Cristóbal Colón* from June 13, 1897, until June 2, 1898.

Another series of journals and logs made available to libraries and scholars everywhere by the microfilm publication program relates to the exploring expedition of 1835-1842 "to the Pacific Ocean and South Seas," under the command of Lieutenant Charles Wilkes.

The ships stopped for considerable time in several South American ports. A variety of backgrounds is reflected in the writings of members of this cruise. Many of the manuscripts today are in private hands, especially those written by the scientific members of the expedition, and a sizable number have been printed. Most of the originals, however, are in the National Archives, where they are a part of the Hydrographic Office records and the records of the Bureau of Naval Personnel.

IV

This report on research opportunities in the National Archives would be incomplete without some mention of the unexpected: that out-of-context item sometimes found attached to a completely unrelated body of records. One example of the unusual is in the records of the Weather Bureau, in a series of about five hundred volumes containing the abstracts of, perhaps, a thousand ships' logs, all organized according to a form devised by Matthew Fontaine Maury. Scribbled across the printed sheets of the "Maury log," kept aboard the *S. S. City of Pittsburgh* during a voyage from New York to California, is an eight and a half page account entitled "The excursion of an Emperor and an Empress on board an American Steamer. Rio de Janeiro, September 10, 1852." The account supports the conventional picture of Dom Pedro as an impressive appearing man of grave demeanor. The writer remarks upon Dom Pedro's punctuality, his light appetite and moderate drinking, and the inordinate courtesy that marked his public treatment of the Empress, and especially upon the Emperor's great interest in machinery, which was his reason for accepting the invitation to visit the *Pittsburgh*. The account ends by pointing out Brazil's superiority to Spanish America despite the handicap of a monarchial form of government.

The written records in the National Archives are supplemented by maps, still photos, motion pictures, and sound recordings. It is desirable usually to store such materials in special equipment designed for the purpose and under the care of special experts, but the materials are separated from the written record only when it is possible to do so without lessening the value of the document they accompany.

V

This paper is in no way a description of the Caribbean materials in the National Archives. It does not even mention by name all the record groups that contain large amounts of materials for inter-American studies. The object has been to illustrate by the use of examples the variety of records in the National Archives and, in the interest of American scholarship, to invite a wider use of them by all of the social science disciplines.

Part V

DIPLOMACY

16

Rexford G. Tugwell: CARIBBEAN OBLIGATIONS

I

PROBABLY a convincing case could be made by a determined partisan on either side of the question: Has the United States been fair to the Caribbean countries? In fact, all of us have seen such arguments set out with considerable force. Such a difference may well have its origin in contrasting interpretations of the past and present. So I may as well say something at the outset concerning the view of this from which I proceed: this is that there has been an obvious progress through the years toward recognizing the obligations created by our interference. Even if it can be argued that there has been unfairness in the past, it seems to me to be well on the way to liquidation in the present.

If history in the nineteenth and twentieth centuries is appealed to for interpretation, progress can, I am certain, be seen quite clearly. There is, of course, the Monroe Doctrine declaring a special interest of the United States in the area. In its original form its limits were fairly well defined. It was intended to exclude European nations who might consider conquest or colonization. There were times when it seemed that our intentions lay in the direction of assimilation; but these were fugitive, and never majority, ambitions. More important was the development of the so-called corollaries to the basic doctrine of protection, especially in the regimes of Cleveland and Theodore Roosevelt. These recognized responsibility on the part of the United States for good behavior on the part of the Caribbean nations which others were precluded from enforcing. On occasion the corollaries went to the length of collecting funds and paying them over to European debtors. The

sole gain to our neighbors was freedom from other interference than
that of the United States.

But under later Presidents, notably Taft and Wilson, new implied corollaries were acted on. It seemed now to be the duty of
the United States to bring about good behavior in quite a new sense.
Disorder and tyranny were to be suppressed and order and liberty
were to be encouraged—with Marines if necessary.

Writing as late as 1928, just after the Sixth Pan American Conference, Mr. Walter Lippmann remarked in an article in *Foreign
Affairs* (July, 1928, pp. 541 ff.), that our chief delegate, the distinguished former Secretary of State, Mr. Hughes, called from
retirement for the occasion, had defined our policy in "very noble
terms." And he went on to say that nobody from Latin America
had either praised or damned the chief delegate's statement: "We
emerged from the conference having endorsed our own solitary
obligation with our own solitary praise." He concluded from this
that, although there was undoubtedly widespread distrust of the
United States, there was no organized movement in opposition. Our
obligation he then went on to define in these terms:

The immediate circumstances which lead to an intervention are
almost invariably due to revolutionary disorder. The lives and
property of foreigners are threatened, and under our latter-day
interpretation of the Monroe Doctrine we take upon ourselves the
obligation of protecting them. But to this obligation we have given
the very broadest interpretation. In the Caribbean we do not intervene merely to save foreigners from being killed or wounded, to
protect property which is threatened with irreparable physical damage. We go much further, and assume that it is our obligation to
insure foreigners a general domestic tranquillity. At times we go
even further than that, and assume that it is part of our obligation
to see that the government in power is friendly to foreign interests,
and that it will not through exorbitant corruption or through radical
legislation interfere too much with the business of foreigners.

It will be noticed about this that there was no hint of another
obligation than that of preserving tranquillity, none even of acting
in the interest of neighbors; nor was there a duty to act in concert
with them in any instance of violent disturbance. The Caribbean
was still regarded as an American lake inhabited by periodically

irresponsible people who had at times to be admonished or cor-
rected—by the government of the United States, acting alone. The
obligation was not to the Caribbean peoples but to those who might
have dealings with them and who were prevented by the Monroe
Doctrine from interfering on their own account.[1]

In this same issue of *Foreign Affairs*, however, Franklin D.
Roosevelt had occasion to comment also[2] on our Latin American
relations; and his statement shows that this was a transition time,
for he spoke of the need to "accept not only certain facts but many
new principles of a higher law, and newer and better standards."
And speaking specifically of our nearer neighbors he said:

The peoples of the other Republics of this Western world are
just as patriotic, just as proud of their sovereignty. The peace, the
security, the integrity, the independence of every one of the American Republics is of interest to all the others, not to the United
States alone. . . . Single-handed intervention by us in the internal
affairs of other nations must end; with the cooperation of others
we shall have more order in this hemisphere and less dislike.[3]

This statement was very different from that of Mr. Lippmann;
it was, indeed, a foreshadowing of what would be, during the
Roosevelt Presidency, an entirely new approach, amounting to a
rejection of the body of old corollary doctrine and the acceptance
of positive obligations, without the unilateral obligation of ensuring
tranquillity. Even this definition of good neighborliness, it will be
noted, stopped short of any suggestion of a duty among a more
advanced people to assist less advanced ones. It remained for President Truman in 1949[4] to say, for the people of the United States,

[1] For an excellent summary of the events during this stage of American
policy, consult Dexter Perkins' *The United States and the Caribbean* (Harvard University Press, 1947), especially Chapters 6 and 7.
[2] "Our Foreign Policy: A Democratic View." *Foreign Affairs*, July, 1928,
pp. 573 ff.
[3] *Ibid.*, pp. 584-585. The good neighbor policy ought never to be
mentioned without reference to the part of Mr. Sumner Welles in its shaping.
Mr. Welles, it is likely, either assisted or influenced the statement of policy
referred to here.
[4] In his Inaugural Address. This was the famous Point Four pronouncement. The transition was less abrupt than is apparent from this brief statement.
For many years American technicians had been loaned freely to Latin America; and in very recent years assistance of this sort had been considerable.

that the time had now arrived for reassessing the duties of the good neighbor. We should, he said:

Make available to peace-loving peoples the benefits of our store of technical knowledge in order to help them realize their aspirations for a better life ... their poverty is a handicap and a threat both to them and to more prosperous areas.

The setting here was wider than a hemispheric one. A recently finished global conflict had widened American horizons. But the historic relationships made it inevitable that the first and most significant application of the new doctrine should be among those who were nearest. And it has proved to be so; up to now the Point Four effort in the Caribbean area, widely defined, had been as great as in all the rest of the world. And in any new advance beyond the conception of Point Four it seems likely that the same sequence will be established. At any rate it may be noted that President Truman's conception of obligation was as great an advance over President Roosevelt's as President Roosevelt's had been over that of his predecessors before 1933.

II

I have always believed that I could see in the expanding concept of good neighborliness—and we see that it has expanded—the natural bent of Americans toward sympathy for others as they struggle toward freedom and well-being. But I have thought, also, that this sympathy might be better expressed in action than it has ever been in the past or than it is being expressed at present.

It has seemed to me that both because of the continuing national strategic interest in the Caribbean and because of a genuine desire to be helpful, a still more positive implementation might be forthcoming. I would, in a word, extend the New Deal, in appropriately modified form, to those nations in the Caribbean who desired it. The analogy between the New Deal's concern for disadvantaged citizens and national concern for disadvantaged nations is not a forced one. I would suggest the elimination of caprice and differences in treatment and the extension of general assistance directed to the laying of those foundations on which social betterment must always depend: the increase of production, first in agriculture and then in industry; the intensifying of vocational education; the betterment of public health; and the gradual establishment of social security. These were the objectives of the New Deal in the United States; they seem to me appropriate objectives throughout the area of special national interest. What else can it mean to be a good neighbor? What else can have been the real meaning of President Truman's pronouncement?

There can, of course, be differences of opinion as to the extent of obligation to neighbors just as there were differences about the extent of obligation to be met by the system of social security at home. And what actually might be done would always be arrived at by compromise. I am not so much concerned with that as with the forthright definition of an obligation which appears to have been generally accepted and the means to meet it, whatever its extent.

In fact the obligation is not denied. The various assistance efforts, of which a long list could be made, amply witness acceptance. But it might not be difficult to establish the point that these have sometimes been, if not ill conceived, at least not directed steadily and accurately to really remedial action. Sometimes they have been distressingly slow or only intermittently pushed.[5] But it is quite another matter to proceed from the vague acknowledgment of obligation to the actual assumption of its demands. This requires debate; and it is this debate which I should like to see begun.

[5] One of the more distressing examples of a good start and then abandonment is furnished by the Haitian-American Agricultural Development Company. This project was begun with the idea of producing rubber from *cryptostegia,* a latex-bearing vine imported from Africa. It was demonstrated that rubber could be produced but by the time the demonstration had been made, rubber from other sources (largely synthetic) seemed to be more economical and many thousands of planted acres were torn out and the project abandoned. The results for the Haitian people were deplorable; and other possibilities for development were either not undertaken or were abandoned. Mr. Jesse Jones's aspersions in *Fifty Billion Dollars* (The Macmillan Company, 1951), were thoroughly unjustified. The management was not at fault. It was the indecisiveness of policy which was responsible.

I have for many years watched with interest the snail's progress made in the Pan American Highway, begun in 1930, which has suffered from intermittent support. The 1950 *Annual Report* of the Bureau of Public Roads indicates that it is still, after twenty-one years, not nearly completed:

"In Mexico it is open and in excellent condition over all the distance from the United States to Guatemala, but in northwestern Guatemala, begin-

This discussion would not center in the utility of any of the undertakings, past or present, for neighborly help. It would center rather in the nature of the obligation and the means considered adequate for its discharge. In the long run the amounts devoted to such a program would be settled by repeated assessment of needs and of available resources. With emphasis turned toward the future it might be hoped to escape from a good many controversies concerning the past, especially those having to do with generosity or fairness.

Perhaps it needs to be said that the recognition of responsibility cannot have any proper reference to concession. It is merely a realistic assessment of mutual interests and of ways to meet them. The federal government is not doing Mississippi or Georgia—or even Puerto Rico—a favor by strengthening the economies and the social structures in those places. It is making itself strong by extending its foundations into the subsoil of a more widely shared prosperity. This extension to neighbors with very much the same relationship, geographically and social, as Puerto Rico, cannot be regarded as novel. There is only lacking the accidental political tie—and that has now been loosened and is quite other than it once was. Having something like this in mind, I would suggest that we might think of extending to other countries assistance of the kind now being extended to Puerto Rico.

---

ning at the Mexican border, there is a gap of 25 miles which is still impassable. In northern Costa Rica there is also a gap of about 65 miles and in southern Costa Rica and western Panama there is another gap of about 150 miles, both of which are impassable.

"Among those sections considered passable there are many which still need improving because of inadequate surfaces, sharp turns, steep grades, and narrow roadway."

Even more discouraging are the following statements concerning current progress:

"In Guatemala no new projects were started and construction has proceeded at a somewhat slower rate on those which were previously under way.

"In El Salvador no work was done except maintenance. . . .

"In Nicaragua the paving of the section from Sebaco to Matagalpa was completed and the section from Jinotepe to Rivas was approximately 40% complete. No new projects were started.

"In Honduras no work was done except maintenance.

"In Costa Rica the only work done was removal of slides and operations to protect improvements already made.

"In Panama an aerial survey was made. . . . "

III

Sporadic undertakings have finally been given up in Puerto Rico for a planned basic program which promises to lay just such a foundation for well-being as would be appropriate to the circumstances of others in the Caribbean. This program is solidly anchored in education, in technical advance, in the development of social security, and in orderly arrangement of productive efforts. Its planning has been carried out largely by Puerto Ricans themselves; and it has called on federal resources only for the same assistance as is given to the various states. It has therefore been possible, merely by extending already tested and familiar devices and methods, to accomplish the same kind of results as in the states. True, the Puerto Ricans are making further efforts on their own and with their own resources; their Development Authority and their Land Authority are extraordinarily brave attempts to overcome quickly some old handicaps. But they could not have been undertaken with anything like the present promise of success if they had not had in the background an expanding system of vocational education, agricultural extension services, credit on the same terms as in the States, technical advice from many federal departments, and reliance on several provisions of the social security system.[6]

It could be argued, I think, that the most significant connection between Puerto Rico and the federal government is represented by inclusion in the state-aid system. The political domination of Puerto Rico by the United States has become by now so tenuous, and self-government is so nearly complete, that the relation is

[6] The cost to the United States of the program in Puerto Rico is roughly 3 million dollars a year. This includes regular grants for agriculture, education, health, and social security. This is for a population of 2,500,000 (figures for 1950). If it may be taken as an adequate meeting of obligation, a projection of like cost to the Caribbean nations might be made. This would be some 60 to 80 millions, depending on the number included. A more realistic projection would include starting funds for only the basic services—planning, budgeting, education, agricultural extension, supervised farm-and-home loans, health, etc. Some nations are better supplied than others with such services already; the start, therefore, would be at different levels in each. The addition of grants in aid for public roads and airports ought to be possible if some such sum as 80 millions could be thought of.

presently one for which there is no precedent. Some ingenuity has been used in finding a name for it; but none of those suggested has so far seemed adequate. The Dominion analogy comes to mind; but its inappropriateness lies in the very services I have mentioned. Commonwealth states have a relation with each other which does not include such organized and continuing efforts on the part of some to bring the citizens of others into equal economic and social status. It has, I think, been concluded by the more far-seeing Puerto Ricans that the name does not matter. What does matter is that every opportunity for advancement shall be fully exploited; and since a special historical relationship exists, and since the services and funds needed are to be found in the federal government, they are accepted.

The case of Puerto Rico, for one who knows something about the struggles of other disadvantaged peoples for improvement, is amazing. The energy, ingenuity, and capacity to plan and administer uncovered in that small island in the last decade represent a challenge to all those who doubt the ability of what are sometimes called, by the patronizing, "backward" peoples, to carry out comprehensive reconstruction.

What has been done in Puerto Rico could not have happened without assistance from the United States; but also it could not have been done by the United States. It is clear to me that much of the success there is owed to the fact that the program has been devised and fitted together by the Puerto Ricans themselves. Their assessment of their own capacities and their adaptation to their own uses of the means made available to them has been a model not only of devotion to a cause but of determined persistence in its service. I say this not to praise Puerto Ricans, who know how I feel about their achievement, but to document my conviction that the same capabilities exist in other Caribbean nations, awaiting only the opportunity to emerge. Indeed they have emerged in various other places, but too often without the resources, or the necessary technical assistance, to proceed in anything like such a spectacular way.

There are problems to be solved on entering into such a relationship. There does, after all, exist a bond between Puerto Rico and the United States. Puerto Ricans are citizens of the United States and they have even served in the armed forces in several wars and so have built up a common loyalty. Their external relations are not within their own control; but otherwise they are—or soon will be—entirely self-governing; but the relations which have grown up through the state-aid programs have become connective tissue which is a very strong bond of union, so strong that there is only a small minority in favor of severing it.

The cooperating members of the Agricultural Department, of the federal credit agencies, of the Social Security Agency, of the Public Health Service, and of the Bureaus of Education or Public Roads —these are not imperialists; they are technicians. And they have no more thought of domination in Puerto Rico than in Minnesota or Tennessee. Indeed the terms of the acts under which assistance is given preclude any such development. There is no difference in the terms of arrangements with Puerto Rico from those with the states of the Union. Indeed Puerto Rico has been brought into successive programs by the simple addition of a clause saying that the "Act is hereby extended to include Puerto Rico."

IV

What I suggest is that the Puerto Rican precedent in giving assistance may be followed in principle in other instances. There would need to be some rather involved diplomatic preliminaries, including a mutual statement of policy which abjured political meanings in any contemplated arrangement. But even this, if it were possible, I should like to see avoided or minimized. The quiet, unostentatious work of the technicians which is the objective would need some framework of agreement; but the less made of such general negotiations the better. There would perhaps need to be a coordinator's office; but it might be pointed out that although such an official was authorized for Puerto Rico, he has never been appointed and seems not to be greatly missed.

The suggestion I make is not, however, that the United States should at once, or perhaps ever, undertake so full-bodied a program of assistance as has been extended to Puerto Rico; it is rather that the pattern and procedure developed there should be adapted to others' needs. In order to see more realistically what this would mean, the contrasts may be drawn between such an undertaking and what is now being done. For much *is* being done at present—enough to indicate that a special responsibility is recognized and that a further development would not constitute something new or unprecedented.[7] At present, assistance

[7] The following summary of the Point Four Program in Latin America was furnished, in response to a request, by Dr. H. G. Bennett of the Technical Cooperation Administration in November, 1951:

"I. *Operations in Fiscal Year 1951*

"The Point 4 program in Latin America in fiscal year 1951 included projects in 19 countries: Bolivia, Brazil, Chile, Colombia, Costa Rica, Cuba, Dominican Republic, Ecuador, El Salvador, Guatemala, Haiti, Honduras, Mexico, Nicaragua, Panama, Paraguay, Peru, Uruguay and Venezuela.

"In individual countries, there are 82 projects in all, of which 29 were agricultural projects, 21 were health projects including maternal and child health, and nine were education projects emphasizing rural and vocational education and the training of teachers of these fields. The other projects covered mineral exploration and mineral resources development, water resources development, highway planning and development, civil aviation administration and various fields of government administration.

"Aside from the individual country projects there were regional projects in natural rubber development, census taking, labor statistics, vital statistics, agricultural statistics and labor law administration.

"In the field on both country projects and regional projects were 584 American technicians cooperating with a much larger number of Latin American technicians. In Brazil, for example, 58 technicians from the United States were working with several thousand Brazilian technicians in projects covering health and sanitation, education, geologic investigations, mineral resources development, agriculture, rubber development, child health and general economic development.

"The total cost to the United States of the program in Latin America in fiscal year 1951 was $11.3 million of which $5.4 million was for the salaries and expenses of United States technicians and $4.7 million for supplies and equipment. The remainder, $1.2 million, was used to bring 482 Latin Americans to the United States to study in various useful fields. The total outlay of the participating countries has not yet been calculated but amounted to considerably more than the United States outlay. In fiscal year 1950, host countries spent $2.70 to every dollar spent by the United States.

"II. *Plans for Fiscal Year 1952*

"The President on October 10, 1951, signed into law an act of Congress authorizing the expenditure of $21.25 million for technical cooperation in Latin America in fiscal year 1952. Legislation appropriating the funds for technical cooperation pursuant to this law was approved by the House on October 11 and was to be considered shortly after by the Senate.

"Provided the funds requested are finally approved, the Point 4 program plans to expand a number of existing projects and undertake new ones. Plans call for an increase in the number of technicians in the field in

is given to specific areas in specific ways on a showing of opportunity to achieve something remedial. Mostly it has been confined to two fields—agriculture and health. These are sufficiently basic and, taken with vocational education, would undoubtedly be the primary objectives of any program. Good as these instances are, however, they are sporadic in nature. The experts are called in to solve a problem and then are expected to leave. It would not be true to say that the effects of their work soon disappear. Often they will have trained local technicians so that their work may be perpetuated. But I would contend that it is not enough; and that a more permanent and continuous effort ought to be made. The field needs to be cultivated, fertilized, and made inherently productive year after year rather than left at the end of a short period to isolated and unassisted local management.

That deeper objective can only be reached in agriculture as it has been reached in the United States and as it is being reached in Puerto Rico—by establishing regional centers of training and research and by developing a permanent extension service as part of a continent-wide system. In health it can only be reached by modern medical training and by an institutionalized public health program similarly related to a larger center. This method is even more necessary to the nurturing of suitable industries. The tendency—so long as vocational education is lacking, and, in fact, so long as a planned series of mutually supporting economic activities related to some great system has not been started—is to foster futile handicrafts and similar primitive efforts. Nodules of modern industry do not survive when they cannot call on a body of trained workers and when the complex of which they are natural parts is lacking. These lessons, again, have been well

---

Latin America to about 900 and for training grants to nearly 700 Latin Americans.

"These increases would require about $18 million in all: $10.2 million for the salaries and expenses of United States technicians, $5.2 million for supplies and equipment and $2.6 million for trainees. The remaining $3.25 million would be divided between the United Nations and the Organization of American States to support multi-lateral technical cooperation projects in Latin America."

learned in Puerto Rico. The training efforts are now reaching many thousands of potential workers and the expected complex of industries runs to hundreds of mutually supporting factories. But of course Puerto Rico has had the advantage also of government credit agencies for assisting new industries and something of this sort would always be necessary.

If agriculture alone is taken as an example, it can be seen what is to be gained by such a change as I suggest. All of the states, and Puerto Rico as well, have agricultural colleges and research centers; they have also extension services officered by college-trained men who carry the results of research to the farms themselves; and they are related to each other and to the whole through the Federal Department of Agriculture. Work and communication goes on day in and day out, year in and year out. Results in productivity not gained in one year are gained in succeeding ones. Results gained anywhere are transmitted quickly to everywhere else. Finally modern practices are communicated to, and put to use by, enough farmers so that the results show in the figures of national productivity. Everyone knows how spectacular these have been in the later stages of this progress. No expenditure of national wealth and effort has paid better than this long, persistent, and cumulative agricultural program.

I would open this system to our neighbors, establishing colleges and research centers first, as was done in the United States, not in every nation but in every region; then, as the men and women trained in the agricultural and household arts appeared, I would follow this with an extension service equipped also with loan funds to be used by farmers under close supervision. Our neighbors, quite aside from financial assistance, would then have open to them all the results of our pioneering, and all the lessons learned in our half-century and more of experience. Something of this has been done. Colleges in the United States have had many students from the Caribbean area who have gone back to their own lands. Many of the results of research have been carried there also by the teams and individuals sent by the Department of Agriculture, first, and more recently, by the Technical Cooperation Administration and the Institute of Inter-American Affairs. These are good beginnings; but they are not a substitute for a permanent system of indigenous training, extension, and research.

They would not be accepted as such in our states; and they are not sufficient to underpin the great increases in productivity necessary to the well-being of the Caribbean peoples.

I have spoken of agriculture. The same method, more or less, is available for industry, for health, and for public administration. Consider, for instance, the enormous usefulness in the Puerto Rican development of the Planning Board supported by the School of Public Administration in the university and by the loan funds of the public bank. The Planning Board has, by envisaging Puerto Rico's own resources, together with the funds available in the various state-aid programs, laid out a program for the years ahead. This is resulting in placing the funds available at the strategic points where they may contribute most to the rounded development of the whole economy. And the expenditure of these funds is directed by a progressively better trained body of administrators emerging from the university. For the planning work and for the industrial program there have been no specific federal grants. The Puerto Ricans have found the resources for these in their own increasing productivity and in the return to them by the federal government of excise taxes on products produced in the island.

I would not press the instance of Puerto Rico too far, but there do seem to be useful anaologies in the nature of the circumstances there and in the other Caribbean countries. I would not, either, make a commitment concerning the terms of the assistance I suggest. The whole program might be gauged to proceed at any practicable level. But I do think it not impractical to insist that the recognized obligation can be met best by an intimacy and continuity of assistance which does not now exist and which cannot be established by present methods. Only by opening our ordinary and continuing system to our neighbors can all the benefits of our wealth and experience be made effectively available to them as they have been to our own citizens.

V

It is true, as I have noted, that much is now being done. There are, indeed, outstanding examples which illustrate, almost as well as the case of Puerto Rico, the method I suggest. There is, for instance, the work of the American International Association and the International Basic Economy Corporation in Venezuela and Brazil especially. This is, of course, a private effort supported by Rockefeller funds and ably administered at the top level by leaders thoroughly conversant with American experience. The American International Association is proceeding outward from experimental centers and training programs to extension services. The peculiar virtue of this effort is its reliance on the thoroughly tested farm-and-home plan device so long used in the United States in rural rehabilitation. This ingenious combination of capital supply in carefully estimated amounts with close supervision of farm and home operations seems to be as successful in Latin America as in the States. It is the intention to carry on this kind of effort temporarily in each country until the Association can withdraw, leaving a going organization capable of carrying on the work.[8]

Similarly, in Peru, the agricultural techniques of the United States have been introduced, adapted to local conditions, and transmitted to something like a million farm people through the *Servicio Cooperativo Interamericano de Producción de Alimentos*. This organization is jointly sponsored and administered by the Institute of Inter-American Affairs and the Ministry of Agriculture of Peru. The basic activity is an extension agent system, working through community committees. The accomplishments of this *Servicio* have been considerable. It happens to be the most advanced among several others—in Costa Rica, Haiti, Honduras, Chile, and Uruguay—and the method used has been admirable. It is described[9] as consisting of three steps—and hopefully a fourth— as follows:

(1) the carrying out of survey, studies, and conferences;
(2) research and experimentation and their adaptation to local environments;
(3) the dissemination of results through extension agents.

---

[8] The International Basic Economy Corporation, the other Rockefeller enterprise, is different in organization and intention. It is directed to supplying goods and services not generally available but for which there is obvious need if the economy of the nation is to be strengthened. It seeks participation of local capitalists in enterprises which may be expected to be profitable.

[9] By Roy M. Hill, associate director, Food Supply Division, Institute of Inter-American Affairs, in an address at the Third Stanford Conference on Latin America, Stanford University, June, 1951.

These, it is hoped, may be followed by a fourth—"The initiating of partially or completely self-perpetuating agricultural developments."

The basic intention of this program, as of the others, it will be seen, is to launch a system which will acquire momentum and which can then be withdrawn from by the assisting agency. This illustrates very clearly, as does the Rockefeller experiment, the difference in intention between this kind of assistance and that which is extended to Puerto Rico. There is no intention of withdrawing assistance from Puerto Rico any more than there is of withdrawing it from one of the states. And I think it can be argued that this is the weakness of all our assistance programs in Latin America. They rest on the assumption—not always definitely formulated—that multipliers can very quickly be found, and an upward spiral started which will then be self-perpetuating. I do not believe this will happen. It would not happen in many of our states if separation should at any time occur. Much of the strength of the state-aid system lies in the organic and continuing connections through which advances made anywhere communicate themselves to everywhere else. It is not assumed—and it would not be true—that technical progress has any end, or that cooperation reaches a point at which it can stop. It needs to go on and on—experiment and research feeding field technology and the gains from these advances supporting a growing system of research and communication.

VI

This is not a process which can get under way quickly. Once under way it does become cumulative; but the dependence on varied sources of discovery and on mutual assistance is considerable. It is indeed so considerable that no one would suggest its rigid regionalization in the United States or its cutting off from those vast laboratories of ideas, invention, and administrative management, the federal departments. It is those very advantages of continuing access to renewable sources of discovery, together with a carefully maintained system for communication to users, which

I would open to our neighbors. It is our most valuable American possession; sharing it would bring advantages, I believe, far greater than the cost.

Sharing it would also discharge an obligation we already recognize. We have entered on a Four-Point Program without commitment to the future. It has been and is admirably administered within the limitations imposed by its temporary nature. But those who administer it must sometimes ask themselves how long it would need to continue before its objectives were reached. If those objectives are defined as a state of well-being comparable with that of people in the United States it must be clear that it cannot be reached in any few years, not, in all likelihood within any few decades; it is a matter of generations. They must also ask themselves whether in a region so divided as to area, resources, and population, it will be any more possible to set up self-contained systems, even in generations, which could then be expected to continue, than could be done in Minnesota, Mississippi, or Iowa.

If administrators ask themselves these questions, as I am sure they must in private, they must yearn for more permanence. The people of Oklahoma or of Nevada are not required to be assisted to a certain level of achievement and then told that they ought now to proceed on their own. They are part of a vast mutually supporting system into which they put what they can and from which they draw what they need. They have confidence that until they reach a more than average level they will continue to be assisted. Thereafter, if there are others who have not reached that level, they will help to assist those others. This is the principle of state-aid. It rests on the assumption that all Americans have an intrinsic value which it is to the interest of other Americans to see developed.

If the people of the Caribbean are brought into that circle of mutual assistance they may for some time be withdrawers rather than contributors; but that has been true of not a few of our states. And I know of no one who regrets the long effort to support their progress. Who knows but that such an investment might be paid back to the temperate-zone peoples with interest in another generation. The riches of the tropics and the creativeness of the Caribbean peoples may be far greater than we have hitherto thought.

VII

Allow me to end with only a brief allusion to what I regard as the greatest gain to be expected from my suggestion. This is that there may be a gradual lessening of the misunderstandings and—let us admit it—the jealousies and ill-feelings among us. There is no price to be put on the achieving of genuine good neighborliness. The enrichment of the American culture which could result from the relief of the hunger and misery we know to exist among any of our neighbors and their freeing for creative achievements would be victories from which we, no less than they, would gain. Our first gain would be in the satisfaction of having really done what we ought to do. The last might be the establishment in one not inconsiderable area of the world of the relations we profess to covet for all nations and all peoples. It is something we can do. I know of nothing to prevent its being done which is in any way comparable with its promise.

17

C. H. Haring: THE UNITED STATES
AND DICTATORSHIP IN THE CARIBBEAN

I

W HAT I AM about to discuss has been a matter of much concern to many worthy citizens of this country: the seeming inconsistency of posing as the champion of democracy in the world at large, on the one hand, and our apparently cordial relations with some less than democratic governments of Middle and South America, on the other. I include South America, for although the title of my discourse refers only to the Caribbean, what I have to say applies to our relations throughout the continent.

We fight a war—two world wars—in defense of a democratic way of life and at the same time we ally ourselves in the Pan American Union (or the Organization of American States, or O.A.S., as today it is called) with some of the most undemocratic, arbitrary, if not unscrupulous, governments in the Western Hemisphere. We frequently hear from the more vocal Left, that with all our democratic protestations, we should not, cannot, stand idly by while the democratic elements in some of the Latin American countries are under the iron heel of military dictatorship. We must give them our moral, if not material, support. We must do something about it. In other words, we must intervene on their behalf in the domestic concerns of their country.

Yet I remember that some twenty-five years ago, when we were intervening in the domestic politics of several Middle American States, from the Dominican Republic and Cuba to Nicaragua and Panama—in accordance with the so-called Roosevelt corollary of

194

the Monroe Doctrine—these same liberals were as vociferously demanding that we desist from intervention in the internal affairs of the Latin American republics. This was imperialism, dollar diplomacy.

When our friends demand that we intervene in support of the democratic elements in nations where dictatorship prevails, one may properly inquire what they mean by "intervention." Shall we revive the policy pursued by our government for a quarter century, between 1904 and 1930—sending marines to help maintain constitutional, representative government? Or shall we refuse diplomatic recognition to governments set up by revolution, by unconstitutional procedure? Or shall Washington exert its influence to deny to such governments economic assistance, either from the United States or from Europe?

II

Perhaps the question may be clarified by brief reference to our experience in Central America and the West Indian republics a generation or two ago. Our policy of "supervision" of the internal, and sometimes external, affairs of the Caribbean nations was certainly well intentioned. Its purpose was to exert to the utmost our power and influence in order to insure public peace, maintain constitutional procedure in these nations, rehabilitate their finances and thus avert intervention by aggrieved governments of Europe, intervention that might jeopardize our control over the approaches to the Panama Canal.

Relations with the new Republic of Cuba were governed by the celebrated Platt Amendment to its constitution, which authorized the United States to intervene for the maintenance of public order, limited the borrowing power of the new state, and incidentally provided for the lease to the United States of naval and coaling stations. The consequence was a period of American rule in Cuba from 1906 to 1909, and threats of intervention in 1912 and in 1917.

The history of the Republic of Haiti had been a long story of arbitrary misrule, revolution, and chronic disorders until in July, 1915, American Marines were landed to avert European intervention. Government finance and the collection of customs were placed under American administration, and the country, although enjoying peace and material prosperity, became practically a dependency of the United States.

Already in 1904, when President Theodore Roosevelt first enunciated his famous corollary, the government of the Dominican Republic was in a condition of hopeless bankruptcy, and European intervention to protect foreign lives and property seemed imminent. An arrangement was then made for a receivership of customs under American control. But political disturbances and financial irregularities continued, and in April, 1916, this small Republic, too, was occupied by American Marines.

I need not enter into our arrangements with the Republic of Panama, for the existence of the Canal constituted them a special case. But intervention in Nicaragua, beginning some forty years ago, was "notorious." Nicaragua had been ruled since 1893 by a truculent dictator, José Santos Zelaya, who aspired to the leadership of all Central America and who to his neighbors was a thorn in the flesh. In 1909 our government rid Nicaragua of him by supporting a revolution of the opposition party, and until 1924 that party (a so-called Conservative Party), with the moral and military aid of Washington, maintained itself in power. American bankers were encouraged to make arrangements for the reorganization of the currency and the foreign debt, and for the economic development of the country. In 1912 a legation guard of one hundred Marines was landed to protect the government from revolution, and they remained there, except for a short interval in 1925-1926, until 1933.

That, by and large, American intervention made for peace, political stability, and financial solvency, I think there can be no question. But that these desirable results were due chiefly to a healthy dread of the North American Big Stick was also true. And it caused bitter resentment, not only throughout Central America but in Latin America as a whole. We were accused of imperialism (that much abused word), of the ambition to dominate by strong arm methods, military and economic, the whole of the Western Hemisphere.

This mounting hostility culminated in the International Conference of American States at Havana in 1928, when it almost destroyed the Pan American movement. There we suffered a virtual diplomatic defeat and were only saved by the rivalries among the Latin American nations themselves.

III

Then Washington began to see the light. We gradually liquidated our commitments in Central America and the Caribbean republics and began consciously to pursue a Good Neighbor Policy—really begun by Republican President Herbert Hoover, but publicized and emphasized by Democratic President Franklin D. Roosevelt. The legation guard was withdrawn from Nicaragua in 1933. Intervention in Haiti was gradually liquidated between 1931 and 1934 when the last of the Marines left the republic. In the same year, 1934, was signed the treaty that freed Cuba from what it regarded as the humiliating terms of the Platt Amendment. The full sovereignty of Panama was recognized by a treaty ratified by the United States Senate in 1939. And in the Dominican Republic, from which American forces had been withdrawn in 1924, the American collectorship of customs was finally abolished in 1940. The results in our relations with Latin America were almost immediately apparent. They appeared at the next Pan American Conference at Montevideo in 1933, and in the Conference at Buenos Aires in 1936, where the American governments agreed, as a matter of principle, to abjure all intervention in the domestic concerns of other American States.

One of the chief aims of our Caribbean policy had been to insure constitutional government, popular control through honest elections. In that we signally failed. The implications, the responsibilities put upon the Department of State, were too vast. They forced the department to serve as interpreter of the constitutions of these countries. Rival political leaders turned to Washington to inquire whether they were eligible for election to the presidency, or which of the political parties in the dispute was constitutional, when in reality neither, perhaps, had much claim to that distinction. If we supported a government as constitutional, it generally meant merely enabling that government to perpetuate itself in power by rigging the elections—in other words, supporting what became to all intents and purposes a dictatorship, as happened in Nicaragua for more than a decade. If we refused recognition to a government as unconstitutional, we encouraged the opposition to attempt to overthrow it by violence—in short, we were encouraging revolution. In any case the party in power, because associated with foreign intervention, was generally opposed by a majority of the people, and the government became really a minority regime. There seemed to be no way out of this morass of contradictions.

And so we slowly liquidated our Caribbean engagements, and joined all the American governments to repudiate formally the right of intervention in the domestic concerns of other American states. This principle found its ultimate expression at the Pan American Conference at Bogotá in 1948, where the problem was discussed of the recognition of *de facto* governments: whether a new government arising by way of revolution should be accorded immediate recognition regardless of its origin, that is, the so-called Estrada Doctrine of the continuity of diplomatic relations. This doctrine was not formally adopted by the conference; the question was referred to the Inter-American Council of Jurists. But in fact our State Department has since acted more or less in accord with that principle.

President Wilson early in his first administration had enunciated a policy of refusing diplomatic recognition to governments coming into power in Latin America by revolution or *coup d'état;* and this policy was thereafter pursued by our State Department in Central America. In conformity with a series of treaties signed in Washington by all the Central American republics in 1923, we furthermore agreed not to recognize any new government, even if elected, that was headed by a leader of a revolution. These efforts to maintain the forms of constitutionalism by denying the right of revolution were abandoned by the administration of FDR as a costly and thankless experiment. And today, in spite of some popular criticism, we seem to be abiding by the Estrada Doctrine.

The Bogotá Conference met in March of 1948. Before the end of the year, two popularly elected governments in South America had been overturned by an army revolt: in Peru in October and in Venezuela in November. In each case the State Department, after appropriate inquiry, recognized the new military regime.

And that is where we stand today.

The past five or six years have seemed somewhat discouraging for friends of democracy in Latin America: in Argentina a constitution, closely patterned on that of the United States, prostituted by a demagogic Perón; military dictatorship in Venezuela, Peru, and Haiti, in all of which countries government by popular election had only recently emerged for the first time in their history; Colombia, remarkable during nearly fifty years for its adherence to democratic rule, driven by factional passions into the dictatorship of a single party.

There is, however, also a brighter side of the picture. Brazil within the same period repudiated dictatorship and returned to popular elections. And although Brazil recently re-elected to the presidency its former dictator, Getulio Vargas, that election in reality was the greatest expression of popular suffrage in its history. Ecuador, classic land of revolutions, few of whose presidents in recent years have been permitted to complete their term of office, seems under President Galo Plaza to have attained to some degree of equilibrium. Chile and Uruguay, too, both of which have lived under dictators at one time or another during the past quarter-century, have retained their democratic institutions intact.

Even in the Middle American area—Central America and the Caribbean—the hopes for democracy are not glimmering, in spite of a Somoza and a Trujillo. The people of Panama have very recently and very forcibly rejected an aspiring semi-fascist demagogue; Costa Rica and El Salvador during the past few years have both fought for free elections; Guatemala five years ago overthrew a heavy-handed dictatorship to restore the democratic process; and even Honduras recently chose a president in a peaceful election.

All of this, however, does not make any simpler the problem of our relations with dictators or democrats. During the recent World War, of course, the contradiction of our fighting for democracy in Europe and consorting with dictators in America was obvious, although it was no more contradictory than our alliance with communist Russia. For both situations the answer is the same: in a time of grave national peril (and after Pearl Harbor it was very grave—we seemed on the brink of disaster) we had to seek help, and especially economic help, where we could find it, regardless, if you will, of political principle.

But there are other considerations, less transitory, more per-

manent, involved. I believe that it is very important that the
Pan American Union, or Organization of American States, be pre-
served for strategic, military reasons, and for the peace of the
world, as a regional organization within the United Nations. That
regional organization is based upon the principle of the absolute
political equality of states, large and small—a unique principle—
for no other international political body, the League of Nations,
or the United Nations, has been able to achieve this equality of
states. Indeed only by adherence to such a principle, among
nations so varied in language, race, culture, and economic power,
has the Pan American concept achieved such notable success.
On our former policy of intervention, which was really a denial
of that principle, the Pan American movement twenty-five years
ago was almost wrecked.

Even under a dictatorship, interference by a foreign power has
frequently stirred the patriotic majority of the nation to rally
behind their own government. A liberal opposition to dictatorship
which welcomed foreign intervention has generally been a minority,
not too popular with its fellow countrymen. In fact, it is a
common phenomenon in Latin American history that dictators or
unpopular governments have deliberately conjured up the specter
of foreign interference in order to rally the nation behind them
and divert attention from shortcomings of the government at home.

Argentina is of course a case in point, both when Spruille
Braden was our Ambassador in Buenos Aires, and today. Mr.
Braden, as ambassador, never attacked the government to which
he was accredited, but he did state publicly that he and his fellow
countrymen believed in democracy and hoped for the ultimate
victory of democratic principles in Argentina. That could doubtless
be interpreted as "moral support" for the democratic elements in
Argentina, moral support for which these elements had been
anxiously hoping. But it just as certainly did not weaken General
Perón's likelihood of election to the presidency. On the contrary,
many believe that popular support for Perón was increased by
what he proclaimed to be gross intervention in the domestic politics
of Argentina. And President Perón has ever since, to this day,
used Ambassador Braden as a whipping-boy to rally the nation
to his support. The issue of the famous *Blue Book* by our Department of State just before Perón's first election, intended to dis-

credit the existing regime in Argentina, was also, and for the same reasons, as the Spaniards say, *contraproducente*.

I am not sure, therefore, that even moral support by our government for the democratic elements suffering under dictatorship in Latin America can be relied on for success. Political interference, either by landing Marines or by denial of diplomatic recognition, we have tried and found wanting. The currents of a jealous nationalism in these countries are running too strong. Pressure of any kind is immediately seized upon by press and politicians, as foreign intervention; and intervention of any kind, the American states were agreed, contravenes the basic principle of the political equality of states.

There are, moreover, other considerations of a collateral nature. There runs throughout Latin America—and our own public is rarely aware of it—another sentiment parallel with Pan Americanism, and quite as strong, if not at times stronger; and that is Latin Americanism. The American nations with a common Hispanic background—and this includes Portuguese Brazil—possess a feeling of solidarity that often transcends the Pan American idea. Indeed, in the minds of many Latin Americans the two are often confused, and when they talk of Pan Americanism they are really thinking in terms of Latin Americanism. This is perhaps quite natural, on cultural grounds and because of the contrast between the Colossus of the North, with its extraordinary economic and therefore political power, and their own meager resources. However, this Latin Americanism, although largely sentimental, is sometimes translated into political terms. The insistence of the Latin American delegates to the Chapultepec Conference in Mexico in 1945, and at the San Francisco Conference later in the same year, that Argentina in spite of its "misbehavior" during the War, be restored to good standing within the Pan American Union and be admitted to the United Nations, is a case in point. It is within the orbit of these ideas that the Organization of American States must function, and it is even more important that the solidarity of the United States with the other American republics be maintained.

There are, however, still other circumstances of a more fundamental sort. It may be questioned whether many of the Latin American nations are prepared as yet for democracy as we understand it in this country. In many of them the rate of illiteracy is high, and land still remains the possession of a relatively few who, fearful of losing their privileged position, are distrustful of democratic institutions. In many of them the mass of the population, Indian or near Indian, remain an ignorant, impoverished, dependent class. In other countries a middle class has advanced in numbers, wealth, and education, and has obtained political and social recognition. But often, owing to lack of experience, political education has lagged behind cultural and economic progress. The consequence is the political crises in Argentina and in Colombia today.

In short, as I have said elsewhere, "no nation can be made to achieve democracy by government fiat, whether at home or from abroad." A functioning democracy is the fruit of a long, hard period of experiment, of trial and error. This is nowhere better exemplified than in the history of our own United States. In some countries therefore, generally the more Indian countries, government at best and of necessity remains in the hands of an educated minority—at worst, in control of a military dictator. And in some of the more advanced republics, either a self-appointed oligarchy of landowners and leaders in industry and commerce manipulates the political machinery set up by the constitution and monopolizes the government, or a demagogic Perón exploits the ignorant proletariat and an inexperienced electorate to set up a semi-fascist dictatorship. Even in Mexico, which has made such extraordinary progress in the past quarter-century, and where the national government in general probably represents the will of the majority, candid Mexicans will freely admit that elections are not, and cannot be, free and uncontrolled.

IV

What, then, is the answer to this problem of the relations of the United States with the dictatorship in Latin America? If we cannot, and should not, intervene openly or covertly in the domestic politics of other American countries, we *can* openly, in our periodical press and elsewhere, condemn injustice and denial of personal and political rights in the more unfortunate republics. Witness the universal condemnation abroad of the rape of *La Prensa* of Buenos

Aires by the Perón regime earlier in this year. We can also assist even undemocratic governments to raise the standard of living of the underprivileged masses, and to provide enlarged educational facilities—a major item in Point Four—and so help create a broader basis for the emergence of an intelligent, popular electorate. We can also provide an example of how a democracy should function by trying to keep our own house in order—not too successfully of late, in view of the disclosures of corrupt practices in both national and local administrations.

And our government should try to avoid even the appearance of condoning dictatorship or the violation of personal and political rights in other American republics. I admit that this is difficult, especially in carrying out the Point Four Program. As Professor Stuart Hughes has said in a recent book, speaking of Italy and Japan: "The United States does not need to support conservative political parties in any overt fashion: these parties simply give their people to understand that they enjoy the blessing of the American government, and their people, far more accustomed than the Americans to think in terms of economic influence on politics, are ready to believe them. American influence can come practically without effort or intuition."*

The same remarks apply to our relations with undemocratic governments in Latin America. The daily press reports that the World Bank has recently granted a credit of a half million dollars to the Republic of Nicaragua for constructing a grain storage and drying plant. Does this assistance imply moral and economic support for a dictatorship? Or is it merely aid in raising the living standards of the Nicaraguan people? I leave the answer to you. The loan of one hundred twenty-five million dollars to Argentina a year ago, although really intended to bail out American business interests, created a very unhappy impression among liberals in it and other South American countries, notably in Brazil, our best friend in that part of the world. And there is no evidence that this "soft touch" approach has even earned us the good will of the Perón regime. The government-controlled Argentine press continues to attack the United States and certain of its respected citizens outrageously. And Argentine inclination to cooperate

* *An Essay for Our Times* (New York: Knopf, 1950).

effectively with the United States and other American republics either in the O.A.S. or in the policies of the United Nations seems to be as remote as ever.

Given, then, the present critical state of affairs in the world at large, and the O.A.S. as at present constituted, intervention by the United States in the countries of Latin America, or the exertion of diplomatic or economic pressures, is out of the question. The charter of the O.A.S. everywhere stresses as fundamental the principles of popular government; yet in fact within the Union there exists an unfortunate division between governments that are narrow oligarchies or dictatorships and governments that are honestly democratic. A policy of intervention by the United States, even "moral" intervention, would merely tend to make this schism wider, and might be resented by all Latin American governments, good and bad. By holding the Union together, we are really working in the ultimate interests of liberalism throughout the Americas, and helping to strengthen the larger world order represented by the United Nations.

W. H. Callcott: THE CARIBBEAN:

SPRINGBOARD FOR HEMISPHERE POLICIES

IN THE TWENTIES

THE HEMISPHERE POLICIES of the United States in the twenties should be considered in the light of the events of the preceding thirty years. About 1890, Secretary of State James G. Blaine entertained somewhat vague, great dreams for the New World but got only so far as to declare a caveat for his country in settling Latin American disputes. This he supplemented by plans for reciprocal trade treaties and for international conferences. His successor in policy making, President Grover Cleveland, was chiefly interested in domestic problems and only took up the Venezuela boundary controversy when his hand was forced by circumstances and by an aggressive Secretary of State. By the turn of the century came the expansionists with their great White House spokesman, Theodore Roosevelt. They had become convinced that the United States should carry the "White Man's burden" in the Caribbean—their special sphere of interest. Rudyard Kipling and Charles Darwin were their philosophical guides and the British Empire their model. Their era waned about 1907.

Secretary Elihu Root's efforts at about this time to introduce sympathetic understanding into Latin American relations were quickly overshadowed by the idea of dollar diplomacy when United States investments skyrocketed in Mexico and other Caribbean republics. Next, Woodrow Wilson became President in 1913. He pleaded for Pan Americanism as "the embodiment, the effective embodiment, of the spirit of law and independence and liberty and mutual service." He endorsed the Pan American Pact which called for mutual guarantees of political independence under the republican form of government, mutual guarantees of territorial integrity, mutual agreements for each country to acquire complete control of manufacture and sale of munitions of war within its jurisdiction, cooling off treaties, and mediation and arbitration agreements. However, this emphasis on cooperation was offset by an actual practice of paternal despotism during the emergencies of World War I.

By 1920, therefore, Latin America reaction to United States policies was one of uncertainty. Due to the exigencies of nationalism, of trade, or of war, the United States dominated the Caribbean. Had not this control been acquired in the name of the Monroe Doctrine? Was not the Caribbean part of the hemisphere? The public response was "yes" to both questions. Then, did not this imply that the application of the doctrine by the great victor of World War I meant domination of the whole hemisphere? Thus reasoned fearful and sensitive souls in Latin America as the twenties opened.

I

President Warren G. Harding, who took office in 1921, has been accused of having no consistent foreign policy, while his successor, President Calvin Coolidge, was said not to have a single international hair in his head.[1] The apparent policy of both men in

1 President Warren G. Harding did not mention Latin America in either his special message to Congress on April 12, 1921, or in his annual message on December 6, 1921. His second annual message briefly endorsed cooperation in an effort to end the Tacna-Arica dispute, and expressed good wishes for the Conference of the Central American states then in session. He then hastily added:

"I would like the Congress and the people of the Nation to believe that in a firm and considerate way we are insistent on American rights wherever they may be questioned, and deny no rights of others in the assertion of our own."

The annual messages of President Calvin Coolidge make the following record:

1923—No comment on Latin America.

1924—Eight lines expressing an interest in peace for the hemisphere and wishing for "increased prosperity" for "our sister republics of Latin America."

regard to Latin America was essentially negative, but the fact remains that very definite developments took place while they were in the White House. Wall Street had become the financial center of a creditor, not a debtor, nation. A short and sharp reduction in exports in 1921 gave way to the ground swell of a boom period as business rose to unprecedented heights. What to do with the profits? Investment in more factories to produce more goods, to build more factories to produce more goods, was obviously unwise. Foreign investments were one alternative and in some years of the middle twenties as much as a billion dollars annually found its way abroad. Statistics can be boring, but also enlightening. In 1913 United States capitalists had about $1,069,000,000 invested in Mexico, Central America, and the Caribbean islands. By 1929 this had increased to over $3,293,000,000, or to more than three times the original figure. But in this same period $173,000,000 invested on the continent of South America in 1913 had increased to $2,294,000,000—or to almost thirteen times the earlier figure. In Argentina the rise was from $40,000,000 to over $600,000,000; in Brazil, from $50,000,000 to over $475,000,000; in Chile, from $15,000,000 to over $395,000,000; in Bolivia, from $10,000,000 to $133,000,000; and in Peru, from $35,000,000 to over $150,000,000.[2]

In general, United States citizens preferred to invest in products rather than in government bonds. The figures quoted, then, meant that certain great products had seized the imagination of the Yankee

---

1925—One sentence endorsing Pan American efforts to codify international law and to outlaw war.

1926—No comment on Latin America.

1927—A brief statement that the United States is scrupulously respecting the sovereignty of Mexico but is endeavoring to protect the interests of its nationals south of the Río Grande. The President further stated that he had sent Henry L. Stimson to Nicaragua in an effort to settle disturbances in that country.

1928—Mentions the Sixth Inter-American Conference at Havana and the invitation extended to twenty New World republics to attend a conciliation and arbitration conference at Washington. It endorses the Inter-American Highway and states the United States is providing its southern neighbors with military and naval missions.

The last entry shows the inevitable rising interest in Washington in developments to the southward and will command attention throughout the paper.

[2] Max Winkler, *Investments of United States Capital in Latin America* (Boston, 1929), pp. 284-285.

investor. These included manganese in Brazil, vanadium in Peru, tin in Bolivia, and copper in Chile. Pressure by petroleum interests seemed to stimulate the thinking of certain senatorial minds which at long last approved the Colombian treaty in 1922. This, in turn, opened that country to Wall Street capital, and a petty investment of $2,000,000 in 1913 mushroomed to more than $260,000,000 in 1929. Venezuelan and Mexican petroleum, Cuban iron, as well as Caribbean coffee, sugar, and bananas, had provided pilot policies that were now extending throughout South America.

The State Department became almost frightened at a situation that was carrying it further and faster than it was accustomed to travel. Great Britain, France, and other creditor nations had long since established *de facto* controls over foreign investments. Now the State Department issued an announcement on May 25, 1921, saying in part:

The flotation of foreign-bond issues in the American market is assuming an increasing importance, and on account of the bearing of such operations on the proper conduct of affairs it is hoped that American concerns that contemplate making foreign loans will inform the Department of State in due time of the essential facts and of subsequent developments of importance....

The department denied the intention of classifying any one offering as a good or poor financial risk, but it did desire to integrate private investments with national foreign policy.[3]

Soon the flood of money became so great that it began to turn to loans to foreign governments in addition to the older commercial investments. A new loan to El Salvador carried the provision that disputes arising from the agreement should be referred to a justice of the United States Supreme Court for settlement.[4] Further southward, a loan to Bolivia was to be administered by a commission of

[3] Herbert Feis, *The Diplomacy of the Dollar: First Era, 1919-1932* (Baltimore, 1950), pp. 7-9. Note that this program contemplated loans from private individuals only. Secretary of State Charles E. Hughes expressed the position of the Department in August, 1923, when he plainly stated that "It is not the policy of our Government to make loans to other governments...." *Ibid.*, p. 6.

[4] *Papers Relating to the Foreign Relations of the United States* (hereafter cited as "*For. Rels.*"), *1922*, Vol. II, *cir.* p. 892, and *1923*, Vol. II, p. 825 ff.

three, one of whom was nominated by the State Department and another by the bankers advancing the money.[5] An application from São Paulo, Brazil, for a loan with which to stabilize coffee prices was disapproved in Washington as tending to establish a monopoly at the expense of the United States breakfast table.[6] The whole continent was alerted.

II

A study of the correspondence of the Department of State for the period shows that a policy was emerging. Above all, there was a desire to maintain peace in the hemisphere. Continuous efforts were made to solve boundary disputes between the Dominican Republic and Haiti; Honduras and Nicaragua; Guatemala and Honduras; Colombia and Panama; Colombia and Peru; Ecuador and Peru; Chile, Peru and Bolivia; and Paraguay and Bolivia. Also in 1923 Washington endorsed the proposal of the Central American republics to insist on *de jure* transfer of power as the only recognizable means of political succession in Central America.

Whenever insurrection broke out there was a rush to secure military supplies from the United States. Shipments were promptly authorized to established governments but restrained or stopped to others. Under an act of Congress of 1912, extended on January 21, 1922, by joint resolution, the President was given the right to proclaim an embargo on shipments of arms and munitions of war to any American state or any country in which the United States had extraterritorial rights. The following embargoes were accordingly proclaimed: Mexico, 1912, 1915, 1924; Honduras, 1924; Cuba, 1924, 1934; Nicaragua, 1926; and Brazil, 1930. The embargoes themselves were supplemented by sharp warnings calculated to restrain warlike activities. However, when Nicaragua proposed a formal alliance with the United States in 1927 and offered to incorporate the provisions of the Bryan-Chamorro Treaty, a custom's receivership and the appointment of a financial adviser in the new agreement, the response was that such proposals were *not* to be encouraged.[7]

[5] *Ibid., 1922,* Vol. I, p. 640 ff.
[6] *Ibid., 1925,* Vol. I, and *1928,* Vol. I.
[7] *Ibid., 1927,* Vol. III, p. 496 ff.

When word reached Washington that legislation was in process to increase the size of the Brazilian navy on the advice of Rear Admiral Vogelgesang, head of the United States Naval Mission in Brazil, the State Department demurred sharply. It admitted that the new construction might be technically advisable but pointed out that it might stimulate competition and suspicion in Argentina and Chile.[8] The United States wanted peace above all and would go to considerable lengths to secure it. True, arms embargoes might mean intervention by abstention. If so, so be it.[9]

Internal political conditions in Caribbean countries were carefully watched. The following incidents were occasions when the State Department showed especial interest: the planning of the Haitian election in 1925 and 1926, the readjusting of the Franco-Haitian treaty in 1926, and the amending the proposed Haitian constitution in 1927;[10] the arranging of terms of a proposed Guatemalan loan contract in 1923, which were characterized as "wholly unsatisfactory";[11] the warning of both candidates in the Honduras election of 1923 to avoid civil war;[12] the scrutinizing of the terms of a Dominican bond issue in 1926;[13] and the sending of a notice to the incumbent president of Nicaragua in 1924 that if he became a candidate for re-election, Washington "would regard his election as unconstitutional, and upon the expiration of his present term would be highly indisposed to extend its recognition to him as constitutional president."[14] At the same time there were continued

---

8 *Ibid., 1924,* Vol. I, p. 323 ff.

Great care was exercised to insure the fact that the naval mission sent to Brazil in 1922 for a four-year term and extended for a like period in 1926, should not offend Argentina (*Ibid., 1922,* Vol. I, p. 651 ff., and *1926,* Vol. I, p. 574 ff.

Feis, *op. cit.,* pp. 30-31, feels that the United States was peculiarly ineffective in preventing private loans which were actually used for military armaments.

9 Henry L. Stimson and McGeorge Bundy, *On Active Service in Peace and War* (New York, 1947), pp. 179-180.

10 *For Rels., 1925,* Vol. II, p. 298; *1926,* Vol. II, p. 396 ff., p. 407 ff.; *1927,* Vol. III, p. 52 ff.

11 *Ibid., 1923,* Vol. II, pp. 381-383.

12 *Ibid., 1923,* Vol. II, p. 424 ff.

13 *Ibid., 1926,* Vol. II, pp. 40-50.

14 *Ibid., 1924,* Vol. II, p. 508.

efforts to reduce the Marine contingents, and later to withdraw them entirely from Santo Domingo and Nicaragua.[15]

Yet such actions should not be taken to imply that irresponsible power resided in Washington. When it was understood that a proposed treaty in 1926 infringed the sovereignty of Panama, the document was rejected in that country. Widespread criticism in Latin America and in the United States then caused the project to be abandoned indefinitely.[16]

Farther south there was less interference with domestic affairs. With the possible exception of the case of the Bolivian loan, there were few or no instances to be mentioned. True, efforts were made to encourage rubber production in Brazil in 1925-1926;[17] protests to Bolivia caused revision of contracts for petroleum extraction in 1924-1926, but only when those contracts clearly discriminated against United States companies;[18] and Chile was persuaded to modify laws which discriminated against foreign insurance companies in 1927.[19] The actions, however, were the normal protection regularly given to insure the fact that a country's nationals received justice and fair treatment in a foreign country. When Chile enacted discriminatory legislation, under the guise of a subsidy to its own shipping through the Panama Canal, Washington merely inquired to verify the fact that the arrangement was a legitimate subsidy.

III

Yet fear did exist, in part because of the pronouncements of President Coolidge. For instance, in addressing the United Press Association in New York he commented on April 25, 1927:

It would seem to be perfectly obvious that if it is wrong to murder and pillage within the confines of the United States, it is equally wrong outside our borders. The fundamental laws of justice are

[15] For typical dispatches on the subject, see *ibid., 1924,* Vol. I, p. 618, and *1925,* Vol. II, pp. 620 ff.

[16] *Ibid., 1926,* Vol. II, and *1927,* Vol. III.

[17] *Ibid., 1926,* Vol. I, pp. 575-577.

[18] *Ibid., 1926,* Vol. I, p. 564 ff.

[19] *Ibid., 1927,* Vol. I, pp. 517-541; *1928,* Vol. I, pp. 115-118.

universal in their application. These rights go with the citizen. Wherever he goes, these duties of our government must follow him.

Please reread the last two sentences. Did not this mean that it was the duty of the United States to protect the property of its citizens to the full? Latin American reaction was emphatic. Blanco Fombona, Manuel Ugarte, and others flayed the imperialism of the Republic of the North, the while they denounced its crass materialism and lack of appreciation of the finer things of life.

In matters of strategic importance, however, it was evident that official interest was specific, not general. For instance, State Department correspondence for 1928 alone showed contacts on behalf of the expansion of United States air lines with Costa Rica, Guatemala, Nicaragua, Honduras, El Salvador, Mexico, British Honduras, Santo Domingo, Haiti, Cuba, Puerto Rico, Venezuela, Nassau, Ecuador, Chile, Peru, Argentina, Brazil, Bolivia, Uruguay, and Colombia.[20]

Beset by these numerous cross currents of commercial and national policy, the Fifth Inter-American Conference, which began its session at Santiago, Chile, on March 25, 1923, accomplished very little. Armaments rivalries between the ABC powers were partly responsible, but a major cause was the refusal of the United States to allow conference consideration of the Monroe Doctrine, of tariffs, and of intervention. Secretary Charles E. Hughes insisted that the doctrine was a unilateral policy to be defined and applied by Washington alone. Tariffs were a domestic matter and intervention was a responsibility of the strong which could not be alienated.

The Havana (Sixth Inter-American) Conference followed in January-February, 1928. Again the issues of tariffs and intervention were suppressed. Yet the Latins argued that they could not pay their debts if tariffs prevented sale of their goods, and that they could not cooperate as equals while fearful of intervention. A pictorial description has been said to have portrayed the conference in the form of a basketball court. The United States delegation on the floor was opposed by a team including the chiefs of five leading Latin American states. The ball in play was labeled "intervention." It had just been tossed toward the goal by a Latin American for-

20 *Ibid., 1928,* Vol. I, pp. 775-830.

ward. Secretary Hughes, playing guard, had climbed the goal post and was sitting in the basket with his venerable whiskers flying in the breeze, with hands and feet outspread to prevent the critical issue from scoring.

Unquestionably such criticism was prevalent and potentially dangerous. However, it can be overemphasized. For instance, many enthusiasts urged Latin American states to join the League of Nations as a protection against Yankee imperialism. Surprisingly enough, only sixteen of the states did so, and three of these sixteen (Argentina, Peru, and Bolivia) hardly became active members. Further, of eighty League conventions, protocols, and agreements requiring ratification by 1934, only one hundred sixty-four ratifications (or scarcely more than two per agreement) were received from the whole of Latin America; and of thirty-three conventions of the International Labor Office only thirty-four (or very slightly more than one for each convention) came from Latin America.[21] Is it possible that as debunkers we have exaggerated our own weaknesses and sold our popularity short?

IV

Let us carry this line of thought a bit further. Some actual progress in cooperation can be discerned. The Gondra Pact was disseminating a beneficent influence in the New World, and arbitration and conciliation commissions were being established. To that peculiarly sensitive post, Mexico City, Dwight Morrow went as ambassador, with his sterling honesty and his rare appreciation of personal values. He gained the confidence of a suspicious people by frankly saying that he would faithfully present just claims of his countrymen but would unhesitatingly try to suppress claims he considered fraudulent. His appointment could hardly have been made blindly, for his ideas were already on record. As early as 1922 he had commented:

"Of course the government of Cuba has been, and is, very bad. It is possible—yes it is probable—that the United States might run Cuba much better. As I get older, however, I become more and

[21] Stephen P. Duggan, "Latin America, the League and the United States," *Foreign Affairs*, Vol. XII, pp. 288-289.

more convinced that good government is not a substitute for self-government. The kind of mistakes that America would make in running Cuba would be different from those that the Cubans themselves make, but they would probably cause a new kind of suffering."[22]

This was certainly not the language of dollar domination. Did the Morrow appointment mean that the sponsors of the program were beginning to doubt its wisdom?

Be that as it may, immediately after the election of 1928 President-elect Herbert Hoover made a tour of Latin America. In his first annual message he advised reduction of the Marine contingents in Nicaragua and Haiti. He called for men of experience and high caliber, who could speak the languages of the countries concerned, to represent the United States throughout the New World. As one observer put it, the "scramble for Latin American posts began." The President publicly deplored "one sinister notion," that is, "fear of an era of the mistakenly called dollar diplomacy. The implications that have been colored by that expression are not a part of my conception of international relations," he said.[23] As a constructive step he appointed a special commission to make recommendations on Haiti. It forthwith decried the "brusque attempt" of the Occupation to plant democracy in that republic "by drill and harrow." Instead, it advised a realistic program founded on humanitarian considerations for an unfortunate people.[24]

Washington also announced that it would follow only the *de facto* basis in recognizing new governments, except in the case of Central America, where the special agreement of 1923 was in effect. The announcement came none too soon. Between 1930 and 1932 revolutionary disturbances beset all but three of the depression-ridden Latin American countries. Scores of dispatches from the State Department to the threatened centers advised the utmost caution to avoid partisanship in local disputes. Following the earlier policy, arms were sold to help established governments resist rebels, and one memorandum of the War Department showed

22 Harold Nicolson, *Dwight Morrow* (New York, 1925), pp. 264-265.
23 William Starr Myers, *The Foreign Policies of Herbert Hoover, 1929-1933* (New York and London), pp. 42-43.
24 *For. Rels., 1930*, Vol. III, p. 198 ff.

sales of over $479,000 of military supplies from United States arsenals to Mexico alone.[25] However, great care was exercised not to aggravate international rivalries.[26]

About the same time, the J. Reuben Clark Memorandum on the Monroe Doctrine was issued by the State Department. This document reiterated that the doctrine was a unilateral policy but asserted that it was merely calculated to protect the hemisphere from external aggression. As an entirely new departure it flatly repudiated the Roosevelt corollary.

International controversies received the special attention of President Hoover. He helped to initiate the final series of conferences that led to the solution of the long-standing Tacna-Arica problem, while other boundary troubles claimed his sympathetic consideration. He extended cordial praise to Ambassador Morrow for his brilliant success in helping to bring the troublesome Church-State controversy in Mexico to an end.

When revolutions threatened in the Caribbean he strove to avoid military intervention (witness the cases of Cuba and Santo Domingo). At the same time, friendly advice and even strong pressures were employed in a number of cases. Elections were supervised and finances reorganized in Nicaragua;[27] Cuban legislation attacking the Platt Amendment was suppressed;[28] President Louis Borno was advised that he would not be an acceptable candidate for re-election in Haiti;[29] and suggestions were made to a new

---

[25] *Ibid., 1929,* Vol. III, pp. 428-429.

[26] To this end no war vessels were to be sold to those nations of the New World engaged in incipient naval rivalries. This policy was made easier by the fact that such sales were forbidden by the provisions of the Naval Treaty signed at Washington on February 6, 1922.

Another detail somewhat beyond the scope of this paper was the well-known antipathy of President Hoover for the Soviet Union. This feeling doubtless led him to be fully cognizant of the Memorandum left by the Secretary of State with the Foreign Relations Committee of the Senate, and also sent to United States diplomatic officers throughout Latin America, denouncing Bolshevik activities in the New World. This seven and a half page document (see *Foreign Relations, 1927,* Vol. I, pp. 356-63), however, is probably more interesting in 1951 than it was in 1927. As a matter of fact, there is no evidence that it aroused much action or comment at the time.

[27] *For. Rels., 1929,* Vol. III, p. 549 ff.; *1930,* Vol. III, pp. 636-708.

[28] *Ibid., 1929,* Vol. II, pp. 894-896.

[29] *Ibid., 1929,* Vol. III, pp. 170-173.

president in Guatemala as to his cabinet appointments and his general policies.[30]

Of course Hoover was a businessman and the successor of Coolidge. As such he firmly believed that peace and prosperity were fundamental bases of progress. During the depression, however, it was considered poor business to exert undue pressure on Latin American debtors, and there was no suggestion of intervention to collect bad debts. The administration simply let it be known that Washington took it for granted that foreign investments in a country would be reasonably safe for the best interests of all concerned.

As yet the Caribbean area was still the chief strategic unit, but with the perfection of methods of transportation the whole of Latin America was obviously becoming a part of that unit. The Pan American Highway project, air line concessions, and increasing use of military and naval missions all bore witness to the fact. Even so, in spite of the businessman's tendency to discount the ability of economically less prosperous peoples, Hoover proved that he wished the Latin Americans to manage their own political problems.

V

While bread lines were forming and industry gagged on its own output in the United States few people thought about hemisphere policies. By 1932 they simply felt sorry for themselves and elected Franklin D. Roosevelt on the basis of his domestic program and by way of demanding a change. Unknown to the public, and largely overlooked in the campaign, was the fact that this man had accepted certain broad principles for a hemisphere program. His ideas had been recorded in an article in *Foreign Affairs* in 1928. Excerpts from this article summarize his thesis as follows: "It is possible that in the days to come one of our sister nations may fall upon evil days" from "disorder and bad government." "In that event it is not the right or the duty of the United States to intervene alone. It is rather the duty of the United States to associate itself with other American republics"; and after "intelligent and joint study," "if the conditions warrant, to offer the helping hands

30 *Ibid., 1930,* Vol. III, p. 184 ff.

in the name of the Americas." Finally, "... with the cooperation of others we shall have more order in this hemisphere and less dislike."

This proposal went much further than Mr. Hoover's program, though it actually carried the Hoover policy to a logical conclusion. Once the new dispensation took office there came in rapid succession the Montevideo and Buenos Aires conferences which provided for the Consultative Pact (no more unilateral interpretations of the Monroe Doctrine), and the war or emergency conferences that adopted joint procedures for hemisphere defense and economic cooperation. Once again, however, most of the testing of the program was to take place in the Caribbean. It was the cancellation of the Platt Amendment with Cuba, the signature of a greatly modified Panamanian Treaty in 1936 giving up the right of intervention, and the withdrawal of Marines from key points that proved sincerity with regard to intervention.

During the strain of World War II, defense requirements dictated the establishment of numerous military bases. Most of these were in the Caribbean area, but some were further afield. Yet even at this time of crisis, consultation preceded action in the case of holdings of European powers which had been overrun by Nazi warlords. True, as a result of its overwhelming responsibilities and of its military effectiveness at the moment, the United States took the first steps, but this was done with prior approval of Latin America. The surprising thing was that after occupation by military force the civil administration was planned through consultation. Truly it is difficult to find other cases where so much consideration was given to weak partners in similar emergencies. But this is leading to another phase of the subject....

VI

Yes, as historians look back on events just after 1920, it is evident that developments in the Caribbean, their successes and failures, their popular and unpopular features, were the springboard and guide to the hemisphere policy of the United States. Here was an area that experienced at first hand the changes from paternal despotism, with all of its benevolent but dictatorial methods, to a program of dollar domination. This domination, in turn, was modi-

fied by its own sponsors, and Hoover turned to many of the cooperative features originally proposed by Elihu Root. Then came the
far-reaching change to a "mutual" program.

With the rise of rapid transportation and the international significance of raw materials in an industrial age, new issues and strategic considerations had developed throughout the hemisphere.
However, though the sphere of action was increased, it was still
the Caribbean region, compact, close at hand, and of immense
strategic and economic value, that was the chief testing ground of
policies. Here, relatively free from outside interference, the real
intentions of the policies of the United States could be best seen
and evaluated.

19

Alberto Lleras: THE ORGANIZATION
OF AMERICAN STATES

I

W ITHIN A WEEK the Charter of the Organization of American States will go into full effect, three years after its signature at Bogotá, Colombia. A long political and juridical process preceded the legal perfection of the world's oldest association of nations. Its historical genesis dates back to the birth of the new republics of America themselves. Many of the founding fathers of the nations that resulted from independence from Spain realized the need for a federation of the peoples of the New World, at the time when the republican constitutions were being drafted. Bolívar wanted to put this bold concept into practice, and he went so far as to call a Pan American congress, in 1826, with the immediate objective of a military and political alliance against any European attempt to dominate part of the hemisphere, including the possibility of joint action to free the Spanish possessions in the Caribbean; and another, more ambitious and nebulous objective, the establishment of a regional American league that might be the first step toward a world association of nations.

Sixty-four years later the United States took the initiative in organizing, cautiously but systematically, and as far as was then possible, the new republican world. The First International Conference of American States was held in Washington in 1890. In 1933 the fundamental obstacle to progress in inter-American relations was eliminated when, at Montevideo, Secretary Hull accepted for the United States the principle of non-intervention. At the end of the Second World War, the Act of Chapultepec signed in 1945 at Mexico City, laid the foundations for hemispheric solidarity by recognizing the fact that aggression against one American nation is equivalent to aggression against them all. In 1947, at Rio de Janeiro, the Act of Chapultepec became the Inter-American Treaty of Reciprocal Assistance. A year later, at Bogotá, the Charter of the Organization of American States clarified and defined the bases for the permanent association of the republics of the hemisphere, and at the same time the American Treaty on Pacific Settlement introduced an original and advanced method of insuring proper legal solution for any dispute that might arise among the American states.

II

As may be seen, the idea that nations can and should live together in harmony, within an organized international society, renouncing the use of force in their relations, just as citizens live within a country, has arisen with growing vigor at various times in the development of the American republics, until at last that viewpoint achieves definitive acceptance. It was one of the very members of this international society—the United States—which proposed a similar organization to avoid war for the entire world, after it had already been tried in our hemisphere. Woodrow Wilson, and later Franklin D. Roosevelt, before taking bold action in international affairs, made earnest efforts to strengthen Pan Americanism. It is no exaggeration, therefore, to say that the League of Nations and the United Nations, whose creation was the sole recompense asked by this country for the decisive part it played in the two greatest wars of our times, were unquestionably inspired by our inter-American organization.

We may also note that the inter-American system was the first significant international political movement of the United States that apparently ran counter to the isolationist advice of George Washington; and that after the First World War, when a disillusioned United States turned once more to isolationism, it went right on practicing with the other states of this hemisphere the principles of international cooperation that appeared to have been repudiated by American public opinion.

Every day, both in this country and abroad, we hear it said that the United States lacks experience in international affairs, lacks a definite foreign policy and good judgment in the management of its relations with other countries. The fact is, however, that in that section of the world in which the United States has had occasion to work out its international course over the longest period of time and under normal conditions, it has produced a genuine master-piece. In its inter-American dealings are to be found intelligence and elasticity, self-control and tact, and the courage to promote great ideals without fear of the consequences. For the difficult thing for a great power to do is to refrain from using its strength, substituting reason for force, without forfeiting its prestige. The inter-American policy of the United States not only has provoked no resistance, but it has been accepted with enthusiasm by the other nations. It has been worked out in close cooperation with the twenty other member states in our organization, and if the rest of the countries of the world really want to know what is the ultimate objective of United States foreign policy, they need only examine the commitments this nation has made in the Organization of American States and its behavior since 1933 in this part of the world, where every development can vitally affect its own interests and its own security.

This policy has not been arrived at overnight, and it has not always been in effect. It is the fruit of experience, and the end result of a courageous rectification. It is not usual for the world's great powers to correct their conduct, nor to learn from the ex-perience of others. That is why the inter-American policy of the United States deserves such high praise. In its early days the intercourse between this country and the other republics of the hemisphere started out very much along the same lines as the course followed by any strong state toward weaker neighbors—the use of military force, ruthless territorial expansion, armed intervention, economic penetration, and diplomatic pressure. One section of public opinion here applauded these tactics which, in a way, could be construed as a sign that the nation had reached the status of a world power. Those were the days of Manifest Destiny. At that time all the nations of Europe dreamed of empire; and in the United States there were those who sincerely believed that the natural limits of its empire should, for the moment, be the two great oceans and the two poles.

From that point of view, naturally, the imperialistic exploits of this country were very successful. All the more credit is due, therefore, to the reaction in American public opinion that put an end to them. This is why today we are not witnessing the liquidation of one more empire, but on the contrary the United States has twenty sincere friends in the world who feel a sense of political solidarity with this nation. It is thereby relieved of continental cares at a time when it must conserve its energies to decide its own fate as well as that of the world at large in these critical times.

III

I have mentioned that a change of course took place in 1933, because it was at the Inter-American Conference that met that year in Montevideo that this nation accepted, for the first time, the principle of non-intervention which the other American republics claimed as fundamental to their foreign relations. Up to then the inter-American system had been merely a faint-hearted exchange of pleasantries, with a considerable admixture of justifiable distrust. But from that day on the American international organization bloomed with new vigor, and all the American states realized that they could sit down and discuss their mutual problems without hesitation, in the comforting thought that juridically they were all equals, whatever their territorial extent, their national population, their material resources, or their military strength. They did not fear that this new deal would be changed, because they counted on its being backed up by North American public opinion. That is, they reasoned that the foreign policy of a democracy would necessarily reflect the collective opinion of its people. The negotiation of treaties, conventions, or other agreements with a dictatorship is a waste of time, since there is no guarantee that they will be honored. A dictatorship is bound by no moral restrictions either at home or from abroad, but is held in check only by force. A democracy, on the other hand, cannot resort to war without having first of all persuaded the thinkers, the clergy, the army, the mothers, the wives, the farmers, the workers, the whole country, in a word, that no other course is open to it. The Latin American republics know very well that the present international policy of the United States cannot suddenly trend toward intervention or imperialism because Franklin Roosevelt did not just make it up. It was created, adopted, and supported by the American people, that enduring force that always welcomes righteous ideas with supporters, defenders, and, at times, with martyrs.

The inter-American system that our organization administers is not a method of international dealing applicable to our hemisphere alone. It could work equally well throughout the world, and would unquestionably be the most generous and wonderful boon that could be bestowed on future generations. In this system there are no privileged countries, none that are immune to the consequences of an adverse majority decision. That is, the veto is unknown in the councils of our organization; not a single nation has the right to employ a veto. It is the democratic way, with all that this implies. The United States, for example, might be systematically overridden at each of the meetings of the organization of American states by the votes of just eleven member nations, even the smallest in the group. But this does not happen, in spite of the fact that in many cases the immediate interests of the United States do not coincide with those of its weaker neighbors. It does not happen because there is a paramount interest in international amity, in maintaining the respect of those other nations with whom one must work and live, and in preserving a set of principles and moral and political rules, thereby impelling the member nations to keep faith with one another.

In a real democracy, moreover, the majorities, merely because they are stronger, do not league together against the minorities, even when the latter are wealthier or happier. And none of the Latin American states can find in our deliberations any sign that the United States wishes to follow a course that would be detrimental to the others. They realize that just as they should and do defend their own special interests, the United States must do the same for what concerns it. The result is almost always a compromise, that excellent formula of active democracy which does not permit the imposition of the majority will by brute force, but which takes into account the strength, interests, and rights of all. One consequence is that the small and weak countries feel very keenly their responsibility to contribute to the common good, and they refrain from deliberately acting as hindrances.

There is one more characteristic of the inter-American system that we do not find in like degree in any other international policy. It is the principle of non-intervention that I have already mentioned. In my opinion the evolution of international life will be retarded until this principle is adopted for the entire world and followed faithfully, as in the Americas. The nations cannot be won over by merely offering them peace and security, for this can be promised by any power with the physical might to guarantee an alliance of the traditional and well-known sort, like the protectorate. Many nations have preferred, and continue to prefer, insecurity to protectorates.

What would induce all the nations to give their sincere support to the international organizations would be an effective guarantee that no state or group of states would interfere in their domestic affairs. But this assurance, unfortunately, cannot be given as long as the veto is granted precisely to those powers that are in a position to interfere. On the contrary, the veto is a powerful weapon for intervention, an insidious weapon superior to the military pressure of former days, because it is less dramatic and spectacular. Around each nation enjoying the veto is formed a sphere of influence that inevitably attracts other states wishing to share in that international advantage, even at the expense of their independence. Furthermore, collective international action against an act of intervention on the part of a nation armed with the veto is utterly out of the question. The American states, including of course the United States, can offer the world as their greatest contribution to the welfare of humanity the example of a hemisphere from which intervention has been abolished, both in theory and in practice. The totalitarian states are interventionists by definition, by their very nature. They can conceive of only their own type of world, and they fully believe that they must incorporate other nations into their system, whose peak of perfection will be reached when it embraces the entire globe.

The inhabitants of this part of the world see it differently. We feel that every state in its international life, even as the citizen in national life, is entitled to preserve a certain sphere of inalienable liberty, which other states, or even the international agencies, cannot invade under any pretext whatsoever. Within that sanctuary they shall not, of course, conspire against the liberty of the others, nor commit any act that would endanger the rights of others. But a nation has its own individual personality, just as a man has, and its preservation from foreign intervention is a standard that is held aloft by the democracies. They must never lower it if they do not wish to lose it forever.

After the creation of the United Nations, many thought that an organization such as that of the American states had lost much of its significance, and that the need for it had been outgrown. This view was also held by some of the delegations at San Francisco, when the United Nations Charter was being written. The American nations fought hard to preserve the autonomy of their system and, thanks to their efforts, Article 51 was included in the charter, recognizing the right to collective self-defense. On this a little later was built the foremost regional pact, the Inter-American Treaty of Reciprocal Assistance, which in turn served as a model for the North Atlantic Pact.

These are the two regional agreements that link this nation with groups of other powers for their mutual defense against aggression; and, in my opinion, prior to the passage of the "Uniting for Peace" resolution by the General Assembly of the United Nations last year, they constituted the only juridical instruments we could rely on to contain the aggression of international communism.

It can also be said, fairly and with juridical authority, that one of the foundation stones of that resolution is an amplification of the concept of collective self-defense embodied in Article 51, since it rests on the principle that there must be effective general action to repel aggression when the Security Council is paralyzed by the use of the veto.

IV

Of course I have referred only to the purely political aspects of the task the Organization of American States has been asked to perform. We can affirm, for example, that the recent policy of technical aid to less developed states is as old, within our organization, as the agency itself. For it was one of the original purposes of the inter-American organization to permit the member states to cooperate with one another by pooling the results of their experience and exchanging knowledge and technicians, in order to convert the development of the new world into a collective enterprise of generous proportions.

We cannot here recount the innumerable services in this and other fields that the organization has rendered from its earliest days. For the present we must content ourselves with a review of the facts that point to the most important political development of our times: international organization, which is one of America's bequests to the human race. Our association of states not only has not yet completed its entire mission, but is destined to continue serving as a proving ground for the brave new ideas that in other parts of the world could not find, and still cannot find, the opportunity to prosper so well as among us.

Wilfred O. Mauck: THE INSTITUTE
OF INTER-AMERICAN AFFAIRS

As A PROFESSOR of history, I used to lecture about international conferences, and the League of Nations, and protocols, and conventions, and diplomatic notes, and wars, and rumors of wars, and ententes, and alliances, and all the stateliness and gobbledygook of diplomacy.

Some of my students seemed to think that all this diplomatic furor was a bit bombastic and futile. They said it was all very interesting (which was nice of them, and always gave me the impulse to raise their grades), but it appeared to me that we were just going around in circles. You build opposing alliances, which agree among themselves politely that they exist just to keep the peace, and arm themselves heavily to do so, and sooner or later come to blows. The war is blamed on the misery of one part of the world or another; and the war creates more misery. And the only way out of the new misery is to regroup the alliances and fight another war to end the misery created by the last one, and create enough new misery to start another. Why not do something to break the circle?

Well, I could reply, much constructive work *was* being done. There had been two or three generations of cooperation along some lines—the International Red Cross, for example, and the Universal Postal Union, and the Hague Court. The League of Nations itself did not wear striped pants all the time and everywhere. It was fighting epidemics, and trying to break up the narcotics trade and slave trade, and encouraging better relations

227

between industry and labor, and doing a dozen or so other things in a direct fight against misery.

But my students were still unsatisfied. And so was I. This was all to the good, but it was still *defensive* action against the social and economic and physical ills of mankind. When would we attack them in a positive way?

If World War II had not come when it did, I think we *might* have taken positive steps. While that war was still going on, many men of good will were planning them. When the United Nations Organization was established at San Francisco, plans were made for international action—not talk—to do something positive about the causes of war, especially those causes which lie in the poverty and ignorance and disease and hopelessness which exist in so many parts of this world of ours.

I think that was largely the inspiration for President Truman's appeal, in 1949, for the more prosperous nations to band together to give a helping hand to the less prosperous among us, and his pledge (the now-famous Point Four) to make it a part of the foreign policy of the United States to do its share in that effort. Point Four recognized a very simple fact. It is not enough for nations to sign agreements pointing out what is wrong with the world. It is not enough to subscribe to international statutes outlawing evil practices. It is not enough to stamp out epidemics and rush supplies to famine areas. It is not enough even to pour out money and supplies to help less developed nations to meet ever-recurring crises. What is needed is positive action to help others to be strong—to increase their own resources so that crises need not recur. That may not prevent war, of itself, but it will help to lessen the chances of war, by reducing some of its causes.

I

When I was asked to forward, in a hurry, the title of my talk, I was a little flustered. Frankly, I do not like to write speeches. I prefer to make some scribbled notes during dinner, and hope I can find a title before I am introduced. I had no idea of what I was going to talk about. So I hastily decided that I would talk about "The Institute of Inter-American Affairs," to which I belong. Our headquarters are in Washington, for we are attached to the

United States Department of State. But our work is in eighteen of the twenty republics to the south of us. The work is that of Point Four—in fact, we are the Western Hemisphere agency for carrying on Point Four work—though as a matter of fact, we have been doing it since 1942, long before Point Four was heard of. But in spite of the subject, it is really about Point Four that I am talking, rather than the institute itself.

Some ages ago, when I was a professor, I used to use popular song titles occasionally for my subjects. I think that if I had had another day to choose a subject, I should have used "Come on-A My House." I don't know the words of the song, but I grasp its general meaning, if any. And I would choose the title just because, when you get into this Point Four work a bit, you get the feeling of friendly neighbors calling to each other to "Come on to my house." And it is a two-way movement, for the more prosperous nations are benefiting from the exchange as much as their neighbors are. It is a little like the barn-raisings and husking bees in which our own frontier families engaged, in the United States, and which many of our rural people engage in today. A man needs a barn, in a hurry. His neighbors all come to help him build it, for he will come to help them, another day. One man does not do the work for another; they all do it together. In a few years, each farmer in the community is standing on his own feet, because the community helped him to help himself, and the whole community is stronger because its members are stronger.

What explains the strength of the more prosperous nations today? Of course, there are many factors involved, but one of the most important is the extent to which they have borrowed in the past from other nations the ideas and the experiences which those other nations have gained, and then applied them to the development of their own resources.

Look at Britain. There has been no more dramatic history than hers. She had from the first an intelligent people, but no very impressive natural resources of her own, except coal—and the development of that resource came late in her history. But she welcomed bankers from Italy, and eventually became the banker of the world (her financial center is still called Lombard Street). She welcomed traders from Germany, and became the leading trader of the world (the Easterlings, as they were called, introduced stable currency, and Esterling and Sterling became almost a world standard). Textile technicians from Flanders, skilled Huguenot refugees from France, imported ship-builders from Scandinavia and Germany—Britain borrowed freely from them all, and made their skill and experience her own.

Look at the United States. The land had great resources, and intelligent people, but few of them. But we borrowed heavily of British money, and we deliberately imported from Britain and France and Germany and the Netherlands and many other lands the technicians who helped us establish many of our industries and our transportation systems, until we could build upon their experience and often improve upon it. We imported our ideas on education not only from England, but from Germany and France as well, and gradually adapted them to our own situation and environment.

I remember a story about an Irish-American who was aroused by the thoughtlessly slighting remarks about foreigners which used to be so common. "Foreigners, is it?" he exclaimed. "I'd like to know who cleared the forests of this country but foreigners? Who built the roads and the railroads of the country but foreigners? Who used to do most of the work in the factories but foreigners? For that matter, who discovered the blessed country in the first place but foreigners?"

II

So we owe a debt, we of the more fortunate nations today, which we must pay. It is not our natural resources which have made us strong. It is the power of ideas and experience which has developed those resources; and as we have gathered many of those ideas and much of that experience from others, so must we pass on our own, when they are asked for. In the process, we shall be further enriched, for we shall gather new ideas and experiences for ourselves.

Two children had an idea about how to get rich.

If I give you sixpence, and you give me sixpence,
We both shall be richer by sixpence the more.
Give me a guinea, I'll give you a guinea—
Let's give each other two guineas, and then we'll have four!

You haven't two guineas? Well, I haven't either;
  We'll have to use pennies if we haven't got more.
So give me your sixpence, and here is my sixpence—
  Now, why do I have no more than before?

So it goes with money. But with ideas! You give me an idea
and I give you one, and we each have two in place of one. The
technical assistance program, when it deals in the realm of ideas,
is a two-way affair.

So technical assistance swings into action. What is its peculiar
value? Not the stopping of epidemics through the action of foreign
health officials, nor the building of hospitals and clinics with foreign
funds; but cooperation in building another nation's public health
service and establishing facilities for the training of a nation's
technicians to do the job for itself—not for the moment, but
forever. Not the dispatch of agricultural experts to demonstrate
the benefits of modern farming, and advise a nation's farmers to
go and do likewise; but the cooperative development of means by
which the nation's farmers, with such resources as may lie within
their reach, may learn for themselves how to grow two ears of
corn where one grew before. Not an educational mission to draw
up a foreign plan for organizing a nation's schools; but a careful
cooperative study of what ideas from outside may be successfully
used for improvement of the existing system, and then a long-
range collaboration to establish means for training the nation's
own technicians to apply them. It is easy to know what to do; it
is not so easy to do it. It has always been so. Some three hundred
and fifty years ago, Shakespeare said: "If to do were as easy as
to know what were good to do, chapels had been churches, and
poor men's cottages princes' palaces." But get two people—or two
nations—to put their heads and hands together on a task, and
"to do" becomes less difficult.

Point Four is a sort of diplomatic activity, in the sense that it
is concerned with the relations between nations. But it is the kind
of diplomacy my students of some years ago were asking for. Its
diplomats are teachers, farmers, doctors and nurses, engineers,
craftsmen, industrial technicians. Very few of the male members
of the group own a dinner suit, and there is probably not a pair
of striped pants among them; and the women tend to leave their

evening gowns at home. For they will be riding to their work on jeeps or mules to isolated towns and farms; they will be walking with dusty shoes across the fields of the Altiplano and the desert stretches of far-off lands; they will be sloshing through the jungle marshes; they will spend long evening hours in consultation with colleagues of other lands in some low-ceilinged room by the light of candle or kerosene lamp; they will shake hands with Peruvian doctors trained in Germany, with Brazilian industrial workers trained in Brazil by North Americans on machine tools from Britain, with Honduran sanitary engineers who may have had to train themselves for the most part. They will be in daily contact with farmers on their home acres, with rural teachers in adobe schools, with children who know neither English nor Spanish nor Portuguese, with local midwives and their patients.

That is the work of this Institute of Inter-American Affairs, and the people who work for it. No—not for the institute, but for America in its broadest geographical and popular sense. Some country says, "Come on to my house"—and for several years that house becomes the home of scores of our best technicians. We say to some of that country's teachers or doctors or engineers, "Come on to my house," and for a year or two they make their home with us, in our colleges or our fields or our factories; then they return, and we are both the richer for their having been here.

It is not an easy job or an easy life. There are hardships to share, out there in the mountains and the jungles and the plains, with people of other lands and speech who are also working on the job. There are sharp differences of opinion and outlook to be reconciled. But the differences are not insurmountable, nor are they always differences in national points of view. I have attended staff conferences abroad, in which the debates have been spirited and heated among the technicians, North American and Latin American; but usually I find a group of North Americans and Latin Americans on one side of the debate and a similar group of North Americans and Latin Americans on the other. The division of opinion, in time, comes to be, not along national lines at all, but simply a division among educators working on a common professional problem. And that is the way it should be.

But in spite of difficulties, headaches, discouragements, frustrations, and delays, the adventure always seems to be a joyous one.

There is fun with it, too, and the growth of a mutual respect, and the stimulation of seeing things happening—slowly, perhaps, but making a permanent impact upon the daily lives of millions of our fellow Americans—and our own. You here are all a part of it, in a way. If any of you should feel the urge to be a part of it more directly, "Come on to my house" in the Institute of Inter-American Affairs, and we'll talk about it!

Index

[Prepared by Walter A. Payne]

235